ASIAN CRUCIBLE

'Will Asia's future be fractured, unified or rebalanced? In *Asian Crucible*, Nick Bisley delivers a sweeping history and clear-eyed roadmap to the forces reshaping the region – and the choices that will define not only Asia's destiny, but the world's.'
Zack Cooper, American Enterprise Institute

'Nick Bisley is one of the world's most perceptive analysts of Asia. With clarity and authority, he illuminates both the dangers facing this pivotal region and the ways they might yet be managed.'
Brendan Taylor, Australian National University

'A succinct and timely book that explores Asia's past and present and offers discerning arguments about its possible futures.'
Jürgen Haacke, London School of Economics and Political Science

'Rarely is the epic story of the making of modern Asia given such thorough treatment as here. Emerging from an imperial past, Asia cohered in the era of globalization. US leadership played a role, but Asia's economies cohered when they became China-centred, albeit not Sino-centric. These vital distinctions are examined with nuance, offering an informed view of Asia's current and future trajectory.'
Samir Puri, Chatham House and author of *Westlessness*

ASIAN CRUCIBLE

Globalization, Geopolitics and the Contest for the Future

Nick Bisley

First published in Great Britain in 2026 by

Bristol University Press
University of Bristol
1-9 Old Park Hill
Bristol
BS2 8BB
UK
t: +44 (0)117 374 6645
e: bup-info@bristol.ac.uk

Details of international sales and distribution partners are available at
bristoluniversitypress.co.uk

© Bristol University Press 2026

DOI: 10.51952/9781529233193

British Library Cataloguing in Publication Data
A catalogue record for this book is available from the British Library

ISBN 978-1-5292-3317-9 paperback
ISBN 978-1-5292-3318-6 ePub
ISBN 978-1-5292-3319-3 ePdf

The right of Nick Bisley to be identified as author of this work has been asserted by him in accordance with the Copyright, Designs and Patents Act 1988.

All rights reserved: no part of this publication may be reproduced, stored in a retrieval system, or transmitted in any form or by any means, electronic, mechanical, photocopying, recording, or otherwise without the prior permission of Bristol University Press.

Every reasonable effort has been made to obtain permission to reproduce copyrighted material. If, however, anyone knows of an oversight, please contact the publisher.

The statements and opinions contained within this publication are solely those of the author and not of the University of Bristol or Bristol University Press. The University of Bristol and Bristol University Press disclaim responsibility for any injury to persons or property resulting from any material published in this publication.

Bristol University Press works to counter discrimination on grounds of gender, race, disability, age and sexuality.

Cover design: blu inc
Front cover image: iStock/freedom_naruk

For my parents, with love and thanks

Contents

List of Figures and Tables	viii
List of Abbreviations	ix
About the Author	xi
Acknowledgements	xii
Preface	xiii

1	Introduction	1
2	Imperialism and Its Aftermath	18
3	Cold War to Long Peace	43
4	Asia Integrated	62
5	The Pandemic Years and the End of Globalization	93
6	Geopolitics and the Great Powers	124
7	Flashpoints and Zones of Contestation	162
8	Sources of Risk and Volatility	192
9	Three Paths to the Future	226
10	Securing Asia's Future	255

Sources and Further Reading	280
References	302
Index	331

List of Figures and Tables

Figures

2.1	Map of British India in 1914	21
2.2	Map of China in 1927	23
2.3	Southeast Asian colonial holdings 1914	24
2.4	Maximum extent of Japan's empire	27
6.1	Map of the South China Sea, with the nine-dashed line	145
7.1	Map of the Taiwan Strait	164
7.2	Map of the Korean Peninsula	166
7.3	East China Sea	168
7.4	Political map of Southeast Asia	171
7.5	Territorial claims in the South China Sea	174
7.6	United Nations map of South Asia	179
7.7	Disputed territories of India	181
7.8	Political map of Central Asia	186

Tables

6.1	Strategic alignment of Asia's states	134
8.1	Asian political systems	216

List of Abbreviations

ADMM+	ASEAN Defence Ministers' Meeting Plus process
AFTA	ASEAN Free Trade Area
AI	artificial intelligence
AIIB	Asian Infrastructure and Investment Bank
ANZUS	(or ANZUS Treaty) Australia, New Zealand and US Security Treaty
APEC	Asia-Pacific Economic Cooperation
ARF	ASEAN Regional Forum
ASEAN	Association of Southeast Asian Nations
AUKUS	Australian, United Kingdom and United States pact
BIS	Bank of International Settlements
BJP	Bharatiya Janata Party (India)
BRI	Belt and Road Initiative
CBM	confidence-building measures
CICA	Conference on Interaction on Confidence Building Measures in Asia
COVID-19	novel coronavirus disease 2019
CPC	Communist Party of China
CPTPP	Comprehensive and Progressive Agreement for Trans-Pacific Partnership
DPJ	Democratic Party of Japan
DPRK	Democratic People's Republic of Korea (North Korea)
EAS	East Asia Summit
EEZ	exclusive economic zone
EIC	East India Company (British)
EU	European Union

EV	electric vehicle
G7	Group of Seven
G20	Group of Twenty
GATT	General Agreement on Tariffs and Trade
GCC	Gulf Cooperation Council
GCI	Global Civilisation Initiative
GDI	Global Development Initiative
GDP	gross domestic product
GFC	Global Financial Crisis, 2007–08
GSI	Global Security Initiative
IMF	International Monetary Fund
KMT	Kuomintang (National People's Party, Republic of China/Taiwan)
LDP	Liberal Democratic Party (Japan)
NGO	non-governmental organization
PACOM	Pacific Command (US)
PLA	People's Liberation Army (China)
PLAAF	PLA Air Force
PLAN	People's Liberation Army-Navy (China)
PPE	personal protective equipment
PRC	People's Republic of China
ROK	Republic of Korea (South Korea)
SAARC	South Asian Association for Regional Cooperation
SARS	severe acute respiratory syndrome
SCO	Shanghai Cooperation Organization
SEAC	Southeast Asia Command
SEZ	special economic zone
SLD	Shangri-La Dialogue
TPP	Trans-Pacific Partnership
UN	United Nations
UNCLOS	United Nations Convention on the Law of the Sea
USSR	Union of Soviet Socialist Republics
WHO	World Health Organization
WTO	World Trade Organization

About the Author

Nick Bisley is Pro Vice-Chancellor for Research and Professor of International Relations at La Trobe University, Australia. He is the immediate past-President of the Australasian Council of Deans of Arts, Social Sciences and Humanities and was elected as Fellow of the Australian Institute of International Affairs in 2020. He served as Editor-in-Chief of the *Australian Journal of International Affairs* between 2013 and 2018 and has been Senior Research Associate at the International Institute of Strategic Studies and Visiting Fellow at the East–West Center in Washington, DC.

Acknowledgements

I am very grateful for the opportunities to present some of the ideas and arguments in this book to various audiences over the past couple of years. This includes a brief but brilliant visit to Victoria University of Wellington, where I spent time in 2022 as a visiting professor; many thanks to David Capie and his colleagues for intellectual engagement and warm hospitality. I would also like to thank John Sidel at the London School of Economics Southeast Asia Centre, Bec Strating at La Trobe Asia, Li Minjiang at Nanyang Technological University, Singapore, Brendan O'Connor at the University of Sydney, Mike Norris at the Australian Strategic Policy Institute and a number of colleagues in government, who need to remain anonymous. Brendan Taylor read a number of chapters and provided his usual sharp observations and helpful advice. Two anonymous reviewers read an earlier version of the text and I am very grateful for their helpful suggestions. My thanks to all who have provided input along the way, the errors that remain are my own.

This book was written while I served as Dean of Humanities and Social Sciences at La Trobe University, where my colleagues have been tireless, resilient and a source of inspiration during some fairly challenging times. My thanks to you all, especially Lorraine Ward and Rachel Laws, who have been supportive above and beyond the call of duty.

Finally, I would particularly like to thank Stephen Wenham at Bristol University Press, who encouraged me to write this book, provided unstinting support and advice and shepherded things through the publication process with consummate professionalism.

Preface

The sheer scale of Asia's population, geographic expanse and cultural diversity has always made it an important part of the world – for thousands of years it has been home to the largest concentration of the human population – but now it has become the epicentre of global geopolitical competition. It is on the cusp of a period of intense contestation that will be of profound importance for its people and for the world as a whole. This book explains how and why this has occurred. It looks back to Asia's past, examining how its experiences of imperialism, conflict and the Cold War contributed to the forces shaping its dynamic present and its perilous future. My aim is to help people understand the forces that have made modern Asia such a success and explain why the region faces such a complex and challenging future. The book is also intended to make the case for Asia itself to be understood as a coherent political, strategic and economic space. In the past, the connections between the continent's component parts were thin. Its different subregions, such as Southeast Asia, had connections that bound them together, but the vast zone was too disparate and loosely connected to be considered as a place in its own right. To make sense of the dynamics at work in the region one needs to understand how it has become an integrated economic and geopolitical system. I hope that readers will finish the book with a clearer sense of how the region is linked together and an understanding of the blend of integrative and competitive pressures at work across Asia.

This book is the product of many years teaching and researching about Asia's international relations. It draws on these experiences as well as considerable interaction with senior officials, analysts and scholars from across Asia and beyond. It will, I hope, contribute to debates within scholarly and policy-making communities, but it is also written for a broader audience curious about Asia's place in today's world. Given this ambition, I decided to keep the referencing of the works on which it draws relatively light in the main text. Readers are directed to the sources for specific facts, quotes, policy ideas and scholarly arguments. At the end of the book, I have included a bibliographic essay that points readers to the literature that has been consulted in preparing the work. It provides more detail about the ideas and sources that influenced my thinking as well as something of a map that readers can follow if they wish to pursue things further.

Nick Bisley
October 2025

1

Introduction

It was hot and muggy as the sun rose over the East China Sea on 7 September 2010. The humidity and heat reflecting from the ocean made the fishing that a Chinese trawler was attempting hard work. But these famously abundant waters are worth the effort and the risk. For the ship was somewhere it really should not have been, just a few kilometres from the jagged cliffs of the islands that in Japan are known as the Senkaku and that the Chinese call the Diaoyu. That area was part of Japan's exclusive economic zone (EEZ); this was not the place for a fishing trawler flying the flag of the People's Republic of China (PRC) to be. And the ship's captain, Zhan Qixiong, knew it. He was taking a calculated risk that the Japanese Coast Guard, which patrols the waters, would turn a blind eye to avoid a clash. The Chinese assumed that the Japanese were likely to be cautious. Prime Minister Kan Naoto had just come to power in June 2010 and his Democratic Party of Japan (DPJ) was known for being less hard line on China than the conservative Liberal Democratic Party (LDP). The chances were, Japan's Coast Guard would leave them be.

This was a mistake. The Japanese authorities ordered the vessel to stop and immediately vacate the EEZ. This began with routine radio communication and escalated to evasive action as the Chinese ship ignored all instructions. Ultimately, Zhan's ship collided with the Coast Guard vessel on two occasions, separated by 40 minutes, and culminated in the arrest of Zhan and his 14 crew members. As word leaked out, the arrest rapidly escalated into a major diplomatic crisis.

Beijing claims the Senkaku/Diaoyu as part of the PRC and argues that its fishing fleet has every right to be there. The islands had been part of Imperial China but were ceded at the Treaty of Shimonoseki that concluded the 1894–95 Sino–Japanese War, a humiliating defeat for the Qing dynasty. It was one of many treaties that Imperial China had been forced to sign, giving away territory and an immense amount of national pride. Since coming to power in 1949, the Communist Party of China (CPC) has made the unification of all the lands and islands that it regards as part of China central to its mission. Consequently, Beijing responded to the incident by exerting pressure on Tokyo, both publicly and privately. The Japanese ambassador in Beijing was summoned by China's foreign ministry multiple times in the days following the event, including reportedly a midnight demand that he attend immediately. The Chinese government allowed anti-Japanese protestors to rampage on the streets of Shanghai, Hong Kong and Beijing, trashing Japan-linked stores and banks and even setting alight cars from well-known Japanese brands. These demonstrations pulsed in several waves in the weeks following the arrests. On 20 September 2010 PRC officials announced that four Japanese executives in China had been arrested for allegedly entering and photographing a military installation illegally. The following day, Beijing let it be known that it would restrict exports of rare earth minerals to Japan. Rare earths are critical constituents of many high technology products and at the time China controlled 97 per cent of the global market. Japan depended on the PRC for 90 per cent of its rare earth imports and the threat followed swiftly on from a period where China had pushed up global prices by constricting supply. Beijing knew that it had leverage and made it clear that it was prepared to wield it. China also made it clear that tourists would not be allowed to travel to Japan. In recent years tourists from the PRC had become a huge component of the Japanese tourism market. The economic threat was very real.

Tokyo faced a confident and carefully calibrated exertion of diplomatic pressure. The Kan government tried and failed to respond meaningfully to China's gambit. It had initially charged Zhan with illegal fishing, then decided instead to seek an indemnity payment from Beijing. While few thought it would escalate into a conflict, the tension between Northeast Asia's two biggest economies was considerable. In the end, Tokyo blinked and released Zhan and his crew on 24 September 2010 without charge, admission of guilt or indeed anything. They were returned home on a jet chartered by Beijing.

Japan's government was badly embarrassed, Chinese nationalists were assuaged and some in the region began to notice that their world was changing. Japan had been a treaty ally of the US for decades and was its most important partner in Asia by some margin. The Senkaku's fisheries are rich, its hydrocarbon reserves are thought to be substantial and the islands are of strategic significance as they are located around 100 km northeast of Taiwan, at the tip of the Ryukyu Archipelago, Japan's westernmost extent. Were they to be in Beijing's hands the military benefit would be considerable. Previously these attributes would have served to see off a crisis; in the event of some friction, it would have been managed without too much fuss. Yet Tokyo was neither able to resist Beijing's campaign nor was the US able to support its ally. While the strained relationship between the DPJ and the US had not helped, it was the wide range of points of pressure brought to bear on Tokyo that had the desired effect. The distinctly new and worrisome development was Beijing's willingness to weaponize its economic ties with Japan. Its rare earths dominance, and the scale of its tourism market, gave China influence that worked rather better than expected. The PRC never even had to choke off supply; the threat was enough.

Asia had become used to decades of peace among its major powers and the economic growth that this allowed had unleashed one of the greatest improvements in human welfare in history. Following the normalization of Sino–American relations in the 1970s the PRC had embarked on a reform programme that, by the end of the 21st century's first decade, had produced a truly remarkable level of economic transformation. During most of that time Beijing followed a cautious approach to its foreign dealings. The business of domestic reform mattered far more than long-term nationalist ambition. But the events of September 2010 showed a new face of Chinese power and a glimpse of Asia's future.

This is a world in which emerging powers have developed the wealth and confidence to make good on their ambitions. Asia is criss-crossed by complex ties of economic interdependence, the webs of trade and investment whose growth had been fuelled by globalization. Those links had driven immense improvements in living standards and had started to tie the region together. But these networks also provide the fuel for more ambitious and dangerous foreign dealings. Beijing showed that international trade, which allows countries to specialize in things that they are good at, creates vulnerabilities. This fact had been known for years. What surprised many was Beijing's willingness to use its trading position to prey on these inherent weaknesses. The win–win world of economic integration through trade now had some very real downside risks as an emboldened China saw economic interdependence as an instrument of political power. At the time technocrats took note and began to draw up plans to reduce these risks in the future, and regional security specialists observed that the PRC was acting in a more assertive manner than previously, but the Senkaku/Diaoyu incident did not seem to be a transformative event. Asia had become prosperous on the back of international trade; the shared interests everyone had in this prosperity continuing would, it was believed, ensure that the underlying international order would remain in place.

INTRODUCTION

Asia comes together

The networks that China threatened to weaponize were part of a thriving China-centred Asian economy that had only recently emerged. Since the collapse of the Soviet Union in 1991, the overarching settings in the global economy had prompted an acceleration of market-led globalization. North America and the European Union (EU), the world's two most important economic centres, embraced openness seeing market forces and not state direction as the best determinants of what was made, at what price, where and in what quantities. The state would act as a rule setter and contract enforcer and, in some areas, would remain a guardian, most notably in relation to agriculture. But elsewhere the market was given free rein in the belief that the efficiencies that this approach creates would be immense and would have pacifying effects even on countries that were deeply mistrustful of one another. Addressing the World Economic Forum in Davos at the start of the new millennium President Bill Clinton articulated this view:

> open markets and rules-based trade are the best engine we know of to lift living standards, reduce environmental destruction, and build shared prosperity. This is true whether you're in Detroit, Davos, Dacca, or Dakar. Worldwide, open markets do create jobs. They do raise incomes. They do spark innovation and spread new technology. (Clinton, 2000)

Asian states saw immense opportunity in this environment. Japan had demonstrated that export-focused industrialization could generate rapid growth and the rest of the region began to follow its lead. As globalization accelerated in the 1990s and early 2000s, shifts in the way international production occurred alongside the dramatic expansion of China's economic capacity and sophistication allowed entrepreneurial spirits across Asia the chance to tap into dynamic economic opportunities.

In the decades between the collapse of communism in the late 1980s and the World Health Organization's (WHO) declaration of the COVID-19 pandemic in early 2020, modern Asia was forged. In three decades, it moved from being a place where a vast population lived but whose fates were separate, operating to different rhythms and with few shared interests, to become an integrated and coherent space. As the Union of Soviet Socialist Republics (USSR) sunk below the horizon, the Asian continent had four components that, while linked to some degree, were effectively discrete centres of strategic, economic and social life. Countries in Northeast Asia, such as Japan and South Korea, were beginning to become more closely connected through trade and investment to Indonesia and Thailand in Southeast Asia, but these ties were in their infancy. In the early 1990s, the nations of South Asia, such as India, Pakistan and Sri Lanka, remained largely disconnected from the two zones on the Western Pacific, while Central Asia had literally just stepped out onto the international stage having been part of the USSR for seven decades.

These four corners of Asia, recognized at the time as relatively discrete areas, were drawn together by the power of market-led globalization. China had launched its economic reform programme in 1978. It slowly and selectively opened itself to international trade and investment and, by the 1990s, was well positioned to capitalize on the acceleration of globalization caused by the high period of global liberalism and technological changes that had transformed the way manufacturing occurred. This spurred a rapid and vast economic expansion and led to China becoming the heart of an Asia-wide economy as well as a critical engine of global growth. By 2020, Asia had a China-centred but not Sino-centric economic system. By this I mean that the region's economic order had moved away from a pattern in which countries competed with each other for inbound investment from the US, Japan and Europe and for exports to those same zones, to one bound together in an integrated production system centred around the PRC. This was no economic replication of Imperial China's dominance of Asia in the 17th and 18th century, the setting that has been described by scholars as Asia's Sino-centric international system. While there had been some minor assistance from state efforts such as the China–Association of Southeast Asian Nations (ASEAN) Free Trade Agreement and the Asia-Pacific Economic Cooperation's (APEC) trade facilitation programmes, Asia's economic integration was the product of market logic, not a political creation. Modern integrated Asia was bound together by economic ties that were created by the opportunities of market-led globalization, not the dominant leanings of a powerful state or the rules of regional organizations.

For the first time modern Asia had become a really existing economic system. It had intraregional trade volumes approaching those of the EU, which is regarded as the world's most integrated economic zone. But it was not just the rational world of manufacturing, trade and commerce that knitted it together. As the events of September 2010 forewarned, the geopolitical ambitions of the continent's major powers had come back to life and turned the landmass, as well as its seas and oceans, into a theatre of competition in which the US, China, India and Russia, alongside many other countries, began to contend with one another to shape the contours of this vast and diverse place.

Market-led globalization and the ambitions and anxieties of geopolitics meant that the sea lanes and landmass of Asia had become what defence analysts call a 'strategic system'. This refers to an international system in which states share a significant set of interests and also have a common sense of military risks and threats. Put simply, a strategic system is a place where the fates of its members are intertwined both economically and militarily. In the recent past Northeast, Southeast, South and Central Asia were not sufficiently linked to share a sense of economic and security interests; now globalization and geopolitics had bound them together.

Globalization was seen as a positive opportunity by virtually everyone. The core of the global economy, North America and the EU, appeared to be forever committed to open markets and free trade. Not even the Global Financial Crisis (GFC) of 2007–08 could knock it from its pedestal. Markets had created turmoil and showed that they needed better regulation, especially with regard to banking systems, but faith in their efficiency and benign social impact remained steadfast. The macro view was that the GFC was, in essence, a very large and complex bank run. It did not warrant changes to the bedrock settings of the global economy. No one of political significance demanded changes to those settings or that political actors should be making key decisions about the core workings of the economy. The state was needed as a firefighter when things went wrong, not as a critical driver of economic decision-making.

The COVID years changed all that. The pandemic shocked markets and politics around the world and fundamentally altered Asia's trajectory. The faith of the wealthy North Atlantic world in markets was shattered. Great power competition was accelerated as confidence in China collapsed. Critically, globalization had previously been seen as a kind of golden guardrail that would keep Sino–American rivalry within manageable bounds. These rails were broken, and geopolitical competition became untethered from the constraints of economic interdependence. This pushed the world's most populous region onto a much more dangerous path.

COVID-19 emerged in Asia and disrupted the world; in an unsettling echo of that pattern, the post-pandemic trajectory of the region's international relations, in which geopolitics is unconstrained, nationalism and illiberalism are on the march, the world is likely to follow the respiratory disease's global pathogenesis.

This book analyses the forces that integrated modern Asia and assesses how they are likely to evolve over the coming decades. It shows how the region emerged out of a history of imperialism, war and economic expansion and how the way in which Asia was able to return to prosperity created the distinctive manner of the vast region's integration. The COVID-19 years were a pivotal period; prior to January 2020, the trajectory ahead seemed clear. By 2022, Asia, and in turn the world, had been wrenched down a quite different path as the underlying balance of ideas changed.

Integrated Asia was a creature of the era of markets. That period has come to an end and a new phase is beginning to emerge, one in which the balance of state and market power is being recast. As we look to discern where the region may go it is critical to understand the dynamics that gave Asia its current shape. The importance of the political and economic choices made prior to 2020 underscore just how important the choices we make today will be for the future. Whether Asia can recover the level of economic dynamism and political stability it had in the 1990s and early 2000s or whether it falls back into patterns of rivalry, fear and conflict will be determined by the decisions made today.

What happened between 2020 and 2022 that is so important for Asia and its future?

Globalization disrupted

In the 1990s and 2000s, market-led globalization held a dominant position in the minds of politicians, business leaders and commentators. In what now seem like quaint debates, scholars and analysts determined that the power of markets and firms was so great that the state was in retreat (Ohmae, 1995), that sovereignty was falling by the wayside (Camilleri and Falk, 1992) and that all that was left for states to do was to get out of the way so that the dynamism of markets and firms could work its magic. While the developed world was the high church of market-led globalization, Asian states were enthusiastic members of the congregation. Or at least they were keenly sitting on one side of the aisle. Asian states had become wholehearted participants in globalization in that they saw great opportunities for exports and attracting inward investment. They remained cautious right up to the pandemic about opening themselves up entirely, instead, the most common path was one of selective integration with the global economy. Asian states were reticent to expose their domestic markets to the full force of international competition. This was not seen as a problem by the wider world as they were either too poor to buy what the rich world exported or they opted to provide some access where they were large enough and there were complementarities.

Asian economies had seen what Japan had achieved by emphasizing export-focused industrialization in the decades after 1945. The country had recovered from the devastation of World War II, when its industrial base had been destroyed, to become the world's second largest economy by the mid-1980s. Taiwan and South Korea had followed suit and, alongside other Southeast Asian economies, including Thailand, Malaysia and Indonesia, they enjoyed sustained levels of Gross Domestic Product (GDP) growth of around 5.5 per cent between 1960 and 1985. The rate and durability of this growth was astonishing, leading scholars and analysts to refer regularly to Asia's 'miracle' economies (Birdsall et al, 1993).

China was a bit later to the game than many Asian economies but it made up for this tardiness by an even more impressive period of economic expansion. Within four decades of launching its reforms in 1978, the PRC had become the world's largest economy in purchasing power terms and the world's largest producer of concrete and steel; it was also the manufacturing hub of the global economy and increasingly a large and affluent consumer market. The transformation was epochal. Consequently, many Asian states had a huge amount at stake politically in continued economic prosperity. The ruling elites of the key countries in the region had sought legitimacy through their ability to deliver stability and prosperity.

INTRODUCTION

Even as globalization first emerged, it prompted a political reaction. In the 1990s, populist politicians, such as Ross Perot in the US or Pym Fortuyn in the Netherlands, appeared and pushed back against its disruptions. Grassroots activism was also evident, such as the violent protests at the 1999 World Trade Organization (WTO) ministerial meeting in Seattle. But these reactions remained at the margins; the political consensus around the importance of open markets, free trade and deregulation was deeply rooted across the North Atlantic world. The risks of globalization and some doubts about its broader social impact began to surface more fully after the GFC in 2007–08 and the long-lasting recession that the crisis left behind. Tighter banking regulation followed as well as more energized social protests, such as the Occupy Wall Street movement, which were fuelled by frustration at the larger inequities of globalization and the sense that the bankers who had caused the crisis had not had to pay for their actions.

The UK referendum to leave the EU and the election of Donald Trump in 2016 showed that the political and popular support for the core assumptions of globalization was much more fragile than many had realized. In the 1980s and 1990s, the UK and the US had been at the forefront of the global embrace of markets and weakening state economic capacity; now they were leading the turn away. The first Trump administration's extensive use of tariffs, its trade war with China and its undermining of the WTO confirmed that the consensus behind market-led globalization was coming unstuck. But it was the pandemic years from 2020 to 2022 that fundamentally transformed the thinking about economic policy settings across the world. This transformation was confirmed by the astonishing direction which the second Trump administration has chosen to take US trade and broader international economic policy.

COVID-19 burst onto the global stage early in 2020 and within weeks had led to draconian lockdowns across China as the CPC sought to contain a deadly disease which spread extremely rapidly, for which there was no immunity, no vaccine and no therapeutic medication. Beijing's response was effectively to shut its society down, prompting a rapid set of contractions in the global economy, most notably a sudden drop in the price of oil. The speed of COVID-19's transmission caused already strained health systems to collapse. Countries around the world had little choice but to copy China's approach of locking their populations in place, closing borders, schools and universities and halting all social movement. The shutdown created the greatest shock to the global economy since the 1930s. In April of 2020 there seemed no end to the catastrophe. Vaccines normally take years to develop, and the fear was that without them, opening up would kill millions around the world. Faced with a global economic collapse, governments found themselves forced to abandon long-held beliefs in the power of the market and the importance of the state staying out of the economy.

The US Federal Reserve Chair Jerome Powell and Treasury Secretary Steve Mnuchin engineered a remarkable programme of economic intervention, including the largest fiscal stimulus in US history. Cash was given to social security number holders, evictions were prevented, debt was put on hold or forgiven and a myriad of programmes that had hitherto been anathema to the free-market absolutist Republican Party were put in place to stave off disaster. Governments around the world followed suit and the collapse of the global economy was averted. The political lesson was unmistakable: markets needed the state to avert catastrophe. Globalization was not an untameable force; indeed, it was a source of immense vulnerability and it had to be corralled.

But it was not just the economic firefighting during the pandemic that brought to an end globalization's dominance. COVID-19 also revealed how vulnerable societies had become because of the way international production now occurred. Before 2020, states had been content to let the market decide what was made where. To be clear, some states tried to protect certain aspects of their economies, usually politically sensitive areas, like cultural industries and agriculture. But manufacturing was, in global terms, a domain where the market was allowed largely free rein. The efficiencies of globalization had meant that countries could import what was made more cheaply elsewhere. This meant, in turn, that most developed economies no longer physically produced anything to do with personal protective equipment, such as face masks, gloves and the like, that suddenly were needed in vast quantities. Nor did most have any ability to produce pharmaceuticals. The pandemic's squeeze revealed the limits of sovereign capability in many areas, and this vulnerability was something that was, in at least some sectors, no longer acceptable.

The pandemic showed just how finely balanced the global economy had become. The complex business of managing international production chains was difficult and rested not just on expertise, careful management and first-rate planning, but on the policy settings that made it possible. The lockdowns showed all too painfully just how fragile these systems had become. The inescapable conclusion was that those risks had to be better managed by political actors. And the anti-incumbent votes in 2024, a year when more than a dozen democracies, including the US, UK, India and Indonesia, went to the polls, showed just how frustrated voters were. Governing parties lost on average 7 per cent of the vote in that year, the largest such collective rebuke in more than 100 years (Burns-Murdoch, 2024). Finally, COVID-19 made clear that some critical technologies had, because of the logic of markets, ended up being controlled by a small number of countries. And as geopolitics heated up further, this reinforced the scepticism about letting the markets determine our collective economic fate. States were no longer content to have prices and firm decisions alone determine where things like microchips or high-end artificial intelligence (AI) developments occurred.

The return of great power rivalry had been announced by the first Trump administration's 2017 National Security Strategy

(White House, 2017). Washington signalled that it now would focus its energy on the old-fashioned business of competing for global influence with other big states, with a particular emphasis on China. As his first term wore on, Trump's administration increased pressure on the PRC, viewing it as a full spectrum threat to US interests and values. The trade war had begun as a largely economic gambit to right what Trump claimed was Chinese misbehaviour but became a broader tool of statecraft as the US adopted a posture of overt competition with the PRC. By the end of the pandemic years, nascent geopolitical rivalry and mistrust had become open contestation. This was illustrated most clearly by the lines of continuity that existed in US policy towards China between Trump and his successor. While President Biden had more sophisticated diplomacy, smoother rhetoric and more effective communication, the underlying direction was the same. The US viewed China as an explicit and long-term threat to its core interests and the overarching settings of the international order. Geopolitics was once again on the centre stage of world politics and it was now a world that no longer saw globalization, markets and the shared interests they created in the same benign light. Indeed, economic interdependence was perceived as a vulnerability against which one must defend oneself. Modern Asia had been made whole, but now it faced a more dangerous world.

Asia's uncertain future

The pandemic years were a catalyst to three major changes that have set Asia and the world down a new path. First, during that period the global consensus about globalization and the neoliberal economic policy that had made it possible broke apart. Following the USSR's collapse, the embracing of a set of policies to do with deregulation, empowering markets and reducing the state's role in the economy through privatization was so pervasive that some analysts have described those decades as the 'era of markets' (Bradley et al, 2022). The COVID-19 years brought that period to a decisive end. Doubts about the balance of power between markets and the state had been emerging in the years leading up to the pandemic but between 2020 and 2022 the political rules about the economy were rewritten. A strong and economically interventionist state returned after the pandemic years and political factors began to play a much more determinative role in the economy. The state is back at the head of the economic table. This entails political scepticism about the ideas of free markets as well as increased intolerance to the vulnerabilities of the supply chains that have become so central to the international production and trading system. The second Trump administration's approach to trade policy is illustrative of just how politicized international economic policy has become. Many Asian economies assumed that the global settings would remain as they had been for decades. Their fates will hinge on how the global economy is reconfigured after the collapse in the consensus about global trade.

Second, during the COVID-19 years, geopolitical competition between the US and China became unambiguously the most significant facet of Asia's and indeed global security concerns. Rivalry had been slowly increasing in tempo and visibility. The pandemic years put a bright spotlight on the competition and the shift in attitudes about the need to give political direction to at least some aspects of international economic relations meant that geopolitics was no longer tethered by economic interdependence. Critically, this period underlined doubts about China's intentions and trustworthiness, most especially for the US and its partners and allies.

Third, the end of a shared belief in the underlying value of a broadly liberal structure to international economic relations has robbed Asia of a set of interests and mechanisms to beat back the atavistic tendencies of nationalism and illiberalism. For all its many inequities, faith in markets and liberal capitalism provided hard-nosed incentives to drive cooperation and mutually beneficial inter-state relations. With the loss of faith, statism and nationalism are unfettered and now Asia faces a much more daunting future.

This book examines how the return of geopolitics and its intersection with the way the global economy is being recast will shape Asia's future and that of the world. The sad reality is that Asia faces a dangerous and uncertain future, in which military rivalry catalysed by nationalism and ambition is here to stay. But just how dangerous that future becomes, how well it is managed and how effectively nationalist chauvinism is kept in check remains open. The purpose of this book is to shine a light on these possibilities so as to understand them better and take steps today to see off the worst outcomes.

The first part of this book, Chapters 2 to 4, tells the story of Asia's making, how globalization and geopolitics knitted this vast and diverse continent into an integrated strategic system. It begins by looking at the region's formation during the era of imperialism when the shape of modern Asia, from the borders on the map to the areas of development, as well as the zones of risk and confrontation, was established. Then it examines the Cold War period when postcolonial states had to reconfigure their economies, construct new administrative systems and forge national identities as the global ideological competition roiled around them. Sovereignty was won, huge economic strides were taken by many and the region moved from being a place of almost endemic conflict to one of remarkable tranquillity. Following the Cold War, the region came into focus as an integrated economic and strategic space. This was made possible by the changes in international production, which accelerated market-led globalization and led to the creation of a China-centred Asian economy. And as wealth and power grew, the ambitions of Asia's major powers began to stir, creating a continent-wide theatre of strategic competition. Where before the risks and interests of countries like Japan and India were disconnected from one another, now they had a shared strategic imagination.

INTRODUCTION

The COVID-19 years pushed Asia down a new path, one in which the balance of political and economic forces is being recast. The book's second part, Chapters 5 to 9, looks forward to the region's future, starting with the reconfiguration of the global economy. It explores the dynamic and complex geopolitical challenges in the region and the long-term ambitions of Asia's great powers as well as the region's many flashpoints. Adding risk to an already fraught environment are the powerful forces of nationalism, climate change and illiberalism that will act as threat multipliers. Chapter 9 looks forward and assesses Asia's future, it develops three scenarios as a means of thinking systematically about the region's future: Fractured Asia, Rebalanced Asia and Unified Asia.

This book argues that Asia's prospects will be determined, above all, by the way geopolitics and the reconstitution of globalization unfold. Asia is a place that is bound to experience military competition, that will be subject to the vicissitudes of nationalism and ambition. However, it must find a way to ensure those forces do not spiral out of control while also ensuring that the ladders of economic opportunity that markets create remain in place for the hundreds of millions of people who remain mired in poverty and social exclusion. The book concludes with a set of recommendations about several short- and longer-term steps that can be taken to ensure this occurs.

2

Imperialism and Its Aftermath

The foundations of contemporary Asia were forged as modern imperialism crashed into the continent. As recent scholarship has shown, European empires behaved in ways that were surprisingly similar to the Asian empires that had dominated much of the continent before the 19th century. They did this by creating systems that were a hybrid of old and new ways of ruling. This entailed incorporating local cultural and political practices and integrating them with those of the imperial power (Phillips, 2021).

Imperialism began to rapidly transform Asia through the 19th century (Copland, 1986). Before then, the Mughal Empire in India and the Qing Empire in China were the dominant political and economic centres. Japan had turned its back on the world in the early 17th century as the military overlord or shogun, Tokugawa Ieyasu, cut the country off from trade. What we now call Southeast Asia comprised a series of kingdoms and sultanates, and central Asia had, by the early 19th century, largely been incorporated into the Russian, Chinese and Ottoman empires. While maritime affairs mattered, most obviously as the means to move goods, military power was primarily focused on land, reflecting the interests of the extant imperial powers.

Asia's modern empires

Europeans had started to appear across the region much earlier. The British East India Company (EIC) started to establish its 'factories', as its city headquarters were known, from the early 17th century, with the first established at Masulipatnam, located around 400 km north of modern-day Chennai on India's eastern coast. The Dutch East India Company's operations in what is now Indonesia also began in the early part of that century (Parthesius, 2010). The Portuguese had established a presence even earlier, in Goa (1510) and Macau (1555), and Spain had acquired the Philippine islands in the middle of the 16th century, the first major European holding in Asia.

Before the 19th century, these outposts were peripheral to the main interests of Asia's empires and polities. Europeans were interested in trade, driven by largely commercial motives, and they operated at a relatively small scale. The presence was in city ports, driven by the logic of mercantile interest not geopolitical ambition or interimperial rivalry. In the 19th century that changed decisively. While trade remained important, Europeans were motivated by competitive impulses with each other as well as by the belief that the expansion of empire was of benefit to the world. And the rapid technological advances of industrialization – advanced ship design, the steam engine, sophisticated armaments, electrification, the dynamics of modern capitalism – gave these new imperial powers the means and force through which they could advance their ambitions.

India

The establishment of the British Empire in India, the most important component of the most significant empire of the modern period, unfolded in a piecemeal, almost haphazard manner over a century and a half (Wilson, 2016). The EIC brought British interests to India in the early 17th century, setting up its factory trading posts in Surat in 1619, Madras (Chennai) in 1634, Bombay (Mumbai) in 1674 and Calcutta (Kolkata) in 1690. Through the second half of the 18th century, the Mughal Empire's breakdown provided opportunities for the company to expand its influence beyond the Bengali territories it had acquired forcibly and its small holdings on India's eastern coast. Providing troops to various Indian interests that were competing with one another to take advantage of the Mughal Empire's collapse allowed the EIC to press further across the subcontinent. Through the first part of the 19th century the company expanded its territorial control across much of what is now India and Pakistan. The EIC was driven not just by the commercial advantages of territorial acquisition, it also sought strategic benefits from participating in the geopolitics of the Indian subcontinent as well as a desire to expand Western civilization.

While technology and modern warfighting techniques had given the EIC distinct advantages, the ways in which the British were able to utilize Indian resources to their advantage was critical to their success. This was most evident in the military forces they deployed, in which Indian labour played by some margin the greatest role (Barrow, 2017). The revolt by Indian soldiers, known as sepoys, against the British ended the curious situation in which a private company was running Britain's Indian colonies, and led to direct rule by the crown, ushering in the period known as the British Raj (James, 2010). But even as British administrators directly ruled much of India until the mid-20th century, there were still significant parts that were indirectly controlled. In those circumstances, such as in Jammu and Kashmir or Sikkim, the local prince or sultan would govern but the British retained influence through trade, finance or defence arrangements.

By the turn of the 20th century, British India (see Figure 2.1) extended from Baluchistan in the west across to Burma, now known as Myanmar, in the east. While it brought aspects of

Figure 2.1: Map of British India in 1914

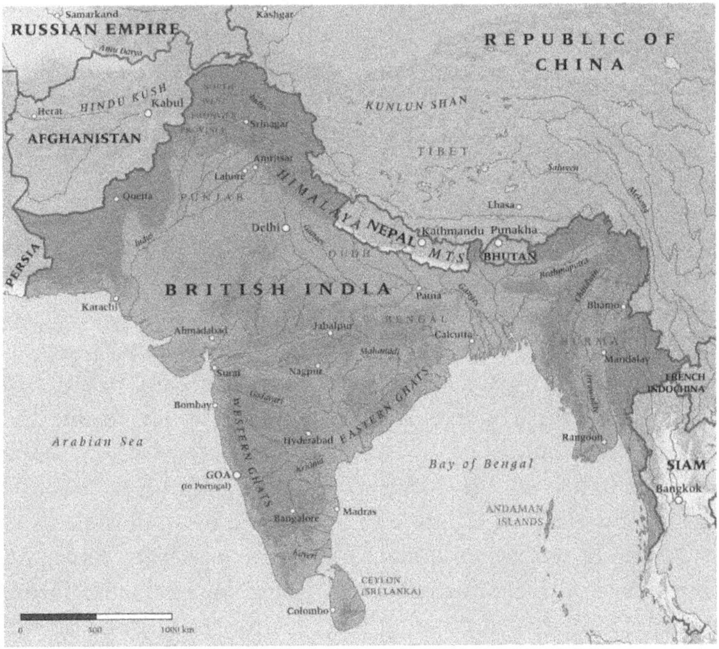

Source: Map courtesy of Geographx and the New Zealand Ministry for Culture and Heritage (https://nzhistory.govt.nz/media/photo/map-british-india-1914)

modernity to the lands it ruled, such as railways and schools, it was structured economically to suit the needs of Imperial Britain and its social structure was increasingly defined by the deepening racism of British rule (Peers and Gooptu, 2012).

China

China under the Qing dynasty (1636–1912) was Asia's most important economic and political power. Its concentration of wealth, sophisticated culture and sheer scale were unlike anything else on the continent and indeed anywhere in the world. The dynasty that had ruled for centuries was among its most successful. In its first 150 years, three long-serving emperors expanded China's empire on a hitherto unseen scale. They improved the economy through increased trade, agricultural innovation and centralized imperial administration. Although Qing China exported goods, notably silk, tea, sugar and porcelain, it imported very little. What was in effect a one-way trade with western powers and especially with Britain, meant that by excluding foreign traders from its large internal markets there was a significant drain on British silver, leading to fiscal imbalances in the empire. After several failed diplomatic efforts to convince Qing China to open up, in the early decades of the 19th century, traders began to work their way around the physical restrictions and they engaged in extensive smuggling operations to access the market. The most significant commodity being brought into China was opium. The empire tightened its controls and completely banned the narcotic, the main supplier of which was the EIC. This prompted Britain to use military force to extract trade concessions and gain territorial holdings (Platt, 2018). This led to a series of attacks from other empires across China's eastern seaboard, culminating in a range of territorial concessions as well as granting effective immunity to many Europeans and Americans from the need to adhere to Chinese laws and rules.

While Qing China was badly damaged economically, politically and diplomatically by foreign powers chipping away at its coast and establishing spheres of influence within its territory, the Qing state remained intact through until its ultimate collapse in 1911. Unlike India, where an external imperial power assumed paramount power, China was never fully given over. When the old empire finally collapsed it was replaced by a republic, led by Sun Yat-sen. It then fell into a civil war as the nationalists, who had established the republic, fought with the communists for the future of a land that was defined by borders

Figure 2.2: Map of China in 1927

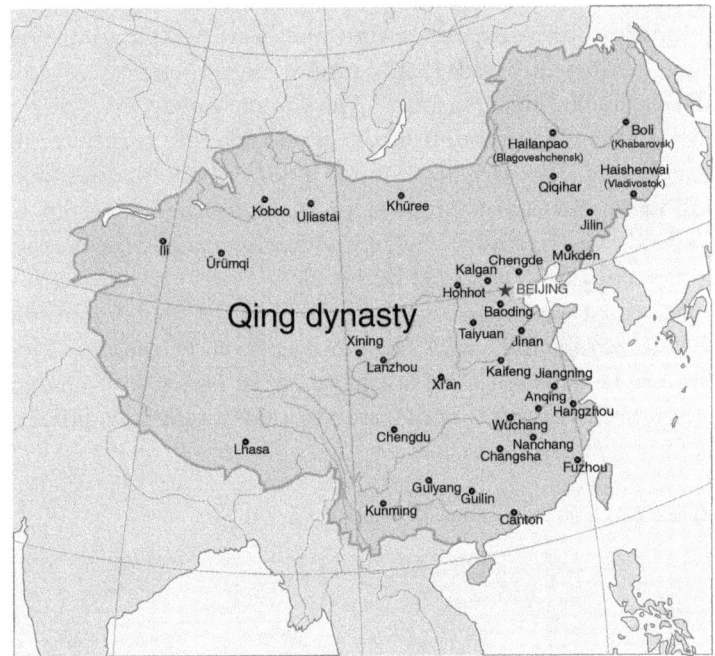

Source: TimeMap of World History

(see Figure 2.2) and a vast population that was ethnically highly diverse created by Qing imperial expansion.

Southeast Asia

In the 18th century, what we now call Southeast Asia comprised a wide range of political systems with kingdoms, such as Chakri Siam and Ngyuen Vietnam, sultanates, such as Aceh, Sulu and Brunei, as well as colonial holdings both expansive, in the Philippines, and toeholds in critical ports, such as Melaka and Pinang.

Within a century, however, this diverse space was overrun by European powers (Tarling, 1992). Britain used India as the foundation for its expansion into Southeast Asia. It controlled Burma from the mid-19th century, then went on to rule Malaya, including Singapore. The Dutch ruled over what is now Indonesia, although in the immediate aftermath of the Napoleonic Wars Britain acquired a raft of Dutch possessions. Following the 1814 Anglo–Dutch treaty, they reverted to Holland, which through the 19th century expanded the breadth of its colony and direct nature of rule.

Indochina was progressively colonized by the French from the 1860s, with the full extent of control achieved by the early 20th century. Perhaps the most notable imperial presence to emerge in Southeast Asia came as the result of a war fought in a different

Figure 2.3: Southeast Asian colonial holdings 1914

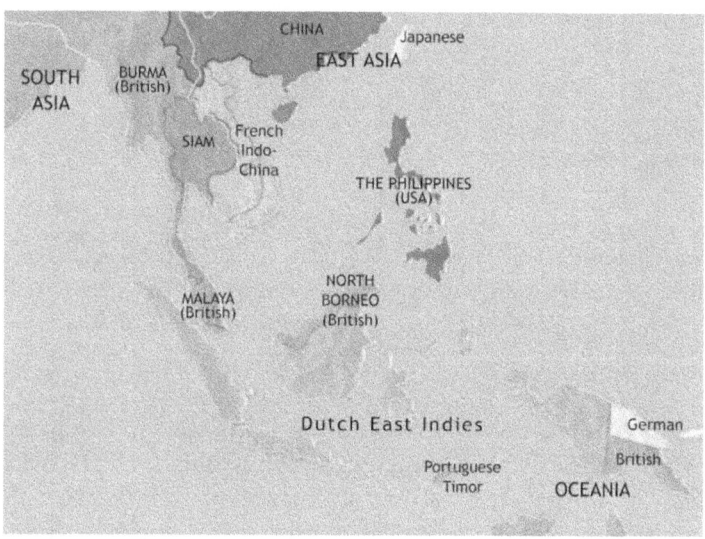

Source: TimeMap of World History (https://timemaps.com/history/south-east-asia-1914ad/)

hemisphere. The Philippines had been a Spanish colony but with America's victory in the Spanish–American War of 1898, the US became an instant imperial presence. What is now modern-day Thailand, then the Kingdom of Siam, was the only local power able to retain its independence from colonial pressures (see Figure 2.3).

In the 19th century the US emerged as a power in Asia, albeit initially at its fringes. Missionaries and traders from the country's western frontiers had been a regular presence across East Asia from the late 18th century onwards. But Washington did not begin to project American power into the region until the second half of the 19th century. This was in part because the country had not yet become the continent-wide power we know today, but also because the task was immensely challenging. America's presence in Asia began when Commodore Perry led a fleet of what the Japanese called 'black ships' and forced the country to open up to international trade in the 1860s. This was followed by the acquisition of the strategically critical Pacific Island territories of Samoa, Wake Island, Micronesia and the Hawaiian Islands. Most importantly, with America's defeat of Spain in 1898, the US became the colonial power of the extensive Philippine archipelago (Green, 2017: 56–113). Yet even as it may appear at first glance to be just another empire, the US' economic power and its attitude towards imperialism more generally was rather different from the Europeans. As a political and economic force, the US shifted from following the old patterns to adopt a much more ambiguous posture by the middle of the 20th century. The anti-imperial sentiments of the Atlantic Charter, driven by US President Roosevelt, sat uneasily with the American position in Asia, but reflected the larger dynamics in which older practices of empire collided with a more modern sensibility.

Japan

Japan's rapid emergence as an imperial power was the most remarkable transformation of the region's political and economic order during this time. Under the Tokugawa shogunate, established in 1603, Japan had cut itself off almost entirely from the outside world. By the mid-19th century, external powers had forced Japan to open up aspects of trade, led by US naval forces under Commodore Perry. These contributed to the weakening of Tokugawa rule and the overthrow of the old order, leading to the rapid modernization of the Japanese state, economy and society under the Meiji emperor (Hellyer and Fuess, 2020).

Through what some scholars have described as a top-down revolution (Trimberger, 1978) Japan was transformed. It rapidly developed a modern industrial economy, restructured its legal and financial systems and swiftly developed industrial infrastructure, such as ports, railways and roads. In its foreign policy it perceived the need to develop a powerful military and an assertive international posture to defend its interests in an international environment populated by highly competitive and predatory powers. Japanese elites formed the view that the country would have to expand its holdings beyond the home islands if it were to secure itself and keep up with the Western empires (Benson and Matsumura, 2001).

This led to increasing friction with Japan's neighbours that ultimately led to the 1894–95 Sino–Japanese War. Japan's victory in this conflict allowed Tokyo to acquire Taiwan in 1895, which was formalized in the Treaty of Shimonoseki, that ended the war. Following its defeat of Russia in 1905 – the first time an Asian power had vanquished a European empire in modern times – Japan absorbed Korea, hitherto a vassal of China and largely isolated from the outside, making it a protectorate of the nascent Japanese Empire. In 1910 it formally colonized Korea and retained the peninsula until its defeat in 1945. In the 1920s and increasingly in the 1930s, Japanese troops expanded their holdings in Manchuria, leading to the 1932 creation of the puppet state of Manchukuo with the last Qing emperor, Puyi, placed as its figurehead ruler. Figure 2.4 illustrates the extent of the Japanese Empire.

Figure 2.4: Maximum extent of Japan's empire

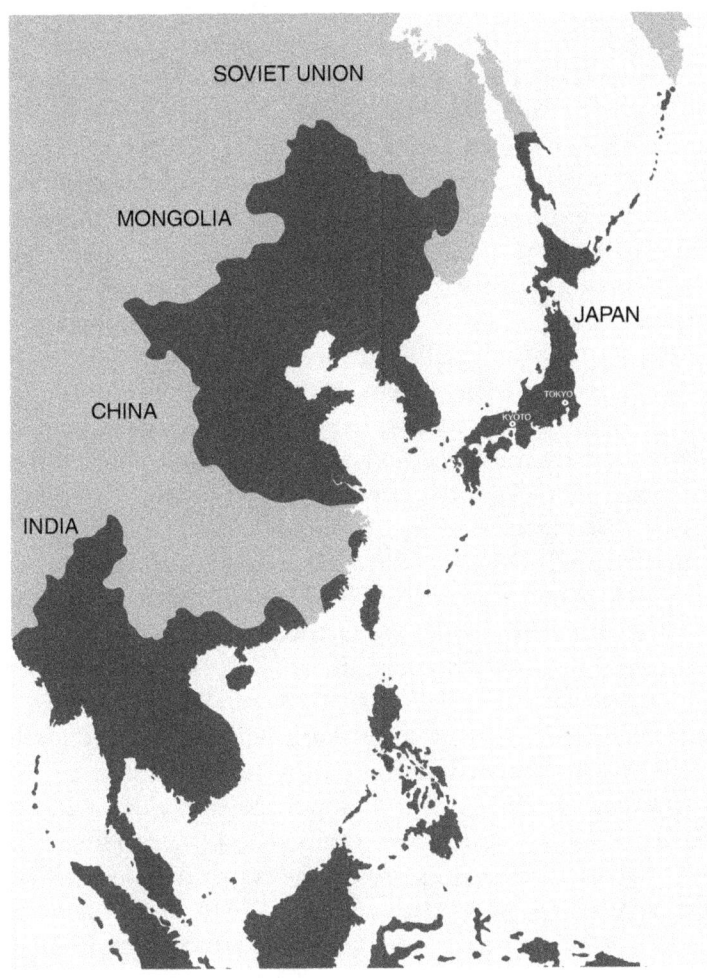

Source: iStock/iSidhe

Asia's war

In the mid-1930s almost all the people in Asia were ruled by other people's empires. British India sprawled from the mouth of the Persian Gulf to the Andaman Sea. Central Asia was locked into the Soviet Union, while the Netherlands, Britain, France and the US controlled virtually all of Southeast Asia. Japan had joined the imperial ranks and was on the march. It had seized Taiwan and Korea, and recently established Manchukuo out of the territories it had occupied in China. Asian peoples had virtually no say in their political or economic futures. But across the continent ideas of self-determination and nationalism were bubbling away, reacting against the cruel hand of colonization and helping to forge Asia as a political idea with which to advance anti-colonial ambitions as well as to carve out a distinct sense of identity. For now, however, these aspirations remained buried under layers of colonial control.

The dynamics of imperialism – the geopolitical manoeuvres of empires jostling for influence and advantage, and the economic systems created by colonial production, investment and trading relations – had drawn Asia into global networks, creating the outline of an incipient region. World War II catalysed a fundamental transformation of Asia's political and economic circumstances; it ended the age of imperialism.

Asia's war was longer than Europe's. Not only did it end in August of 1945 with the twin atomic bombings of Hiroshima and Nagasaki, whereas in Europe the war had ended in May of that year, but it also began before the 1939 Nazi invasion of Poland. Japan's imperial ambitions had led to conflicts through the 1930s. These became more significant as it pushed from its colony in Korea into Manchuria in 1931. Full-scale hostilities commenced in 1937 following the Marco Polo Bridge Incident (Frank, 2021). Just outside Beijing a relatively minor clash between the Imperial Japanese Army and China's republican forces swiftly escalated into open warfare. Japanese forces then pushed through to occupy large swathes of Northeast and Central China. Their rapid gains were achieved not just because of superior military technology and war-fighting techniques, but also because of the weaknesses created by the Chinese Civil War that was entering its tenth year. Although successful in China, Japanese forces never controlled all of what had been the Qing Empire.

Until 1941, the conflict was understood to be essentially a Sino–Japanese war. After Tokyo joined the Axis Powers in 1940, the US and the UK embargoed Japan in mid-1941, prompting the country to move rapidly to attack Southeast Asia and the Western Pacific. Starting in December of that year with the Pearl Harbor bombings, followed by swift assaults, humiliating the British, French, Dutch and Americans as Japan seized Malaya, Indochina, parts of Indonesia, the Philippines and a string of islands in the Pacific. Ultimately, Tokyo was overstretched and under-resourced, and despite a tenacious and unrelenting approach to combat, it could not maintain its gains in the Pacific. The US and its allies broke the Japanese Navy and through this established the capacity to attack Japan's home islands, leading ultimately to defeat (Hastings, 2008).

Japan was a transformative power in this period. In the early 1860s, it was largely closed off to the outside world; within 50 years it had started to seize territory to meet its needs and self-styled identity as a global empire. It followed the European imperial playbook, ruthlessly exploiting its advantages, expropriating wealth, treating subject peoples terribly and using racial and cultural hierarchies to organize the imperial project. Its approach was inspired by the same callous logic of expropriation and subjugation that was at the heart of British, French, Dutch and American rule. Japan showed that empire was not just something that only white Europeans did (Beasley, 1991). Yet the very fact of its non-Western origins and the speed with which it had dispossessed the UK, France, the Netherlands and the US helped to undercut European imperialism while also undermining the idea of empires as a legitimate enterprise.

War as a catalyst of change

Empire was the dominant fact of life until the late 1930s, but after the war circumstances were transformed. Beyond the obvious devastation that it brought, the conflict destroyed three critical facets of empire. In material terms the war undercut the ability of imperial powers to rule in the old way. The British, Dutch and French simply could not afford to retain the pre-war modes of operation, although it took some time for them to recognize these realities. The nature of reconstruction at home, the creation of social welfare states and the changing political economy of Europe meant that colonial holdings could no longer be sustained. From the cost of the military required to defend widespread interests to the desperate need to focus on the home country, empires had literally become unaffordable.

Even though Japan had been a cruel occupying force, its rapid success and the ease with which it seized Europeans' holdings helped prick the bubble of racial superiority that had been central to imperialism. The fall of Hong Kong and Singapore were particularly emblematic of the hollowness of British power and prestige. Empire is necessarily built on a pedestal of hubris and that was inflated by the racial and cultural assumptions of the European powers. The war wrecked not just the sense of superiority that Western powers had in themselves, but the horrors of war and Nazism in particular put paid to the idea that Western culture and civilization were inherently and necessarily superior to all others.

The war ended the idea of empire as a legitimate idea or way of ruling. The anti-colonial sentiments that had been stirring prior to the war were invigorated by Japanese invasion as well as the role of subject populations in the fighting. These become powerful forces after 1945. In part this change was driven by the US and the USSR sharing a desire to see Europe's enemies unwound. While this was to a degree self-interested; the weakening of Europe's empires strengthened the respective hands of the US and the USSR internationally. There was also a genuine sense that the imperialism of the old kind was no longer the order of the day.

After the war

World War II in Asia ceased with the armistice of 15 August 1945. The nature of the war's conclusion was unlike Europe's and not just because of the atomic weapons that ended the fighting. In Europe, Nazi forces had been physically repelled from the territory they had occupied. By contrast, in Asia, the allied strategy was to cut off Japan's supply lines across the Pacific and attack the home archipelago (Renzi and Roehrs, 1991). This won the day strategically but left the curious situation in which Japan's imperial forces remained in place across China, Korea and Southeast Asia. In some famous examples, Japanese troops refused to surrender and stayed on for years and, in some cases, decades. But the overwhelming majority surrendered and handed over authority to the allied command. The question of to whom the allied military authority should then be turned over was vexed. France and the Netherlands, for example, expected that things would revert to how they had been before the war. In Indochina and Indonesia, however, nationalist forces demanded to be given their freedom.

For the old imperialists, the challenge of what to do after the war was twofold. They had depended on their colonial holdings for economic growth and prosperity prior to the war and, as they sought to rebuild their industrial base as well as, in most cases, begin to create modern welfare states, the need for the economic capacity that the colonies provided had never been greater. Yet to retain empires was itself not just an extremely costly endeavour after the anti-colonial nationalism that had been accelerated by the Japanese occupation, they would very literally have a fight on their hands to keep hold of what they had taken.

Although it was not yet clear in the mid-1940s, the war had fundamentally reset the global economy. In a basic sense the old power centres had been wiped out, with the US and the USSR coming out of the war as the pre-eminent economic players. Washington had an unparalleled concentration of global GDP because the country's physical isolation from the conflict had protected its economy. As the empires began to crumble, so too did the trade, investment and production networks that they had created and sustained. Postcolonial elites started to think about how to make their way in the world, and the opportunities and risks of the global economy were being reshaped by the newly established Bretton Woods system, the structures of the Soviet economic bloc, as well as the dynamic way that the capitalist economy developed after the war.

From 1945, the geopolitical and geoeconomic space of Asia began to be viewed differently by actors on the international stage. It was no longer a zone of imperial conquest and rivalry, instead it had become a place of significance in its own right, increasingly on its own terms. This change in perspective had been shaped directly by the experiences of war in which allied combat in the Pacific Theatre, as it was styled by global command, had been organized into three zones of operation: the Southeast Asian Command (SEAC), the Southwest Pacific Area Command and the China Command. The China Command was essentially a means to support the Kuomintang (KMT) and CPC efforts to resist and repel Japanese forces. The Pacific Command was the main operational component to prosecute the efforts to crush Japan's navy, remove its forces from key islands in the Pacific and attack Japan's home islands, while SEAC was designed to combat Japan's imperial forces in Burma, Malaya and Sumatra. Following the armistice in 1945, SEAC's remit broadened to include the Dutch East Indies and Indochina, and shifted from military operations to government and transitional political arrangements. What began as a logistical war-fighting division of labour to manage the huge combat operations in Asia had become a mechanism that was responsible for millions of people who had, in relatively short order, shifted violently from one colonial regime to another (Dennis, 1987). SEAC was also tasked with decommissioning Japan's war machine and its colonial administrative apparatus in Southeast Asia. But SEAC's most contentious role was to act on the expectation among the allies that it would oversee the return of the colonies to the European powers in the face of the demands of anti-imperial nationalists.

The war also completely reconfigured Asia's balance of power. Japan had been wiped out militarily. It was then occupied by the Americans who forced a democratic constitution on the country that required Japan to renounce war and not maintain a military. British forces would never again be able to project meaningful military force in the region, while the French and the Dutch had themselves long been subordinated to British power. Most importantly, the Pacific had effectively become an American lake. In the decades prior to the war, Asia had experienced what scholars call a multipolar geopolitical environment. That is a situation in which power is spread more or less evenly across multiple countries, with each having distinct advantages and none being able to dominate. In 1945, the US stood alone. While the USSR was a resident power and its military had, very late in the piece, joined the war against Japan, it was ultimately a second-order armed force.

America, however, did not expect to remain the primary power indefinitely. Even with its wealth and industrial capacity, Washington wanted to demobilize much of its army, navy and air force. Policy planners anticipated that the end of Japanese imperialism in China would mean the return to civil war between the nationalist KMT and Mao's communists. The expectation among elites in Washington and across the region was that the numerically superior, better funded and supported KMT would ultimately prevail. No one expected that a KMT-ruled republican China would be a liberal democracy, at least not under the leadership of Chiang Kai-Shek, but it would assuredly be aligned to the US. From Washington's point of view, nationalist China would act as a strategic anchor for the region that would allow for the scaling back of the US presence. Mao's 1949 victory meant that a cornerstone of US planning was swept away. Having concluded that Asia was a theatre of strategic significance for Washington over the longer term, America needed to swiftly develop a new strategy (Munro-Leighton, 1992).

On 2 September 1945 the USS Missouri was moored in Tokyo Bay. It hosted a stellar array of dignitaries, including US Supreme Commander General Douglas MacArthur, US Fleet Admiral Chester Nimitz, Soviet Lieutenant General Kuzma Derevyanko and Australia's General Sir Thomas Blamey among others, who had gathered to witness Japan's signature of the instrument of surrender, formally bringing to an end not just World War II but the age of imperialism in Asia.

The backdrop to the ceremony on the Missouri was a Tokyo in ruins, still smouldering from the firebombing inflicted in the first part of the year. The USSR remained an ally of the West, but relations had already become testy, with the USSR seizing islands to the immediate north of Hokkaido against Washington's wishes. Moscow ultimately signed a separate armistice with Tokyo. The Cold War was not far over the horizon. The age of imperialism would soon be replaced by a turbulent period of decolonization, with its attendant conflicts. States had to be constructed out of the remains of empire. Disparate nations and ethnicities knitted into coherent modern societies and economies reorganized to provide newly independent peoples the means to make their way in the world. The Soviet–American competition, with its terrifying nuclear shadow, would swiftly become a critical determinant of life in this part of the world. Asia remained little more than a large expanse on the map, with disparate peoples and cultures linked in uneven and at times highly limited ways. But as the Cold War's ideological and geopolitical contest became the driving rhythm of world politics, Asia's subregions begin to coalesce, and one could make out the first faint traces of the integrative forces that would come to forge modern Asia within two generations.

Dynamics of decolonization

If empire was the region's defining characteristic going into World War II, it follows that the ways in which those empires were unwound would be of critical importance to the region's future. Once Japan's overextended supply lines were snapped, most expected things to revert to how they had been for many decades. Against those complacent expectations the imperial structures were unpicked and, in some cases, violently overthrown after many years of conflict.

A distinction should be drawn between the unravelling of the Japanese Empire and the holdings of the Western imperial powers. When it was defeated, Japan had the most extensive imperial possessions in East Asia. To its colonies in Taiwan and Korea it had added large parts of China, French Indochina, Malaya, the Dutch East Indies and the Philippines.

The four decades of Japanese rule in Korea came to an end with the US military forces seizing critical parts of the peninsula. The viciousness of Japanese rule had generated nationalist resistance and there was no shortage of ideas about what an independent Korean republic might look like. In 1943, the Allies had determined that Japan would be deprived of all the territory it had conquered when it was defeated. During the war's closing months, the allied powers agreed that a liberated Korea would, in time, become an independent state, but they deemed that an international trusteeship would rule until the Koreans were thought to be able to do so for themselves; North Atlantic condescension remained powerful. The Soviets had only joined the war against Japan at the last moment – on 8 August 1945, between the two atomic attacks – and the Red Army rapidly moved down the peninsula. The US was concerned that Soviet forces might occupy all of Korea and expand its sphere of influence, as was already becoming evident in Europe. Washington hastily devised a plan to divide the peninsula into two zones of occupation, akin to the four zones controlling defeated Germany. Two colonels, Dean Rusk and Chris Bonesteel, determined that Korea would be divided in half, with the 38th parallel serving as the dividing line. This line was chosen essentially because it meant that the peninsula was roughly in two equal parts and that Seoul was in the American zone. The two zones reflected neither existing historical or administrative boundaries nor a logical economic division.

The US proposal was swiftly accepted by the Soviets, which surprised the senior American officials by all accounts. Neither the Korean people nor Korean elites were consulted about how their land would be split (Lee, 2006). The intention was that there would, as in Germany, be a four-power trusteeship for the whole peninsula but the suspicions between West and East and the hostility of Koreans to the trusteeship closed that down swiftly. Between 1946 and 1948 the Soviets and Americans occupied their zones but their efforts to negotiate a post-occupation future failed. The question was then turned to the United Nations (UN), but the USSR would not accept the fledgling institution's suggestions. Elections were held in the South, with Rhee Syngman becoming the first president of the Republic of Korea (ROK), which was formally established on 15 August 1948. The Soviet-backed Democratic People's Republic of Korea (DPRK) was founded on 9 September that year and Kim Il-sung installed as its leader.

Taiwan had become part of the Qing Empire in the late 17th century. Following the Sino–Japanese War of 1894–95, it was ceded to imperial Japan even though it had not been a point of conflict in the war itself. Unlike Korea, where Japan's defeat immediately threw into relief the geopolitical challenges of decolonization in the context of a nascent Cold War, Taiwan's standing was given little consideration. The island would revert to China and, during wartime planning, it was nationalist China that sat at the negotiating table with the allied powers. With the signature of surrender in September 1945, Japanese forces were instructed to hand over occupied territories and the KMT established control over the island. The Chinese Civil War recommenced in 1946 and Taiwan was of little concern to either side until 1949 when, upon its defeat, the KMT found itself with a redoubt to which it retreated and from which it hoped to eventually return and rule all of China. To this day, the CPC regards the independence of Taiwan as the last remaining remnant of China's division and occupation by foreign powers.

Following its victory in the Spanish–American War, the Philippines was ceded to the US in 1898. After the three-year American–Philippines War, a civil administration was established by Washington in 1902. Filipino political elites pressed for representation and eventual independence from American rule and, in 1935, the Philippines Commonwealth was established with a plan for a ten-year transition from self-rule to independence. Japan attacked the Philippines shortly after Pearl Harbor and controlled much of the archipelago until the 1945 surrender. Japan's colonial period was particularly brutal and the extended battle to liberate the country was by some margin the largest and deadliest of the Pacific Theatre, with fighting continuing right through until September 1945. On 4 July 1946, the US recognized the Philippines' independence, and the two established a mutual defence treaty in 1951 (McCoy, 1981).

Japan had ruled French Indochina through a combination of direct military administration and collaboration with some French colonists linked to the Vichy regime. Upon its defeat, Japan handed over the territory to SEAC in 1945 and specifically to General Douglas Gracey, who had landed in Saigon (current-day Ho Chi Minh City) with 20,000 British and Indian troops in September of that year. France made clear that it intended to re-establish its colonies, but that it was prepared to give some concessions to self-rule. This plan was stoutly resisted by Vietnamese nationalists, who had been emboldened by Japanese occupation as well as by communist forces. Vietnam had declared its independence on 2 September 1945, before the SEAC forces had landed, and, in 1946, there appeared to be a tentative diplomatic equilibrium struck between France and Vietnam. This did not last, and open conflict broke out late in the year. The First Indochina War was fought, primarily between French and Vietnamese forces, until 1954, when the Geneva Accords created four independent states out of what had been French Indochina: the Democratic Republic of Vietnam, the State of Vietnam, the Kingdom of Cambodia and the Kingdom of Laos (Waite, 2012). The cartography of the division mapped almost precisely the administrative boundaries of the French colony.

The Dutch, like the French, saw Japan's occupation as an interruption of what it hoped would be continued colonial rule of the extensive archipelago that was richly endowed with natural resources. The Japanese had actively encouraged nationalist sentiment and administrative structures to facilitate their rule. Following the announcement of Japanese surrender in August 1945, pro-independence leaders Sukarno and Mohammed Hatta declared Indonesian sovereignty. A self-styled preparatory committee for Indonesian independence elected Sukarno president and Hatta vice-president, it drafted a constitution and created a national committee to assist Sukarno as a quasi-interim government (Dahm, 1969). The challenge of ruling an underdeveloped postcolonial state spread over thousands of islands was immense to begin with. Added to that was the fact that Dutch rule had often been through local intermediaries, who stood to lose out economically and politically from the creation of a republic. This created a fragile and combustible political environment. The Dutch requested help to reclaim its holdings and SEAC forces arrived in September 1945, leading to a series of conflicts between those attempting to resist the reimposition of Dutch rule and various allied forces. Struggle and, at times, intense warfare between republican forces and the Dutch lasted nearly five years before UN mediation allowed Indonesia to achieve complete independence in 1949.

British India was the world's largest colonial operation and, as it was never taken by Japan, it followed a distinctive path unwinding the imperial project. While most of India had been directly ruled by British administrators since the mid-19th century, this was not universal. Many parts of the country were indirectly ruled through local intermediaries themselves a mix of princes, kings and administrators. While formally sovereign, they were ultimately subordinate to British power. In the 1920s and 1930s, independence movements had gathered political momentum following a 1919 reform that gave some limited responsibility to regional governments. The nationalist movement led by the Congress Party and Mohandas Gandhi prompted a mix of reform and repression by the British, leading, in 1935, to changes that gave much greater autonomy to regional governments. Elections in 1937 consolidated Congress' power in key provinces across much of India. Although Congress was the dominant nationalist grouping, the Muslim League was also growing in influence, particularly in the parts of India where adherents of Islam were a majority. The League's aim was to establish a separate state for Muslim Indians.

World War II further exacerbated tensions between rulers and subjects as India's resources were necessary to support the war effort, and the prospect of Japanese invasion seemed possible in 1942. The British effectively conceded that independence would occur after the war and the election of the Labour government in 1945 ensured that the move would be relatively swift. While the British had wanted to retain a unified India, the political dynamics of anti-colonial elites and the imperative to move quickly meant that British India became two independent states in 1947, India and Pakistan (White-Spunner, 2017). Pakistan itself was in two parts, West Pakistan and East Pakistan. The latter would become Bangladesh after a civil war in the 1970s. Partition, as the division of British India into the two successor republics was known, led to one of the largest movements of population in history. Hindus fled Pakistan and Muslims moved in huge numbers in the other direction, due to the communal violence that had accompanied the independence struggles. Ceylon, which had never been part of British India formally, became independent Sri Lanka in 1948. Burma, which had been administratively carved out of British India in 1937, also achieved independence in 1948.

Conclusion

Following the cataclysm of the war, empire was defeated as an idea and imperial powers lacked either the will or capacity to carry on in the face of formally subject peoples fighting to chart their own course. With remarkable speed states were forged out of the shells of empire. Decolonization left several critical markers on modern Asia. Perhaps the most visible of these are the maps; the region's modern political cartography is a direct product of colonialism. Many of today's borders, such as those between Burma and India, or among the states of Indochina, for example, were lines drawn by colonial administrators. Other boundary lines were newly created by imperial powers as part of the rapid-fire post-war imperatives to decolonize, such as the 38th parallel between North and South Korea and the borders between India and Pakistan.

Decolonization is a bland word to describe what was in many cases a violent and deeply traumatic process. Millions were killed in Vietnam's wars. Indonesia's struggle to stand on its own, while not as large-scale, was nonetheless violent and created a legacy of trauma, resentment and social cleavage. The partition of British India unleashed communal violence, if not a formal conflict, that also killed millions. The process and outcome of decolonization cast a long shadow, creating enduring resentment, geopolitical tensions and a sense of 'unfinished business' that continues to percolate to this day.

The division of the Korean Peninsula and Taiwan are the two most significant illustrations of this. The cartographic fact of Taiwan's existence was and remains unacceptable in the minds of CPC leaders. In the 1950s this led to a number of crises in the Taiwan Strait and the fact that the island republic's leadership held the China seat at the UN in those years further rankled. The Korean War's bitter legacy of death and destruction was augmented by the long-standing fear that the war, which has never formally ended, could reignite at any moment. India and Pakistan were set on a path of rivalry and antipathy that has erupted regularly into military clashes and political violence. In Southeast Asia, anti-colonial conflicts persisted for years, including not just the wars in Indochina but also low-intensity conflict between Malaysia and Indonesia over the borders that were drawn between the two. Malaysia had been created out of British Malaya, Singapore and the separate British colonies of North Borneo and Sarawak. The latter two on the island of Borneo shared a border with Indonesia, over which the conflict was fought in the mid-1960s.

Prior to colonization, Asia in general and Southeast Asia in particular had long experienced fluid movements of religious and ethnic groups pursuing economic opportunities and the expansion of faith. Colonial administrations froze that movement and locked populations into colonial structures that, when they became successor states, created in many parts of the region ethnic and religious tensions that persist to this day.

Asia was, like many parts of the world, dragged into the structures of the modern global economy. In both its political and economic structures, the colonial encounter established the basic contours of the modern region. The war that brought the era of imperialism to an end, and its aftermath, laid down the bedrock of some of Asia's most enduring disputes. If imperialism and war created the foundations for the making of modern Asia, the arrival of the Cold War's ideological and geopolitical competition established the structural centrepiece of the region we recognize today.

3

Cold War to Long Peace

For elites in the West, the Cold War made clear that Asia was a zone of critical importance to the dynamics of global politics. The Cold War here refers to two distinct but related things. First, it was the geopolitical and ideological competition between the USSR and US, and their respective allies, partners and subordinate powers, that was the master strategic dynamic of international affairs from the late 1940s until the early 1990s. Second, the Cold War was a global contest for military supremacy and at its heart it was a struggle about how human societies should be organized. It waxed and waned in intensity over five decades, beginning with the breakdown of the grand alliance that had been formed to defeat the Axis powers and ending with the collapse of the USSR in 1991. It was 'cold' in the sense that there was no direct conflict between the two main protagonists, but it was an intense affair that entailed many wars, in which the two sides fought indirectly.

The Cold War is critical to the story of Asia's formation and its futures, for a number of reasons. First, it was during this period that Asian states became fully sovereign actors on the global stage. Second, after the European continent, from which the conflict first burst forth, Asia was the most important zone of competition and where the Cold War's hottest conflicts were fought. Third, the dynamics of the Cold War competition played a critical role in determining how Asian states and societies developed. Without providing an overview of this period of Asia's development one cannot fully understand the manner in which the continent became bound together in the 1990s and 2000s.

Cold War

Asia's Cold War had two distinct phases, with the normalization of relations between the PRC and the US as the hinge point between them. The first of these, from the late 1940s through to the late 1970s, was a time in which the notion of a 'cold' war in Asia seemed like a cruel joke, given the scale of conflict and communal violence in Korea, Indochina, Indonesia and South Asia. The second period, from the late 1970s to the early 1990s, is notable for the almost complete absence of major conflict and the dramatic period of economic growth which this made possible. In a remarkably short period, Asia moved from being the most war-prone part of the world – from the 1950s through to the mid-1970s Asia endured the highest numbers of people killed in war zones, both combatants and civilians – to one of its most peaceful. The idea of an Asian miracle was borne from the remarkable expansion of economic growth that occurred in this period, and the speed with which it moved away from large-scale violence should be recognized as at least as miraculous as the achievements in material prosperity.

The Korean War brought the Cold War to Asia and, in turn, ensured that the continent would be ensnared in the global Soviet–American competition (Haruki, 2014). American planning for post-war Asia had been scrambled by the communist victory in China in 1949. US leaders had anticipated that Chiang-kai Shek would defeat Mao's communists and that his strongman rule in China could be an anchor for the region's strategic balance. Rather than being able to rely on nationalist China, Washington faced a unified communist block that stretched from the Baltic to the South China Sea. The US had hoped to reduce its military forces based in Asia after Japan's defeat, and it now had to hastily devise a new approach to maintaining a strategic balance in a geographically complex and widespread theatre of operations. In response, the US developed the idea of establishing 'a defensive perimeter', which was a line across East Asia that would have to be held in the face of communist expansion. In January 1950, US Secretary of State Dean Acheson sketched out that line at a National Press Club address which ran, he said, 'along the Aleutians to Japan and then ... to the Ryukyus ... from the Ryukyus to the Philippine Islands' (Acheson, 1950). The Korean peninsula was not included in the defensive perimeter. This led the North Korean leadership to conclude that their ambitions to spread DPRK rule over the entirety of Korea would not meet strong American objection. They decided to launch an attack on the South, prompting a long and bitter war. At its conclusion, after three years, with millions dead, the geopolitical circumstances had not been changed at all. After the war, the North and South's borders were as they had been at the start of the conflict in June 1950 (Cummings, 2011).

If the efforts to unify the peninsula failed, they did succeed in confirming in the minds of Washington's political and policy leaders that communism in Asia was an expansionary force and that an active strategy would be needed to see off its challenge. The Korean War also meant that American attitudes towards Japan changed. US forces had occupied the fallen empire from 1945 and, in 1947, imposed a hastily written constitution that stripped the emperor of all but a symbolic role in a liberal democratic system (Dower, 1999). That constitution renounced Japan's right to use military power so as to ensure that militarism did not return and that the US would not have to fight back some kind of resurgent fascism in Asia. The US wanted and indeed needed a democratic Japan, but it did not want an independently minded one that had a meaningful military capacity. Attitudes in Washington began to change in the face of communism's expansion. A wide-ranging communist challenge in Asia meant that US forces based in Japan would need to be able to deployed across the region. That might leave Japan vulnerable, as the earlier idea had been that US forces would defend a militarily denuded Japan. Reluctantly, US elites recognized that Japan would have to rearm so that it could defend itself as US forces would be required across a broader strategic canvass than had previously been imagined.

This first part of the Cold War has been described by scholars as one of bipolarity (Yahuda, 1996), reflecting the dominance of the two centres of military power: the US on the one hand, and a Sino–Soviet bloc on the other. While this first phase did indeed comprise two main components, there remained a considerable degree of strategic and ideological complexity across the continent. Some countries were clearly attracted to the ideals of one or the other side and sought to use the Cold War to their advantage, but others saw the dangers of being caught up in this rivalry. The Soviets and Americans each represented distinctive models of economic development, one based on Leninist politics and command economy industrialization, the other on liberal democracy and market principles. There was a starkness for some that was disconcerting as Washington and Moscow viewed the choices of the postcolonial states in zero-sum terms. In response to this, many Asian elites tried to carve out a distinctive path. This was in part to avoid the treacherous waters of military competition as well as to try to find some middle path for their political and economic systems that might better suit their needs than the transplantation of Soviet industrialization or free market capitalism to vulnerable circumstances. Many states in the region began to position themselves in a posture that came to be known as non-alignment. Although it did not formally launch the non-aligned movement, the 1955 Bandung Conference that established the Afro–Asian People's Solidarity Organization was an early effort to open space between the Cold War poles and it was also an attempt to forge diplomatic solidarity among postcolonial states trying to navigate a challenging international environment.

In Southeast Asia this effort would ultimately fail, at least in the terms originally conceived. This was partly due to the low-intensity conflicts between Indonesia and Malaysia in the early 1960s, as well as the inability to wall off Cold War dynamics from the domestic and foreign policy priorities of newly independent states. The cost of constructing the basic administrative function of statehood, as well as developing an economic structure to support large and growing populations and defending one's interests in a contested security environment was immense. It was impossible to ignore the appeal of one side or the other. Equally, divisions within postcolonial states about the paths they should take mirrored the larger international division. Few Asian states were especially fond of democracy, with India and Japan being the only real exceptions, but sharp lines were drawn in many states between communist and anti-communist forces.

The US and its allies established the Southeast Asia Treaty Organization (SEATO) in 1954 to try to contain the communist challenge in that corner of the region. Yet the grouping, in spite of its name, failed to include any Southeast Asian states except Thailand and the Philippines and reflected a colonial era outlook, whereby external powers would handle strategic affairs on behalf of the local population. Its other members were the US, Australia, France, the UK, New Zealand and Pakistan. They dedicated very little resourcing in military terms and, although the alliance was cited by the US and Australia for their involvement in the Second Indochina War, the grouping had little longer-term impact (Buszynski, 1983). That war, however, was much more consequential.

This conflict, known as the Vietnam War in the US and other allied countries, was the Cold War's longest conflict. The 1954 Geneva Accords had created a communist-ruled North and a US-aligned South, as well as Laos and Cambodia. The North had never been satisfied with the division and, by the late 1950s, had begun an insurgency campaign against the fragile rule of Ngo Dinh Diem. Almost from the moment the Geneva Accords were signed, the US was convinced that the South had to be kept from being swallowed by communism because of fears of the advantage it would give Moscow. It also believed that the rest of Southeast Asia would swiftly follow South Vietnam down the road of communism.

Initially, US decision-makers thought that effective economic and political governance in the South, along with some support against insurgency, would suffice to see off the threat posed by the North. This failed and steadily the US escalated its involvement, leading to US forces playing a major combat role. Washington's perception of the conflict as a geopolitical and ideological one underestimated the nationalist motivation of Vietnamese leaders and combatants. Equally, as scholars have shown, the US approach to the war was marked by a failure to link its larger regional interests with the particularities of that conflict (Green, 2017). A war of national liberation in a relatively small and not strategically significant country should not have been the focus of so much blood and treasure for the US.

The intersection of Cold War global dynamics with regional ambitions and aspirations created an international environment in Asia that was much more uneven and fluid than in Europe. This was in part due to the different ways Asian states were positioning themselves. Some countries, notably Japan, South Korea and the Philippines, had formal alliances with the US, while others, such as Indonesia and India, positioned themselves between the Soviets and Americans. During this period of the Cold War, the PRC was aligned with the Soviet Union, yet it retained agency and independence in a way that was quite different from the USSR's satellites in Eastern Europe: Beijing was by no means another Bucharest.

The US' approach to the region was critical. How it would approach its contest with Moscow in a physical environment that was very different from Europe's was not at all clear. The mix of maritime and continental interests, the sheer distance from American power and the combination of a small number of very large powers and a larger number of smaller powers made determining a strategy difficult. In the first instance, the US developed a vision associated with Dean Acheson, that the US should develop positions of strength in the region that would dissuade Soviet adventurism. These were centred around the alliances the US had signed in the 1950s that helped it overcome the problem of distance by providing bases from which to project power (Hara, 2015). Yet Washington was unable to develop a coherent way of distinguishing between its larger interests in the region and the specific challenges of a given crisis, leading to the mistake of Vietnam. Policy elites had a clear sense of the larger objective, to prevent a power hostile to the US from dominating Asia. However, in this first phase of the Cold War, the US failed to devise an effective way of advancing that goal in a manner that was affordable, both politically and economically.

One of the most important and overlooked dimensions of the Cold War crashing into the region was the effect the conflict had on the region's economy. Without the Korean or Second Indochina wars, it is difficult to imagine Asia becoming the economic success story with which it is associated today. Even though Japan's rapid modernization following the Meiji Restoration in 1868 had shown that non-Western economies could move swiftly to become powerful industrial economies, in the shadow of World War II the prevailing economic wisdom asserted that it was essentially impossible to break the chains of economic dependence that colonialism had created. The difficulty of accumulating sufficient concentrations of capital and creating a skilled workforce to fuel industrial production was fearsome, given their circumstances. By the 1990s, however, Asia's 'tigers' had created their economic miracle (Birdsall et al, 1993). How had first Japan and then South Korea, Taiwan, Hong Kong, Thailand, Malaysia and Singapore achieved sustained levels of economic growth? The take-off had occurred in the 1950s for Japan and then in the 1960s and 1970s for the others, with Thailand and Malaysia being the last to join the 'miracle' club in the 1980s.

Much scholarly work has examined the success of these economies, with many pointing to the beneficial role played by a strong and interventionist state that was able to drive the development of an export-focused model for industrialization. There needed to be markets into which these economies could sell their goods, and an open American market that was willing and able to absorb the exports was also important. Prudent fiscal policy, high savings rates, strong work ethics and cultures of entrepreneurship and thrift were also seen as important by scholars. Yet a vital factor, that is sometimes forgotten, was one normally associated not with economic growth but with destruction: war.

Asia's hot wars in Korea and then Indochina played a pivotal role in priming the pump of economic growth that in time became synonymous with the region (Stubbs, 2018). The wars had two effects, one directly economic and the other institutional. Economically, the prosecution of the Korean War required immense organizational and supply efforts. Japan's location, its industrial base and managerial capacity meant that it was able to become effectively a logistics hub and resupply centre for the US war effort. This provided a dramatic acceleration of the country's re-industrialization and drove capital investment into critical sectors of the economy. The economic pump-priming was to be replicated in parts of Southeast Asia with the Second Indochina War, with Korea and Taiwan this time able to benefit from what was, in effect, a kind of military Keynesianism. Equally, war helped drive the development of strong and effective centralized states that were able to promote industrial policy, develop export substitution models and attract capital investment. Without the prompts of war, the likelihood of this occurring so swiftly would have been much lower.

During the first few decades of the Cold War, Asia's distinct subregions had varying levels of economic success and there were very uneven connections between them. Central Asian states were subsumed within the Soviet system, which was itself largely isolated from the capitalist economic order. Japan enjoyed the greatest level of economic growth during the Cold War period, rapidly rebuilding from the ashes of war. Taiwan and South Korea also grew, following Japan's model of selective protection of its economy, strong industrial policy with close relations between the big industrial conglomerates and the state, and a heavy emphasis on export-focused industrialization. They also benefitted from Japanese firms moving production facilities to those economies to take advantage of lower costs as well as other locational benefits to do with tax, regulation and market proximity. Southeast Asia's tigers followed this example, also supplemented by Japanese inbound investment. Economic ties between Northeast and Southeast Asia would not begin in earnest until the Cold War's second phase. And once those economic connections were made, the links between Northeast and Southeast Asia were primarily investment and development assistance; trade, whether components or finished goods, was limited as the states of the region largely competed with one another for investment from and exports to Western Europe and North America.

During this early period, India and South Asia's other states settled into a pattern in which their economic and security interests operated quite separately from those in Northeast and Southeast Asia. The Cold War roiled in South Asia as well, leading to hot wars and amplified strategic and ideological contestation. India and China's border war in 1962 and the war that created Bangladesh out of East Pakistan in the early 1970s were driven by specific bilateral clashes of interest as well as interwoven with the dynamics of Cold War competition. Bangladesh's creation shifted the strategic balance in South Asia, strengthening India's hand considerably due to the obvious reduction in size and influence of Pakistan. The US had diplomatically and military supported Pakistan for some time due to India's collaboration with the USSR; Bangladesh's independence consequently also reduced American influence in South Asia. That said, Washington did not place anywhere near as much importance on that part of Asia as it did with the Northeast and Southeast regions.

If the US had been keen to separate China from the USSR in the 1950s, by the time of the actual divorce of the two communist partners that came to the surface in a short sharp border war in 1969, it was so preoccupied by the conflict in Vietnam that it was unable to act on the division in the short term. Around that time, however, the mood in Washington turned, particularly following North Vietnam's successful 1968 Tet Offensive. By 1970 or so, the US recognized that it could not achieve its aims and had to work out how to extricate itself without ceding too much geopolitically or suffering too much humiliation. The acrimony between China and the USSR provided the opportunity to change the strategic balance in Asia and thus to allow Washington to get out of a costly and embarrassing war. And this diplomatic manoeuvre would transform Asia and, in turn, the world.

ASEAN was also established in this period, with the Bangkok Treaty bringing it into being signed in 1967 (Narine, 2002). The group was established to improve political and diplomatic ties among the five founding members, Singapore, Malaysia, Indonesia, Thailand and the Philippines, and to reduce the chances that Cold War geopolitics would destabilize their state and nation building efforts. Its creation had been made possible by the overthrow of Indonesia's president Sukarno by General Suharto in 1967. Suharto's seizure of power meant that all five ASEAN members were led by anti-communist nationalists, all had varying kinds of authoritarian political systems and all were keen to advance economically on broadly capitalist lines. While the group ultimately served to reinforce elites' domestic agendas, it provided an institutional reflection of the incipient sense of regional identity and political purpose. In time, it would contribute to Asia's more stable strategic setting.

Asia's long peace begins

If the first part of the Cold War in Asia was marked by major wars and frequent violence, the second half was noteworthy for the almost entire absence of conflict. For around three decades after World War II, Asia had been the world's most war-prone region. From the late 1970s that ended abruptly. The key reason for this change was the diplomatic grand bargain struck between the US and the PRC (Kirby, Ross and Li, 2006).

When Henry Kissinger, then President Richard Nixon's National Security Adviser, appeared in Beijing in July 1971 to begin negotiations to reset Sino–American relations, it shocked allies and foes alike. The trip's secrecy had been absolute, leaving many close partners feeling a sense of betrayal. Kissinger paved the way for Nixon's meeting with Mao the following year that, in turn, led to the rapprochement between the US and the PRC, one of the 20th century's most significant diplomatic agreements (Tudda, 2012). As the terms of the rapprochement were not all worked out in the Nixon–Mao meeting, it took considerable diplomatic effort, sustained in complex times – Nixon resigned because of Watergate in 1973 and Mao died in 1976 – before being fully realized with the exchange of ambassadors in 1979. But the essence of the deal was straightforward. The US recognized the PRC; previously it had favoured Taiwan as the legitimate China. This recognition gave the revolutionary state not just prestige and standing, but a capacity to operate in international affairs that had largely been denied by the diplomatic deep freeze that came from Washington's support of Taiwan. In return, the PRC would accept Asia's international order as it was and would cease trying to subvert it through the export of revolution and the support of communist forces in the region. The question of Taiwan was the most complex component, with the US agreeing to a subtle One China policy that gave Beijing the standing it sought without affirming China's desire to resolve the matter on its own terms. Congressional leaders in Washington were furious at the deal, arguing that the island nation should retain its standing and US protection. In response, US Congress passed the Taiwan Relations Act, that requires the US government to provide Taiwan with the capacity to defend itself from the PRC (Javits, 1981).

The reconciliation with China had been started by Nixon, but it was completed by Jimmy Carter. In finding a way to live with the PRC, the US had reoriented the central tenets of Asia's strategic balance. Where previously Asia was divided between the two main poles of the Cold War, now there was a three-way division of power and influence, and, critically, two of those poles, the US and China, now saw the benefits of positive diplomatic ties and a concerted diplomatic engagement. Even though the region remained one of significant political diversity – in the late 1970s, democracy remained unusual, autocracy was the norm and various forms of communist regimes remained – ideological division was essentially removed as a source of conflict and contestation. While legacies of the Cold War's origins remained visible and very real points of risk, the dynamic of Cold War competition and ideologically infused geopolitical rivalry ended in North and Southeast Asia in the late 1970s. The USSR's invasion of Afghanistan in 1979 would propel Soviet–American tensions back to heights they had not experienced in decades, ensuring South Asia was still firmly in the Cold War's grasp, but the eastern parts of the region began to operate to a different rhythm than that which was evident in Europe or the Middle East.

The change in US–China relations provided the necessary international environment in which the PRC could undertake the economic reforms known as the 'four modernisations' led by Deng Xiaoping (Vogel, 2011). These produced the most dramatic period of economic development in modern history as the CPC sought to move away from Maoist models of economic growth and embrace export-focused industrialization, following in many ways the model pioneered by Japan and the other Asian tiger economies. China mirrored its domestic economic reforms with a long-running foreign policy normalization programme that entailed resolving almost all its territorial border disputes with neighbours (Fravel, 2009) and a concerted effort to improve diplomatic ties with almost all countries in the region. While the US recognition of the PRC and move away from Taiwan had not removed the island as a point of risk, it established an effective diplomatic equilibrium that reduced the volatility of the island as a source of conflict.

Normalization of relations with China also allowed the US the space to devise a durable and effective strategy in the region. Washington's basic goal had, since the Korean War, been clear: Asia was to be kept free from domination by a hostile external power. This was part of the larger Cold War aim to have Western Europe, the Middle East and Asia free from Soviet influence (Walt, 2005). Yet it had not worked out an effective means of prosecuting the strategy in this part of the world. Its desire to push back an active communist menace, as Washington perceived it, wherever it was, informed by the sense that freedom threatened somewhere was a threat to it everywhere, had served neither to deter communist advances nor to secure regional stability. With China no longer tied to the USSR and focused on internal matters, Washington could focus its strength on maritime dominance, overlaid with overwhelming nuclear superiority. Stability would be reinforced by Washington's regional partners playing a greater role, with a particular focus on Japan's place as the 'unsinkable aircraft carrier' in East Asia. This meant that Japan would have to increase military expenditure and expand the understanding of the post-war constitution. In Japan's Prime Minister Nakasone, they had a leader who was more than willing to support this approach (Hattori, 2023). This allowed the US to achieve a military primacy that was accepted by virtually all and which had a stabilizing effect on Asia's strategic balance. And this geopolitical dominance was backed by America's economic role as the biggest destination market for Asian exports and the largest source of inbound investment. For Northeast and Southeast Asian states, many of which had embraced export-focused industrialization, there was a remarkably close fit between their economic and strategic interests.

In the early 1970s, Asia was a war-torn place, subject to great power rivalry and Cold War contestation with millions killed in wars and communal violence. By the early 1980s, it had become almost entirely free of international conflict. This ushered in a remarkable four-decade period of peace and stability. This transformation had been made possible not only by the fact that China and the US worked out how to live with one another but also the acceptance of the geopolitical deal that had been struck, one which rested on US primacy, by virtually every country in that part of Asia. This acceptance came from the fact that while not all states were thrilled with American leadership, they preferred it to the uncertainty and risk of unfettered competition among countries like Japan, Korea and China. These states were also able to benefit by not having to take steps to provide international public goods that US primacy provided, such as ensuring sea lanes were kept open for commerce, and thus could afford to spend less on defence than they otherwise might have. This, in turn, meant that they could focus almost entirely on the domestic priorities of economic and social development and state building. The programmes of economic improvement helped to create networks of trade and investment that started to bind disparate parts of the region together. It was the deal struck by the great powers as well as the choices made by the rest of the region to focus on domestic priorities that underpinned the beginning of Asia's long peace.

For most of the Cold War period, ASEAN was the only multilateral institution in East Asia. As the region began to settle into a longer period of stability, and as the global multilateral trading system established as part of the Bretton Woods arrangements began to struggle with a changing global economy, states in Northeast and Southeast Asia, as well as in the Americas determined that a regional mechanism was needed to advance economic cooperation in general and trade liberalization in particular. The APEC grouping was founded with its initial finance minister level meeting held in Canberra in 1989. This was the first institutional expression that linked distinct corners of Asia into a larger 'Asia-Pacific' conception. Indeed, it connected not just the ASEAN members with trade partners in Northeast Asia, it also included Canada, the US, Australia and New Zealand. In 1991, as the Cold War was being put to rest, it expanded further with three 'Chinas' joining: the PRC, Hong Kong and Taiwan (under the auspices of Chinese Taipei). APEC managed this neat diplomatic trick by having member economies and not states and reflected the reality that each of the three operated as discrete custom zones with their own currencies, fiscal policies and tariff regimes (Ravenhill, 2001).

The Soviet invasion of Afghanistan served to strengthen ties between Pakistan and the US as Washington sought the country's support in its efforts to pressurize the Red Army. Equally, Pakistan's ties to China meant that it was also able to benefit from Sino–American normalization, particularly as India had, in the early 1980s, opted to strengthen its relationship with the USSR to ensure its advantage over its military rival Pakistan (Ganguly and Pardesi, 2009). That rivalry dominated the region and led to South Asia largely being peripheral to the dynamic developments in Northeast and Southeast Asia as well as to broader global affairs.

The Cold War's end

The USSR retained ambitions to be a serious force in Asia into the mid-1980s – it is easy to forget that Soviet hopes to become the Pacific's dominant naval power were real and worried US planners at the time. The USSR's sudden collapse had profound implications across Asia. Had the USSR somehow limped on and been able to reap the benefits of the early 21st century commodity booms, then Asia's recent history would have looked very different. Most immediately, the Soviet collapse meant that several states in the region lost a critical partner and supporter. Of those, North Korea had come to depend the most on Soviet assistance in the form of aid, military equipment and markets for exports. The departure of the USSR led directly to the nuclear crisis with the US and the famines that followed as the policies that the DPRK had developed to respond to the shock of the USSR's disappearance had disastrous consequences (Haggard and Noland, 2005).

Vietnam too had been a close partner of Moscow and, while the loss of this ally was unsettling – the Soviet Union had been the ruling communist party's longest supporter, and Vietnam had fought a short war with China in 1979 – unlike Pyongyang, it not only coped with the loss of a great power ally but also thrived in the new international environment. This was in part because of its 'Doi Moi' market-based reforms that had been adopted in 1986, which were already producing dramatic effects. By the early 1990s, Vietnam had become a food exporter where it had for decades struggled to feed its own populace (Tuan, 2009). Internationally, the absence of the USSR allowed the country to chart its own course, leading Hanoi to normalize diplomatic relations with China in 1991 and with the US in 1995.

India also suffered a significant shock when the USSR imploded. The lodestar of Delhi's approach to the world had been non-alignment but it had leaned towards Moscow for several decades. The American victory in the Cold War wrecked that means of orientation. The USSR had been a supplier of critical military weapons but also, through the Council of Mutual Economic Assistance, it was one of the few export markets in which India was competitive; these were now lost. This was compounded by a severe economic shock caused by the 1990–91 Gulf War that prompted India to adopt significant economic reforms. The end of the Cold War directly drove India to adopt a much more pragmatic foreign policy orientation as well to begin to reorganize its economy on more liberal lines (Ganguly and Pardesi, 2009).

Central Asia's states were throughout the Cold War part of the USSR. As the Soviet Union's political integrity was being challenged by elite division and nationalist sentiment, the Central Asian republics began to push for greater sovereignty. Following the failed coup of September 1991, they declared their independence and, with the state collapse at the end of that year, stepped out into international society as independent players for the first time.

Asia's Cold War had always operated to its own distinctive tempo as the global contest collided with the ambitions and rivalries of its numerous peoples and states. It was the place of greatest conflict for several decades after 1945 and, in East Asia at any rate, the Soviet–American rivalry moved away from centre stage much earlier than in Europe or the Middle East. Yet the Cold War remained important and with the demise of the USSR and the idea of communism that the Bolsheviks had institutionalized over seventy years, Asia entered a new period. This was one in which great power competition had disappeared, in which there was near-universal recognition of the importance of foreign markets for economic prosperity and a growing self-confidence among Asia's states and societies.

Conclusion

In the five decades or so after World War II, Asia was transformed. From a place of imperial domination, it had become a dynamic and increasingly confident set of sovereign states. For the Central Asian republics, that independence was extremely new, having slipped the Soviet yoke just a few years past, but for virtually all, sovereignty remained a precious thing that had been hard-won in the living memory of much of the population. Economic development, particularly in Northeast and Southeast Asia, was the most visible change, with an acceleration of economic growth that was one of the most dramatic ever seen. Tokyo, Seoul, Taipei and Singapore had become high technology metropolises, centres of cutting-edge industry and finance. And for the first time scholars and analysts began to reflect on the prospects in which Asia might become a dominant factor in world affairs.

Yet as the 1990s began, the two giants, China and India, remained in the very early phases of their economic reform and development. Chinese growth had begun to pick up but in 1991 its economy was only a tenth of the size of that of the US. India was years away from realizing the economic benefits of reforms that were launched in that same year, and both economies were still largely isolated from global markets.

Northeast Asia was also notable for the continued security tensions of Taiwan and the division of the Korean Peninsula. This ensured that the US military focus in Asia, while framed in larger terms – the Pacific Command had a sphere of operations that went from Hawaii to Pakistan – was dominated by Northeast Asia. Southeast Asia, for its part, had largely resolved its longstanding security concerns, with the Cambodian peace agreements brokered in 1991 finally bringing an end to the simmering Vietnam–Cambodia conflict that had been festering since Hanoi had overthrown the Khmer Rouge in 1978. Where divisions that had their origins in the Cold War remained visible in Northeast Asia, they were essentially banished in Southeast Asia. Consequently, ASEAN began to consider further expansion, having accepted Brunei as a member in the mid-1980s.

Asia, thus, appeared to be coming into view. Yet its four component subregions remained discrete and, in some cases, almost entirely walled off from one another. South Asia shared few links with the states and economies on the East Asian littoral, while Central Asia was equally poorly connected. Northeast and Southeast Asia had some shared economic and security interests respectively, and some growing trade links between themselves. The newly formed APEC, with its emphasis on the Pacific Ocean and trans-Pacific connectivity, and the enthusiasm of members and those wanting to join, gave an indication of how, at that point, the Asian region was perceived. In the early 1990s, the gaps between South and Central Asia were so large and the dynamism of the Western Pacific economies such that the dominant way of thinking about the region was as a place that bordered the Pacific, not as a coherent set of states and economies based on an immense landmass.

The Cold War had been momentous for Asia's states and societies. They had found their independence, but millions had had to fight and die for that privilege. Some had found great prosperity, while for others it remained elusive, with poverty still being the lived reality for most of Asia's population in 1991. The imprint of colonialism remained visible in the borders of many countries, as did the longer resentments that imperialism had stoked. But Asia's states were now all sovereign, free to determine their paths, not subordinate to colonial dictates. The Cold War had energized economic development, driven violent conflict and been a period of immense national progress for so many. By 1991, it had become clear that the continent was going to be a place of importance to the globe and not just because of the sheer scale of its population. But what this would look like – in terms of the locations of power and influence, and the expanse and spread of interests – was much less clear. The coming three decades would forge an immense integrated region of great prosperity but also growing geopolitical risk.

4

Asia Integrated

The death of Communism led political leaders in many corners of the world to conclude that the liberal economic settings of the global economy were essentially inevitable. Faith in private property, the profit motive and price signals, and the belief that markets were better at and often more powerful than states, created a near-global ideological consensus in the early 1990s. While the different experiences of Sweden and Japan showed that capitalism was flexible, its universality seemed inevitable (Hall and Soskice, 2001).

In significant parts of Asia, this was old news. In its Northeast and Southeast, states were already enjoying a peace dividend that the Nixon–Mao grand bargain allowed. Sino–American normalization in the 1970s had transformed the region from one of the Cold War's bloodiest theatres to a place where conflict was essentially banished (Bellamy, 2017). It provided the external conditions necessary for China to introduce sweeping market-oriented reforms that led, in time, to a dramatic expansion of economic prosperity. When the hammer and sickle was lowered for the last time from the Kremlin's flag poles, East Asia was already some way down the path defined by unparalleled US military dominance and the embrace of liberal capitalism. Many parts of Asia were a decade ahead of the rest of the world.

At the start of the 20th century's final decade, Asia remained a term that described a place where its subregions and major powers could be found; it was not yet a coherent region in its own right. Northeast and Southeast Asia were becoming increasingly linked through trade and investment and a growing realization of a shared set of threats to their security and well-being. At that time, this could be observed in the way policy elites, analysts and even firms talked about being part of an emerging 'Asia–Pacific' region. Northeast and Southeast Asia were physically connected by the waters of the Western Pacific, and many thought the emerging links between those two dynamic parts of Asia would be paired with strengthening ties across the Pacific Ocean. The expectation at the time was that growing integration between East Asia and Canada, the US and Latin America was of much greater prospect than links to the more geographically proximate South and Central Asian regions. Those two parts of the world remained, in the early 1990s, on very different economic and strategic planes than the countries of the Pacific littoral. The post-Soviet Central Asian republics had just stepped out as fully sovereign states while India and the other countries of South Asia were economically isolated and, in security terms, almost entirely focused on internal and intra-South Asian problems.

The chapter will chart how, in the three decades after the Cold War's end, Asia was finally bound together to become a China-centred but not Sino-centric economic and strategic system. This was made possible because of two tectonic forces, globalization and the return of geopolitics.

The opportunity to plug into global markets for goods and investment that market-led globalization opened up was seized by many Asian states. But it was not just the dynamism of global markets and the wealth it generated that was important, it was the way in which market-led globalization prompted a change in the nature of international production that allowed the creation of proper pan-Asian networks of trade and investment. This knitted together the discrete subregions into a modern Asian economy, with China as the regional centre of gravity.

The second force, geopolitical competition and rivalry, was fuelled in turn by the growing wealth and power of Asian states. The US had long been focused on ensuring that Asia would not become home to a dominant power hostile to Washington's interests. As the region became more economically dynamic, American interest in sustaining that ambition did not recede. Once Washington and Beijing had worked out how to get along in the 1970s and the USSR slipped from view in 1991, sustaining that goal was relatively straightforward. But as China became more affluent, and especially as Xi Jinping crafted a more ambitious and assertive foreign policy following his rise to power in 2012, the US faced overt competition from a country wealthier and more powerful than any it had faced before. India also started to develop regional and global ambitions, on which it could now act. Like Washington, it wanted to ensure that Asia was not subject to the dominance of a sole power, which it perceived had interests that cut across its ambitions. And Russia, a country with a substantial physical presence in Asia, a source of much of its weaponry and energy, began once again to view Asia as a critical theatre to advance its broader strategic interests to push back against the US and undermine Western influence globally.

In the years leading up to the pandemic, great power competition had become increasingly visible. In 2017, the first Trump administration's national security strategy made major power rivalry the key focus of its efforts, replacing terrorism as its primary concern (White House, 2017). This was the first time a genuinely pan-Asian sense of strategic interaction had existed in the modern era. Previously, there was nothing that bound all of Asia's states together in strategic or security terms; the contest for its future geopolitical order now did exactly that. Prior to 2020, however, that competition remained within the guardrails established by the shared interests of globalization.

This chapter examines the process through which globalization and geopolitics created an integrated Asian region.

The Asian economy

At the start of the 1990s, the volumes of trade and investment between Asian countries were not especially substantial. Links between Northeast and Southeast Asia had started to grow in part because Japanese and South Korean firms had begun to move production away from home and into lower cost locations (Urata, 1993). But in the main, countries in those parts of Asia largely competed with one another for inbound investment and outbound markets. For example, the southern Malaysian city Johor Baru might compete with the Thai capital Bangkok to attract a Japanese automotive factory, using tax holidays and other incentives to make themselves more appealing. Equally, manufacturers across the region competed with one another for markets into which they sold their goods.

North America and Western Europe were by some margin the largest of those markets, and thus economic development plans predicated on export-led growth were of necessity focused ultimately on selling things to Americans and Europeans. This put limits on the scale and depth of economic integration among Asia's economic component parts. To the extent that economic connectivity among economies was occurring, it only happened at this point in East Asia. The paucity of South Asia's international trade at that time is hard to overstate. In the 1990s, trade by value from South Asia – a region then accounting for around one sixth of the world's population – was around US$1.8 billion, compared with the total value of the world trade of US$66.2 billion. Of that, about half went to ASEAN countries, plus ROK, Japan and the PRC, and only around 3 per cent of that modest value was traded amongst the country's South Asian neighbours (Mishra, 2015).

By the time of the pandemic years, this situation had fundamentally changed. Nearly 60 per cent of trade in Asia was between countries from the region, approaching the levels of the EU, the world's most economically interdependent place (Economist, 2023). Investment from Asian sources to other destinations within the region had leapt, following the well-established pattern that once trade flows start, investment swiftly follows. And Asia had become an important final consumption market as hundreds of millions of people joined the middle class.

How did this happen? The short answer can be found in the selective but nonetheless enthusiastic embrace of market-led globalization by virtually all of Asia's economies. This shift in orientation – and for China and India it was a significant break with the approaches they had pursued since the late 1940s – was made possible by the confidence that US military predominance created and the sureties of what appeared to be a post-ideological world.

Japan had pioneered the model of export-focused industrialization as it rebuilt its economy after World War II. It showed that attracting foreign capital, collaborating with multinationals and focusing on export markets could generate dramatic and sustained growth (Forsberg, 2000). China had effectively walled itself off from the outside world after 1949, while India's approach to economic development after independence was predicated on self-reliance, keeping foreign competition at bay and tightly managing the economy. Decades of the General Agreement on Tariffs and Trade (GATT) regime had reduced global barriers to trade, the end of the Bretton Woods system had created a dynamic global financial system and Japan and Taiwan had shown that non-Western powers could do well out of integrating into the global economy. The tiger economies began to seize these opportunities, and countries in North and Southeast Asia began to develop swiftly.

This economic acceleration by those East Asian economies was supported by a range of policies put in place in Asian countries.

Central among these were the careful calibration of state policy to promote industrialization. This included providing some protection from foreign competition, subsidies to support key industries and the effective use of industrial policy. Industrial policy refers to a range of policies that governments put in place to shape market and firm behaviour. This was also supported in informal ways through close and collaborative relations between economic elites and government (Stiglitz and Yusuf, 2001). Here major firms would work closely with government departments to advance shared goals. The benefits that these countries enjoyed due to integration into international markets was not simply a story of letting market forces rip. Rather, globalization provided the possibilities for rapid industrial growth and East Asian elites provided a policy context that allowed firms and states to benefit. China's tentative steps into the post-Mao economic world were guided by these principles. The PRC followed the example led by Japan, South Korea and, indeed, Taiwan, in which market forces and international markets were a key component but the interaction between these and the Chinese state and society were carefully managed by Party-state elites.

The settings of market-led globalization provided opportunities for economic growth, something desperately needed across the region. But Asia was knitted together not just because of growing economic growth but because of the particular way in which globalization evolved. The critical development that allowed Asia's disparate economies to be woven more tightly together was a major transformation in the way international production occurred. Without this important change Asia's subregions would probably have remained separated, essentially competing with one another for markets and investment.

When companies decide to manufacture their products outside of their home country the phenomenon is described by scholars as 'international production'. For several decades after 1945, firms moved internationally to produce goods in a relatively fixed pattern. During that time, industrial production remained driven by the basic tenets of mass production known as 'Fordism', so named because it was modelled on the pioneering work of the Ford Motor company in the early 20th century. In this model firms broke down the assembly process of complex goods, such as automobiles or industrial appliances, into a series of simple steps to increase the speed with which things could be made and lower the cost of manufacturing.

Companies built large production facilities, and they would seek to maximize their output. In this approach, a firm looking to increase its markets by setting up a factory or plant internationally entailed essentially replicating what they did at home in a foreign location. There were three main reasons why firms would choose to go abroad and not just build another factory at home. The primary one was to take advantage of the benefits of having a facility in that foreign locale. These were mainly about the way a new location could help reduce costs, such as accessing cheaper labour than what was available at home. It could also include other factors, such as proximity to a market or to the components that go into the products. These factors could help reduce transportation costs associated with gathering the elements of the product and getting the finished item to consumers. A second reason was to get behind tariff barriers. Tariffs are the technical name given to taxes imposed on the importation of goods or services from other countries. They are normally used to defend local markets from competition by forcing up the prices of imported goods. After World War II, the GATT was established with the express goal of reducing tariffs to allow market forces a greater say in shaping the international economy. The GATT regime was successful at reducing tariffs on manufactured goods, although in some sectors, such as motor vehicles, many barriers remained. So if a producer wanted to sell its cars or other goods where tariffs were in place, it could only do so in a cost-competitive way if it established a presence within that market. For example, Australia maintained high tariffs in the automative sector until the early 2000s. This was to protect manufacturing jobs by pushing car companies to build vehicles there to sell into the local market. This led foreign firms, such as Toyota and Mitsubishi, to establish manufacturing plants in the country to serve the local market. The third reason firms would go abroad was to seek regulatory benefits from producing in different jurisdictions. Here, environmental regulations, labour standards and other rules might provide incentives to produce in a new location. But whatever the motive, having cheaper workers, circumventing tariffs or benefitting from different regulations when establishing a factory in another country, the mode of production itself did not change. Some inputs might be sourced from different places than before, the laws might be beneficial to the bottom line but establishing an international production facility did not change the basic productive process, which remained largely following a model established in the first part of the 20th century. Notably, the firms that went abroad in those early post-war years were almost all from the advanced industrial economies and particularly from the US.

The transformative development of international production, and the change that was critical for the creation of a China-centred Asian economy, was the move away from an integrated Fordist model and towards a complex and highly disaggregated 'value chain' or 'value network' model of production. In the 1990s, firms began to move away from the business of making things and became focused on the process of production. This may seem like a semantic difference, but the shift was one of real substance. Where in the past the making of things entailed designing and building a product, such as a television, a car or a machine, such as a metal press, that is used in industrial production. The company would acquire some components, usually of low value and complexity, but it would make many elements itself and then assemble the final product. The value chain approach changed things considerably. Instead of an integrated production process within one firm, the whole productive process was broken down into its constituent components and the making of things became a question of design and logistics (Riad et al, 2012). That is the design of the good itself, as well as the structure and organization of suppliers who were able to produce the many components and parts, such as gears, wiring, microchips, screens and memory boards, that would comprise the finished product and to ensure their integration into a single process. It also put a high emphasis on branding, marketing and international distribution.

Suppliers were knitted into complex chains that linked together across considerable distances to assemble the final product. The constituent components were sourced from wherever the best price-quality match could be found (Dicken, 2015). That process itself might entail its own disaggregated process. For example, the solid-state memory drives that are critical components of smart phones or games consoles are themselves products of international supply chains. This hyperspecialized disaggregated form of international production meant that firms that were famous for making things did not themselves actually have factories that produced anything. The Apple iPhone is perhaps the archetypal example. Apple designs the phone, both the physical device and the software system that makes it work. It then manages a highly complex chain of components, which are assembled into the final product in massive facilities primarily undertaken in the PRC, oddly enough by a Taiwanese firm. Famously, the products all carry the reminder that they were 'designed in California' but assembled in China. Critically, despite not making anything physical, Apple captures by far the largest share of the price the consumer pays for the device (McGee, 2025). This is a way of doing business that would have been literally unimaginable to the Fordist multinational managers of the 1950s and 1960s.

The turn towards disaggregated production provided opportunities for specialization that widened the range of ways that Asian states could take advantage of globalization and they began to adjust their policy settings accordingly (Coe and Yeung, 2015). Where in the past the emphasis was on trying to get productive facilities established, requiring large concentrations of capital and expertise as well as dependence on multinational corporations, under a disaggregated supply chain model firms could become exporters with smaller investments and focusing on intermediate goods. This created a much wider range of opportunities for Asian firms. They were not stuck just making low-value basic items with little prospect for dynamic growth because they could not muster the capital or managerial know-how to compete with large complex production processes. Now they could specialize on components, which were themselves becoming more complex and valuable, that could be plugged into the production networks that were weaving modern manufactured goods. And it was the PRC that became the most significant player as its scale as well as policy settings meant it was able to benefit more than any other.

The economic growth that China experienced because of its 'reform and opening up' programme was created in the first instance by moving large populations from the countryside to cities and getting that labour engaged in low-skill export-focused production. This was focused primarily on relatively simple manufacturing such as clothing, plastic goods and basic electronic goods. Initially, this occurred within special economic zones (SEZs) such as Shenzhen next door to Hong Kong, where Mao-era economic policy had been eased, private property and profit motives were introduced, and where market-based rules incentivized economic activity (Garnaut, Song and Fang, 2018).

During the first dozen years or so of the reform era, growth was in relatively basic manufactured goods, such as clothing, sporting goods, footwear and toys. Here Hong Kong firms were critical players, transferring their operations from what was then still a British city. Just 25 km away was Shenzhen, one of the first SEZs (Song and Sung, 1995), and this move was an important first step for China. But the model of growth remained simple, both in terms of the basic mechanics of manufacturing and distribution and in the relationship to the larger global economy.

This began to change through the 1990s. While the first generation of labour-intensive production continued, a second generation emerged that was focused on the assembly of more sophisticated manufactured goods organized by large firms, which acted as the coordinators of complex supply chains. The PRC was particularly successful at assembly for machinery and transport equipment. Critically, China's success was built on its role as final assembler for a network of components that were largely based in East Asia, so as it became a more successful producer and assembly hub it also began to shift the dynamics of the region's economy. The PRC was able to capitalize not only on its huge pool of cheap and relatively skilled labour but the reforms that had created the SEZs and focused on attracting inbound investment meant that the requirements for facilities to work effectively as part of larger regional and global networks, such as communication, transport and managerial coordination, were in place to support this move. Those links, between Chinese firms and the producers of components in Taiwan, South Korea, Thailand, Singapore, Malaysia and Indonesia, began to form the basis of a more integrated Asian economic system.

China's importance grew not just on its success as a place where highly complex global production processes could be coordinated, finalized and shipped to market, but it also began to become part of the value chain process as the home of firms that also produced component parts. The first generation of economic growth was limited to simple manufactures like clothing, and the second generation of firms focused on the final assembly of more complex goods. Through the 2000s a third generation of Chinese firms, as well as foreign firms based in China, began to play a greater role in the intermediate processes. They would themselves draw inputs from others in China as well as the region and then ship those components on through the value chain. Finally, as economic development continued and as incomes and savings grew, China also became an important final market for many products, with consumer electronics being the most significant. China now assembles goods, produces components and is a major market for finished goods. Perhaps the most striking example of this is that the PRC has overtaken the EU as Apple's biggest market outside the US for its iPhone (McGee, 2025).

The beginning of the supply chain model in East Asia can be seen in the 1980s as Japan began to shift production to lower-cost locations, including Hong Kong, South Korea and Singapore. But the much more complex supply chain system started to develop in the mid-1990s and accelerated through the first 15 years of the 21st century. While the specifics of the chains are very complex, they are visible at the national level in terms of trade growth and among Asian states and the increases in 'value-add', whereby each stage of production increases the value of the good as it makes its way along the chain. Economic data shows that China's share of manufacturing increased significantly during this period and the value-add increased in China, Malaysia, Thailand, Indonesia as well as South Korea, while trade volumes between each of these countries and China grew, as well as trade between China and the lesser developed economies, like Cambodia, Vietnam and Laos (Berger-Thomson and Doyle, 2013).

China's size as well as the sophistication of its many firms and the immense infrastructure that the government had invested in gave it huge advantages. Firms across the region were able to capitalize on opportunities that had now become possible. They were also assisted by some regional initiatives that ASEAN had driven and which helped provide momentum for the interlacing of Asia with trade networks. The ASEAN Free Trade Area (AFTA) arrangement was established in 1993 and led to relatively high levels of liberalization among ASEAN economies by the early 2000s, helping to reduce the costs for Southeast Asian firms to begin to take advantage of the emerging supply chain opportunities (Ishikawa, 2021). This was supported by the China–ASEAN Free Trade Agreement, which came into force in 2010 and has helped drive a substantial increase in trade between China and Southeast Asia (Chiang, 2019).

These developments most immediately tied the economies of East Asia into strong and mutually beneficial trade relationships with the PRC. But these dynamics have also helped overcome the metaphorical trading barrier of the Himalayas, as China has become increasingly important to South Asia, and India most particularly.

After India's liberalization reforms of the early 1990s, China swiftly became its most important trading partner, quickly outstripping Korea and Japan, a pattern followed by other South Asian economies. This trade was dominated by the assembly goods that had become the centre of China's economic dynamism and at the heart of the region's new economic structure (Boillot and Labbouz, 2006). India was very much plugged into the China-centred regional economy in a way that it had never been under the policies put in place by the Nehru government and that had dominated the post-independence period.

In the decades following the Cold War, Asia's economy was transformed. On the strong foundations established by Japan and the tiger economies, changes in international production processes provided opportunities to enhance export-focused growth in ways that aligned with reforms that China had created. Its scale, policy settings and the skill level of its workforce allowed the country to capitalize on these opportunities. China became the world's largest economy, at least measured by purchasing power, and its most dynamic. Its role as the lender to whom Western Europe came begging following the GFC in 2007–08 was illustrative of just how far it had come. These changes had, for the first time, created a genuinely Asian economy where trade and investment between firms and states across the region was happening in ways and in volumes that had not been seen in the modern era.

Within a lifetime the PRC had moved from being barely able to feed itself to the most important player in a regional economy on whose success much of the world depended. A simple illustration of its importance is the number of countries for whom the PRC is its most important two-way trade partner. That number exceeds more than 120 countries globally, including the EU. And it is by some margin the most important trade partner in Asia. The region accounted for 57 per cent of global GDP growth between 2015 and 2021. In that year, its trade was 53 per cent of the world's trade in goods, and 49 of the world's most important trade routes are either between Asian ports or have an Asian end point (Seong et al, 2023). Asia has become the most important economic region in the world, and China is its most critical component.

Strategic competition returns

Globalization led to the creation of a genuinely Asian economy. But it was not economic forces alone that turned the Asian landmass, its littoral and oceans, into a coherent strategic space. Regions are formed when states and societies in specific parts of the world are tied together by shared interests and a common sense of risk and threat. As the forces began to pull Asia's economy together, the region's major powers also began to compete with one another. This strategic competition was in part fuelled by rising prosperity and in part by their growing range of interests and the inevitable clashes that follow from such expansive countries. As China and India have more at stake in the global economy, such as the networks of trade that make their growth possible, they have a greater interest in the smooth operation of those networks and their vulnerability to disruption. And it is the relatively rapid emergence of this competition, which had only recently come to the surface before the COVID-19 pandemic broke, that consolidated the sense of Asia as a coherent whole. The US' desire to retain the strategic setting established in the final decades of the Cold War and the PRC's ambition to change it are at the centre of this dynamic. As well, India and Russia have ambitions for the region that are different from the status quo, while the second-tier powers, such as Australia, Indonesia, Vietnam and Japan, also recognize the ways in which their interests are being challenged by an unstable strategic setting and taking steps, both military and diplomatic, that act in region-creating ways.

America's Asia

While the US has been a significant presence in Asia for centuries, it was during the Cold War that it became the dominant military power in the region. As the post-Cold War world emerged, the main question for Washington, and its allies and partners, was whether the country would change its approach, allowing it to seize the opportunity for a 'peace dividend'. Checking Soviet power and stabilizing a regional military balance had led the US to establish bilateral alliances across the region and to use these to manage a significant forward deployment of military force. Around 100,000 personnel had been based in the region for decades, concentrated heavily in South Korea and Japan, as were significant military assets, including aircraft carriers, bombers and fighter jets. And while the host governments contributed to the costs of having the US military presence, the price that the US bore was considerable.

The USSR's demise meant that Asia's geopolitics began to take on a different complexion. China had embraced moderation in its foreign policy and was busy getting on with its economic reform programme. By the early 1990s, that programme was beginning to show signs of success. China's economy was growing rapidly, it was courting foreign investment and its diplomacy showed all the hallmarks of a country trying to make the most out of globalization. It joined APEC in 1991 and resolved almost all its border disputes with its neighbours (Fravel, 2009). The USSR was gone, and Russia was clearly a second- or even third-tier power. It was not at all clear that there was a need for the US to maintain a Cold War structure to its approach to Asia while its straitened economic circumstances at home also seemed as if it might drive a change in approach. The recessionary environment that had catapulted Bill Clinton to the Oval Office in the 1992 election meant an American retreat from Asia was a real possibility.

The US ultimately opted to retain the purpose and structure of its Cold War strategy (Sutter, 2002). This was articulated in two reports authored by academic turned Under Secretary of Defense Joseph Nye. The first report definitively answered the question of whether the US would change its approach to what was then described as the 'East Asia–Pacific Region'. It explored a range of options for US strategy, from retrenchment to the fostering of a local balance of power, and concluded that the US would retain a long-term presence in the region arranged through bilateral alliances; it would not adopt a multilateral structure. While there was some gesturing towards building regional institutions and strengthening allies' capabilities, the inescapable reality was that the US had looked at a part of the world that had been transformed and determined that that which existed as it was would be best over the longer term. The report noted that Washington was committed to the existing force structure of around 100,000 troops, basing this number on modelling that sought to estimate what would be needed in the region to fight a war there as well as one in Europe or the Middle East at the same time (Department of Defense, 1995).

It is tempting to see inertia as a driving force of what was essentially a decision not to change things to any great degree. The administration recognized the decisive role that US power had played in maintaining a stable setting and facilitating economic growth in the region. Any significant move from this would create instability, at least in the short term. Even at the time that the reports were being drafted, American analysts were beginning to express concerns about China's rise (Brown et al, 2000). In less than two decades the PRC had increased its GDP by more than threefold and fears about what this might mean for the US and its partners, most especially Taiwan, were real. North Korea had revealed its nuclear weapon ambitions in the 1992 nuclear crisis and lingering Sino–Japanese acrimony meant that it was not difficult to see that, without the stabilizing force of US military might, Asia's future might be dangerous indeed.

The principal problem for US policy then, as it had been for decades, was how to approach the PRC. While few serious analysts saw the People's Liberation Army (PLA) as a credible military around the turn of the millennium, equally few thought it would be forever weak. Just how powerful it might become was entirely unclear. Also, Taiwan's importance to the CPC leadership – which then as now saw the island's independence as an infuriating reminder of the Chinese Civil War – meant that the China challenge was a live issue even in the mid-1990s. But China was also acutely interested in international economic engagement and its prosperity then was dependent on foreign markets. Equally, US firms were especially attracted to the potential that the massive and growing Chinese market represented.

These were liberal times and there was considerable optimism about how economic interdependence with the PRC might influence the country's long-term behaviour. No one then thought that trade or investment with China would make it a democracy, the Tiananmen Square massacre was too fresh in the memory for such naïve thinking, but there was some confidence that the PRC's economic interests would act as a moderating force on its foreign policy. Yet even the most optimistic assessment of the prospects of economic interdependence recognized that risks remained, and that the US and its partners needed to retain the ability to deter Chinese threats. To reconcile these trends the US eventually adopted an approach known by the unlovely term 'congagement'. The mashing together of containment and engagement represented Washington's efforts to try to make the most out of the economic opportunities presented by the PRC's growth while also sustaining a strategic presence to prevent Beijing from taking dangerous steps. The Clinton administration devised congagement; it had good support in the private sector and was continued by the Bush administration when it came to office in 2001. Following the 9/11 terrorist attacks and the major reorientation this event prompted in US policy, that led to the 'global war on terrorism', it remained the central idea animating Washington's approach to the PRC through until the election of Barack Obama. This was despite the arguments of a number of conversative scholars and analysts who had put the case for a harder edged approach to China's growing power (Friedberg, 2011).

After a short period in which the newly minted Obama administration tried to develop a more cooperative relationship with China, from 2010 the US launched what it described as a 'pivot' to Asia. Announced by Secretary of State Hillary Clinton in a speech to the East–West Center in Hawaii, Washington set out to reorient US foreign policy away from its emphasis on the long-running conflicts in Iraq and Afghanistan which, in the eyes of the new administration, had distorted American priorities and weakened Washington's position in the region. As pointed out repeatedly in several speeches, Obama declared that Asia had once again become the world's most significant zone and that it was a vital American interest to remain not just engaged in Asia but for the US to retain its position as the pre-eminent power, militarily, economically and diplomatically (Campbell, 2016). The policy was a response not just to the ways that the war on terror had distorted US foreign and defence policy but also the realization that China's power was beginning to reorient the region and required a more focused approach from Washington.

While the pivot was probably the most significant single element of Obama's foreign policy, it was notable that its major features remained in keeping with the long-term trends in the US' Asia strategy. First, the goal was to retain the circumstances in which the Asian continent would be kept free from a hostile dominant power in the face of a rising China. Second, the means through which the US would achieve that ambition were largely as they had been: bilateral alliances and partnerships, forward deployment of military force and active diplomatic engagement. The Obama administration put a renewed emphasis on multilateral institutions and sought to be much more engaged than the US had been. It also gave the economic dimension a stronger push. The most notable element was its decision to join the Trans-Pacific Partnership (TPP) negotiations. The TPP had been started by a number of small liberally minded economies, namely Brunei, Chile, New Zealand and Singapore, in 2005. Other larger economies had joined in and, when the US entered the negotiations, Washington chose to frame the putative agreement as one that would ensure that the US and like-minded countries would write the rules for trade in the region and not China.

For all its much-touted novelty, the pivot entailed continuing a congagement approach with an attempt to strengthen the containment side of things. At the time these efforts were seen by many observers in the region, as well as in the US, as somewhat underwhelming. Washington had recognized just how much Asia's economic and strategic setting was changing, but the policies they introduced seemed inadequate to the task. Surely, realizing that China had become the most important economy in an integrated Asia and was in the midst of a very significant military modernization programme would lead the US to do a bit more than adjusting the disposition of littoral combat ships and sending a few thousand marines do six-month training rotations in Australia. Not for the first time was there a considerable gap between Obama's rhetoric and his administration's foreign policy actions (Turner and Parmar, 2020).

The election of Donald Trump promised the possibility of a radical break with US regional strategy. The president-elect flirted with a realpolitik-infused shift in policy towards Taiwan, adopted a trademark bombastic approach to China and indicated that he would not care if long-standing alliances were junked in favour of a much more self-interested and transactional approach to US foreign policy. As the administration settled down, however, it became clear that Washington would not fundamentally change course, but it did do a few things differently from its predecessor (Bisley, 2020). Most critically, the administration explicitly endorsed a national security strategy that turned its back on terrorism and focused instead on great power competition and particularly the challenge presented by the PRC (White House, 2017). The US imposed significant tariffs on Beijing and forged a new bipartisan consensus that the PRC was a full-spectrum threat to American interests. It formed the view that China's role in advanced technology was an acute threat and took out a series of measures to block PRC firms' ability to compete with US and other Western firms.

The Trump administration also adopted the 'Indo–Pacific' as a strategic construct. This was introduced by the US president in a speech at an APEC business leaders' summit in 2017. It marked the beginning of what is now the standard way the US government talks about its interests in Asia. It is most symbolically visible in the rebranding of the command structure that oversees American regional power from PACOM – short for Pacific Command – to INDOPACOM – short for United States Indo-Pacific Command. PACOM, the unified military command, was created out of the various structures that had fought in the region during World War II and was formally created in 1947. The renaming was instituted in 2018 and sought to reflect the way the US increasingly saw the two oceans as integrated even though it had long operated with a unified theatre of operations between the two zones.

The US approach to Asia has been consistent over a long period of time. Trump's taste for bellicose theatre notwithstanding, the US made clear that it intended to maintain its long-term ambition that Asia should not be dominated by a power hostile to US interests and values. That challenge was now plainly identified as the PRC. What was more puzzling was that the main features of US strategy had barely changed from the character it had adopted in the late Cold War period. This involved forward deployment of large but limited forces, organized through bilateral alliances and the 'natural' advantage of its economic size and dynamism. For the four decades after Sino–American rapprochement, the economic and strategic interests of most countries, including the PRC, remained in line with American preferences. But, as the 21st century proceeded, that began to change. The reconstitution of economic interests has made the business of retaining US regional dominance that much harder. US policy towards the region can be understood as a slow-motion realization of the scale and substance of changes in Asia. In the sharp turn to competition and the widening out of the aperture of American strategy from a Pacific focus to a two-ocean approach one sees the sudden realization of just what it is that Washington faces in the new Asia.

China's ambition

The most significant change in Asia's geopolitical settings has been the shift in attitude and approach from Beijing. After all, as Washington elites liked to remind anyone who cared to listen, China had benefitted more than anyone else from the stability that US power and strategy had created. Why, they complained, could Chinese leaders not see that it was not in their interests to change things? While this revealed a good deal about the inability of American elites to see things from others' perspectives, few could have anticipated how much and how rapidly Xi Jinping would alter the PRC's approach to Asia and the world.

From its rapprochement with the US in the 1970s until the end of Hu Jintao's term in 2012, the PRC's foreign policy was centred on an acceptance of the broader regional arrangements established by the diplomatic deal struck between Mao and Nixon. Moderation, caution and a low profile were the hallmarks of its foreign policy. Even though there was never any great enthusiasm for a set of regional arrangements centred on US primacy, the priority the party put on domestic reforms and economic growth meant that the PRC operated as an ordinary member of international society during this period. Of course, Taiwan remained a neuralgic issue for Beijing. Its clumsy attempts to intimidate voters in the island's first democratic elections in the mid-1990s and the consequent dispatch of US carrier battle groups to the Taiwan Strait was a reminder of the priority Beijing put on this piece of 'unfinished business' and its international ramifications. But the party had hitched its wagon to national economic development and for around four decades this led to a leadership style that, in its regional behaviour, would not challenge the international arrangements that had become so important to the success that it sought.

The transition from Hu Jintao to Xi Jinping initially followed the post-Mao template. Xi had been identified as the anointed successor and groomed for the role, taking on various positions in the party and state structures in the lead up to the 2012 transition. China had acted in uncharacteristically risky ways at times during that period. This included the sort of more assertive actions in the East China Sea mentioned in Chapter 1, and most famously, commenced the reclamation works that produced more than 2,000 acres of artificial islands in the contested waters of the South China Sea. But analysts at the time assumed this was linked to internal machinations within the PLA and the CPC as part of the changing of the guard. Most thought that Xi would continue with the pattern established after Mao, which had, after all, served the country so well.

Xi was thus a surprise both to the party elites that had facilitated his rise to power and to the region and world (Tsang and Cheung, 2024). Internally, Xi consolidated power and moved decisively away from the collective leadership model established in the 1970s. He instituted a massive anti-corruption campaign that was intended to marginalize opponents as well as root out what he perceived to be the biggest threat to the party's long-term rule. Xi also reinvigorated party ideology; Deng's pragmatism was replaced by a demand for rigid adherence to party doctrine linked personally to Xi for all of Chinese society.

Internationally, Xi has brought a more ambitious and assertive approach to China's policy. Even from relatively early on in his tenure, Xi made clear that he perceived the international arrangements in the region to be created by Washington and designed to serve Western interests. In May 2014, Xi's speech in Shanghai to the Conference on Interaction and Confidence Building Measures in Asia (CICA), a regional grouping focused on Central Asia, he declared that: 'it is for the people of Asia to run the affairs of Asia, solve the problems of Asia and uphold the security of Asia.' (Xi, 2014) This came not long after two 2013 speeches, one in Astana and the other in Jakarta, which launched the ambitious Belt and Road Initiative (BRI). In the context of a China that was taking risky and assertive steps in contested maritime and territorial spaces in the East and South China Sea, the new leadership was signalling that it was not content to live in what it believed to be America's shadow.

The opacity of the Chinese political system makes discerning the specific aspects of the country's long-term strategy difficult. Equally, it is hard to see the diversity of views that exist about both the ends and means of Chinese policy. However, in the public speeches and pronouncements on these matters, as well as China's actions, one can discern a clear outline of PRC ambition (Rudd, 2024). By 2020, the following components were visible.

Xi stated repeatedly that the country would not only be an advanced economy by the centenary of the PRC's founding in 2049 but that it would be at the forefront of countries in terms of national power. But it is not just that China seeks to have military capacity commensurate with its scale and its own sense of its civilizational standing, it wants to reshape the rules of the international game. In the past, China had to accept the existing rules, norms and standards. By the time the pandemic roiled the globe, its ambition to change these rules and create an international environment more conducive to its interests had become clear.

Beyond the higher order ambition to change the basic operating system of international politics, China's more ambitious policy is motivated by a widening conception of China's interests. This derives from the growing stake it has in the workings of the global economy. The country's dependence on foreign trade also gives it a critical stake in the means through which goods traverse global markets. It requires hydrocarbons, iron ore, coal and critical minerals from Africa, the Middle East and Australia to propel its economic growth. The components that are part of production networks move through Guangzhou, Ningbo, Tianjin and its other major ports. In turn, the finished goods it assembles and ships out to the world all make use of the maritime bonds of integrated Asia. These vital interests reinforce the geopolitical imperatives driving Xi's ambition.

One of the most noteworthy examples of China's ambition is the BRI. The initiative is ostensibly intended to advance infrastructure capacity across Asia and beyond. But there is more to it than that, as the BRI is both about strengthening economic ties between the PRC and the region, but also about increasing Beijing's geopolitical influence and aligning the interests of states across Asia with the PRC (Clarke, Sussex, and Bisley, 2020). By driving economic connectivity through financing and supporting the building of pipelines, highways, ports and train terminals, among other things, China hopes to improve economic development in its periphery. This would be helpful because of the economic opportunities it would create as well as the way in which development would help advance political stability. Just as the Marshall Plan's economic reconstruction of Europe after 1945 was intended to align the economic and political interests of that continent with Washington's, China believes that helping Asian states to achieve their development aspirations will improve its diplomatic ties and its standing more broadly. The BRI also aims to increase the ways in which goods and commodities can move in and out of the PRC. At present, the vast bulk of trade travels via China's major ports on its eastern seaboard. This provides some vulnerability to its economy, particularly given US naval power. If it can create more diverse ways for things to move in and out of the country, China will reduce this risk.

Between Xi's ascension to power in 2012 and the onset of the COVID-19 pandemic, Beijing's behaviour made clear that it wanted to reshape the international environment to better suit its interests. The PRC moved away from accepting what it felt was a subordinate position in the region and set out on a long-term path to compete with the US for regional and indeed global influence. But during this time, it remained unclear just what exactly the PRC was trying to achieve, what price it was prepared to pay and what risks it was willing to take to advance those goals. The direction of travel had become clear, but the destination and timelines were much less so. While it was taking more risky steps than previously, it appeared that it did not have the appetite to undertake dramatic and highly destabilizing moves.

China's newfound economic prosperity was matched with an ambitious leadership that set out on a path to contest American leadership in the world and its strategic dominance in Asia. Washington recognized the challenge for what it was and determined that it would attempt to sustain the regional order that had been in place for some decades. A competition for the region's future was set in place. While the Sino–American rivalry was by far the most important element in the lead up to the pandemic years, at the time, both India and Russia were beginning to make clear that they too had ambitions to shape the large strategic balance in Asia. An era of geopolitical competition among the region's great powers beckoned. Globalization had bound Asia together and made it prosperous. But it also fuelled ambition and anxiety, and this geopolitical contestation created a properly Asian strategic imagination.

Asia's new institutions

Evidence of Asia's growing integration could be seen in the relatively rapid-fire formation of new regional institutions. During the 20th century multilateralism – where groups of states get together to collaborate on shared policy goals – became a central feature of international relations and a vital means through which geographically proximate states managed their increasingly shared opportunities and risks (Lavelle, 2020). As multilateral institutions began to proliferate after 1945, most notably in the North Atlantic world, where the nascent European Communities were rapidly transforming that war-torn continent's economic and security landscape, Asia was notable for its lack of such initiatives.

ASEAN was the only significant grouping established in the Cold War period, created in 1967 at the height of the second Indochina war (Narine, 2002). Its focus was firmly on intra-elite solidarity among the five founding members, Thailand, Indonesia, Philippines, Singapore and Malaysia, and not policy coordination. These relatively poor and authoritarian states wanted to find their way in the complex geopolitics of Cold War Southeast Asia, where the risks of being caught up in that conflict were all too visible in Vietnam and Cambodia. Consequently, ASEAN's remit was deliberately narrow. The South Asian Association for Regional Cooperation (SAARC) was founded in 1985, as the Cold War was in its final years, and it too had a decidedly compressed set of interests and geographic scope.

As the forces of globalization were beginning to assert themselves, the region began to make up for lost time and went through a period of rapid and, to a degree, uncoordinated construction of a wide range of institutions (Gill and Green, 2009). This flurry of institution building was the product of the growing realization that Asia's states needed to cooperate to advance their interests in a world of increasing economic connectivity. Also, even though the overt competition between the US and China was years off, it was clear that the stability of the Sino–American rapprochement period was at risk as the certainties of the Cold War ebbed away. APEC, whose first ministerial gathering was held in Canberra in late 1989, was the first to be founded. Its focus was on economic cooperation with a particular emphasis on trade liberalization.

At the same time as ASEAN was expanding its membership in the mid-1990s to include Cambodia, Laos, Myanmar and Vietnam, it was also beginning to establish a set of forums and institutions with non-ASEAN members. The group was swift to recognize that the collective fortunes of its members would be shaped by forces emanating from outside Southeast Asia. They established the ASEAN Regional Forum (ARF) in 1994 to bring together foreign ministers from across Asia and beyond, including all of ASEAN's Dialogue Partners, to improve communication and diplomacy in relation to broad security concerns. It also established the ASEAN+3 framework in late 1997 following the Asian financial crisis of that year, bringing together ASEAN, the PRC, Japan and South Korea. Originally intended to improve economic coordination and cooperation, the group has developed an extensive cooperation framework over a wide range of policy areas.

In 2005 ASEAN launched the East Asia Summit (EAS), a process that was designed to bring the top political leaders of its members together annually to discuss the full spectrum of policy issues. The foundation membership was the ten ASEAN members, the '+3' (PRC, Japan and South Korea), as well as Australia, India and New Zealand. In 2011 the US and Russia joined, making the 18-member group a formidable club, including three of five permanent members of the UN Security Council and the world's three biggest economies, the US, PRC and Japan. For the first time the region had a multilateral grouping that spanned Northeast, South, Southeast Asia and, with Russia, aspects of the central Asian landmass as well. Alongside the EAS, ASEAN also created the ASEAN Defence Ministers Meeting Plus process (ADMM+), which has the same membership as the EAS but operates at defence minister level and has a remit focused on military cooperation.

This is an expansive catalogue of bodies, with impressive memberships and, on paper at least, a wide array of areas in which the countries from many parts of Asia, and indeed beyond – the ARF counts the EU as a member – can work on shared issues of concern. The substantive areas of meaningful policy coordination emanating from these many acronyms have not yet been as significant as many might have hoped (Bisley, 2009). Indeed, one of the driving forces behind the creation of both the ARF and the EAS was the sense that the post-Cold War environment threatened the return of great power competition, yet the bodies were unable to prevent the deterioration of Sino–American relations.

China has also shown some leadership in this area. In 2001, it established the Shanghai Cooperation Organization (SCO). Originally comprising China, Russia, Kazakhstan, Kyrgyzstan, Tajikistan and Uzbekistan, the group was designed to provide a means to stabilize the post-Soviet central Asian space. It was intended not just to be about combating the narcotics trade and terrorism, but it was also an effort by China to provide some structure to a region with relatively weak state capacity. The SCO has since expanded to include India, Pakistan and Iran. China has also sought to use the CICA platform to advocate for a distinctively Asian face of security cooperation and Beijing also established the Asian Infrastructure and Investment Bank (AIIB) in 2016. The bank is a major multilateral lending institution that has an extensive membership and was established to support the need for massive infrastructure investment across the region. When it was first being put together, the US argued against its formation and strongly encouraged its allies and partners not to join. Washington perceived that the AIIB was not just a threat to the lending standards of existing international financial institutions but also a risk to the institutional framework established at Bretton Woods in the 1940s. The US was acting in ways that seemed to confirm the suspicions of anxious Beijing policy elites that the US was intent on containing PRC influence.

As well as these formal bodies Asia has a vast array of dialogue forums which meet regularly and provide a space for policy signalling through speeches, diplomacy and coordination across a range of areas from geopolitics to public health, technology to humanitarian disaster relief. The Shangri-La Dialogue (SLD), held since 2002 at the Singapore hotel of that name, is run by the London-based International Institute for Strategic Studies and is perhaps the highest profile of these. Modelled on the Munich Security Conference, the dialogue process itself has no particular political valence, but it is perceived by China, Russia and some others as favouring the US-centred status quo. China's 2014 creation of the Xiangshan Forum, run by the China Association of Military Sciences and China Institute of International Strategic Studies, is intended to provide what it purports to be a more open and inclusive forum to discuss shared security threats and challenges. India also hosts a forum along similar lines, the Raisina Dialogue, which met first in 2016 and is run by the Observer Research Foundation, a Delhi think tank. While each of these platforms is technically run by independent groups, they are strongly funded and supported by governments and are styled as 'Track 1.5' processes, reflecting their existence as somewhere between the informality and independence of 'Track 2' meetings and official 'Track 1' gatherings. China also created the Boao Forum, an annual gathering in the city of that name in Hainan. It is modelled directly on the World Economic Forum, which gathers in Davos, and, like that body, is focused primarily on economic matters with an emphasis on economic development and integration in Asia.

As Asia has been brought together into a meaningful strategic system it has developed an institutional infrastructure reflecting this larger character. The complex discussions and work programmes illustrate the nature of those pan-regional ties and the ways states across the region are trying to grapple with their shared challenges. And as they do so they are not just evidence of the integrative forces, they are also helping to further link the states and peoples of the region together.

Integrated Asia

In a generation or so Asia has gone from being a convenient fiction to the most important strategic system in the world. Even in the decade after the USSR's demise, there were neither economic ties nor strategic issues that bound the states of the vast continent together. While the two Koreas had been on a hair trigger since the armistice of 1953, China and India had fought a short but bloody war in 1962, and Indochina was traumatized by decades of brutal conflict, the disparate security threats and risks did not cohere into a larger strategic landscape. Equally, for much of the postcolonial period, Asia's economies were either autarchic, or close to it, and those that were not had little do to economically speaking with their neighbours. Those countries that did engage with the global economy followed export-focused industrialization models that led them to compete with one another for inbound investment and final export markets. And the region had no institutions to encourage economic links or the managing of shared risks because there was no sense of purpose on an Asian scale.

All that has changed. Asia has coalesced into a coherent region that is centred on China but it is not Sino-centric in the way that East Asia's international environment functioned prior to the colonial period. The PRC's role at the centre of the region's economy, the ambition it has shown, albeit in vague and unclear ways prior to 2020, to remake the region and the contestation of that by the US, and the broader ambitions of India and Russia, forged an Asian strategic imagination. No clear-eyed observer could fail to notice that, by early 2020, Asia's future was one in which geopolitical rivalry was going to play a major part. Notwithstanding the very real risks that the return of great power competition presented, most analysts and decision-makers took comfort from Beijing and Washington's extensive set of shared economic interests. Globalization's golden guardrails would act as a constraining force, reducing the prospects of competition getting too far out of hand. Trump had made noises in his first term about getting manufacturing jobs out of China and back in the US but had had little success. The implacability of global market forces seemed very real and, from a geopolitical point of view, the source of some basic comfort.

Then the COVID-19 pandemic hit, shattering the political consensus supporting market-led globalization that had made modern Asia possible. It also turbocharged Asia's geopolitics and destroyed the economic guardrails. Asia's future is now very different from the one that we all imagined prior to the pandemic years. The remainder of this book will examine the scrambling of Asia's trajectory caused by the pandemic and the forces that are likely to shape the future of the world's most important region.

5

The Pandemic Years and the End of Globalization

Asian states were among the most enthusiastic supporters of the opportunities that market-led globalization created (Beeson, 2014). Few were free-market absolutists, indeed, most countries, both large economies, like China and Japan, and smaller players, like Vietnam and the Philippines, showed a flair for selective and carefully managed integration with global markets. Internationalized production and supply chains provided many ways to benefit but all were careful to protect home markets. While plenty of state constraints remained in place in terms of their domestic economies, their underlying approach was clear: growth was to come from finding international markets for goods and inbound investment. They took this position confident in the belief that governments around the world would maintain their support for economic integration based on a faith in the power of markets, most especially the major export destination economies on either side of the North Atlantic. Asia's states also benefitted from the stability that American military dominance had fostered in the Western Pacific. The period that brought integrated Asia together was one in which the power and benefits of the market seemed all-pervasive. To describe the period between the Berlin Wall's collapse and the onset of the pandemic as the era of markets was no piece of hyperbole.

The years of the COVID-19 pandemic brought the curtain down on market-led globalization and the international consensus about economic policy on which it rested (Goldberg and Reed, 2023). Doubts about some of its elements had come to the surface after the 2007–08 GFC, and these began to crash into mainstream politics in the 2016 shocks of the Brexit vote and Trump's election victory. But these concerns did not fundamentally challenge the foundations on which the global economy rested. The pandemic years changed things much more dramatically and the balance between economic and political forces was and remains scrambled. States are no longer content to let market forces decide what is made where. Politics has returned to the workings of the global economy with a vengeance. The simultaneous turbocharging of geopolitics has accentuated this trend. Where in the past many felt that market integration would prevent or at least constrain Sino–American rivalry, it now appears to be unchecked by shared economic interests. Even during Trump's most anti-China moments in his first term, observers felt that the two countries' economic interdependence would ensure that unalloyed geopolitics would not prevail. That is no longer the case. Beyond geopolitics, market power is being restrained as states seek to re-engineer their economies, deepen resilience after the pandemic and adapt to a changing climate.

This chapter explores the ways in which the COVID-19 years marked a critical juncture and set Asia and, indeed, the world, on a different path. During this time the slowly building scepticism about globalization erupted as the pandemic revealed in stark terms the vulnerability of tightly connected economies and a global system in which the decisions about what is made where and by whom are left largely in the hands of market forces. But it was not just that the offshoring of manufacturing left countries unable to provide personal protective equipment (PPE) or viral testing kits that was seen as an intolerable product of globalization. As geopolitical temperatures have risen, the hawkish argument that the ties of economic interdependence between the US and China were a source of vulnerability (CSIS, 2018) became entirely mainstream in Washington and among its allies. This gave further impetus to the recasting of economic relations to serve political goals and served to reinforce geopolitical competition. This chapter examines the COVID-19 years and explores the ways in which globalization is being reconstituted, shaped by a much more explicitly political set of forces than existed before the pandemic.

A fraying consensus

From the 1980s, most of Asia began to embrace the basic tenets of market-led globalization, at least as they related to the opportunities for growth that it promised. This began with an emphasis on export-focused industrialization, as pioneered by Japan and then South Korea, and was accelerated by the transformation of international production and the adoption of complex supply chain management by multinationals in the 1990s. The opportunities of globalization were made possible because of the consensus that existed across the advanced economies that markets were the best way to allocate resources (see, for example, Micklethwait and Wooldridge, 2000). There were no meaningful alternatives that had any degree of plausibility – the old command economy models had been discredited and even the more statist inclinations of the capitalist economies from the 1960s and 1970s of having national champions, industry policy and capital controls seemed to be from another era. To argue for the need to limit the movement of capital across borders or that states ought to be able to produce certain goods themselves, whether petrochemicals or pharmaceuticals, was not just out of touch with the times, it was almost embarrassing. The faith in markets and their eternal openness was deep and profound among the advanced economies (see, for example, Woolf, 2004).

There was good reason for this faith. Costs of products across the spectrum dropped dramatically during this period. The price of a flat screen television is illustrative. First introduced in the early 2000s, a 42-inch screen sold for nearly US$20,000 when initially released. In 2024, a cheap version could be acquired for a few hundred dollars and even a premium branded set cost around US$700. While not all price reductions were as dramatic, the economic benefit of allowing market forces their head was plain to see (Dreher, Gastons and Martens, 2008). And it was not just that consumers could buy cheaper vacuum cleaners or retailers could acquire clothes to on-sell at bargain prices, the growth opportunities that it realized drove an expansion in incomes and prosperity at a speed and scale that had never been seen before.

Asian states' interest in market efficiency and the growth that it propelled was as much political as it was economic. The growing prosperity of many economies brought with it a cycle of entrepreneurship as well as expectation. These more spontaneous factors – firms seeking to grow, consumers responding to market signals – were reinforced by political interests. Put simply, states that had displayed faith in access to global markets became politically beholden to their continuing success (Rock, 2017). Increasing wealth and improved living standards legitimated governments and political systems. And Asian leaders lived with the fear that a failure to continue to provide economic success and material improvements in people's lives would lead to political and social unrest, if not complete upheaval.

They had good reason to be fearful. The Asian financial crisis of 1997–98 that tore through South Korea, Malaysia, Thailand and Indonesia remained seared in the memory of many in the region. The crisis set back economic growth in those countries and sent political shock waves across Asia (Haggard, 2010). Most famously, the Indonesian autocrat Suharto, who had ruled the former Dutch colony since the mid-1960s, resigned amid massive social protest and the country swiftly launched a transition into a vibrant liberal democracy (Aspinall, 2005). The crisis sent a clear message to many Asian leaders: mishandling the economy and pushing back living standards risked societal upheaval and political revolution.

For the PRC this was especially important, given the extent to which it had tied its political fortunes to economic management. The reforms launched by Deng Xiaoping were a conscious effort by the CPC to move away from Maoist orthodoxies and into a more pragmatic approach where market forces could be harnessed to advance the party's goals of national rejuvenation (Liu and Zhang, 2010). For decades Beijing was fixated on ensuring economic growth, not just to improve the economic and social fabric of the PRC but to maintain social stability and legitimate party rule. Outsiders might be forgiven for assuming that economic growth was simply a trade-off for political freedoms – people would put up with Party-state authoritarianism in return for prosperity. To a degree this quid pro quo was part of the story, but the PRC was a country that in living memory had barely been able to feed itself and that had endured the brutal chaos of the Cultural Revolution. Economic wellbeing had an imperative beyond a legitimation strategy. It meant being able to hold the country together and ensuring the vast land of unimaginable population could be managed. For rapidly growing countries across Asia the interest in sustaining prosperity was profound.

When globalization was first recognized as a social phenomenon in the early 1990s, its transformative impact on economies and societies created an initial political backlash (Sassen, 1998). Dutch populist Pym Fortyn, US independent presidential candidate Ross Perot and Australian MP Pauline Hansen all rode political waves created by globalization's social dislocation (Mudde, 2016). The GFC of 2007–08 in the US, and the Eurozone crisis that followed, created some cracks in globalization's political foundations (Mason, 2012). Mainstream political parties had recognized some of the symptoms. The UK's Labour Party had tried to use stagnant middle-class wages for political advantage in the years after the GFC but failed to gain any electoral traction (Eatwell and Goodwin, 2018). The twin political shocks of 2016 showed that the global tide was beginning to turn. But in Asia, faith in globalization's larger benefits remained, understandably so, given the benefits it had created.

The Brexit referendum starkly revealed how big a gap existed between elite policy consensus about markets and globalization and public opinion. British Prime Minister David Cameron's cavalier approach opened the door and the anti-EU forces, nationalists and populists, barged through (Clarke, Goodwin and Whiteley, 2017). Several months later, the election of the reality TV star Donald Trump to the US presidency confirmed that the political foundation of contemporary globalization was seriously fractured. The two most substantial proponents of free-market capitalism had experienced convulsive political shocks. To be clear, Trump's rise to the presidency was fortuitous. In 2016, he ran in a large and divided Republican field, where the 'winner takes all' rules for the primary election meant he could turn a plurality of votes into a substantial outcome. The US electoral college provided disproportionate influence to the voting groups that supported him, and he ran against an unpopular Democratic nominee. Yet, while more than 2 million more Americans voted for Hillary Clinton, he won around 46 per cent of the vote and more than 64 million people cast their ballot for a complete political neophyte. His strident, xenophobic and anti-globalization message plainly resonated with a substantial part of the US electorate (Sides, Tesler and Vavrek, 2018).

Central to the 45th president's message was a visceral articulation of the belief that the years of globalization had made most Americans worse off. By that Trump meant not just that wages were frozen, industries lost and the ladder to middle-class prosperity removed for many working families, but that the fabric of American society had been shredded by the social and cultural changes that globalization foisted on the US. Political scientists have analysed Trump's electoral support and shown that it was motivated more by grievances about cultural changes than it was about economic deprivation and exclusion (Norris and Inglehart, 2019). Trump's shrewdness lay in fusing these related but disparate concerns into a coherent and energized voting coalition that was concentrated in just the right places on the electoral map.

In his first term government, Trump was often chaotic and incoherent in action; he did little to improve the lot of those in the cities and towns that globalization had ravaged. To address what he described memorably in his inaugural address as 'American carnage', he targeted China, which he depicted as a pantomime villain that had been stealing American industries, jobs and ideas. But the venom was not only rhetorical. In October 2018, in the lead up to the mid-term congressional elections, Vice President Pence's speech at the Hudson Institute made it clear that the administration was taking a much more aggressive approach to China, of which the tariffs were only the first part (Pence, 2018). Elements within the administration, most notably Peter Navarro, sought a significant rupture in Sino–American economic ties. 'Decoupling' began to appear as a term to describe the efforts to disentangle the complex interdependence that had developed between the world's two most important economies. Trump's trade assault was intended to damage critical PRC industries and drive businesses to bring back factories and plants to the United States. The tariffs were introduced over several years and across a wide range of areas from solar panels to steel, so that by 2019 trade worth around US$250 billion was affected by major new impositions. The most hard-hitting of these were in intermediate goods, such as car parts and components in electronic goods; the impact on trade volumes was stark (Brown, 2022).

As the presidential election year loomed, Trump appeared to feel confident. The US economy was booming; low interest rates combined with massive tax cuts had stoked investment and consumption. US consumers seemed unconcerned by the administration's tariff policy. While allies and partners would have preferred less bellicosity from Trump, they shared anxieties about China and were supportive of Washington's more muscular approach. The political scepticism about unfettered globalization, manifest so vividly in the 45th US president, was beginning to gain traction. Interestingly, after Trump's election and just before his inauguration, Xi Jinping gave a speech at Davos, presenting China as the defender of economic globalization, which he said was not the source of problems that some claimed (Xi, 2017). And the Democratic Party seemed in disarray, with many candidates seeking the nomination but with no strong and compelling figure among the group. In January 2020, four more years for Trump looked a safe bet.

The pandemic

While Trump's scepticism about globalization was embodied in his unlikely presidency, it was the pandemic years that coalesced the disparate concerns about market dominance, inequality, the hollowing out of industrial capacity as well as the ways supply chains had created acute vulnerabilities into something politically transformative.

The story of COVID-19's emergence in Wuhan and its rapid global spread is reasonably well known (MacKenzie, 2020). In February 2020, it looked like a major problem but one that, like the severe acute respiratory syndrome (SARS) crisis of 2002, would ultimately be contained within China and perhaps one or two other countries. This swiftly proved to be wildly optimistic. The absence of a vaccine for and the lack of immunity to the highly contagious new respiratory disease led to medical facilities being overwhelmed in the countries where it struck first, in China, then Italy and spreading swiftly across Europe and then the wider world. On 11 March 2020, the WHO declared a global pandemic, but by then the disease was loose in the world. The CPC had responded in February by implementing largescale shutdowns of major cities, forbidding travel, closing workplaces and implementing draconian measures to try to halt the physical spread of the disease. Outside observers looked on but could not imagine that such things would be possible outside an authoritarian regime. By slamming the brakes on its society, the PRC dropped a brick on its economic growth, which had dramatic knock-on effects on the global economy, the first sign of which was the collapse in oil prices. At one point, tankers were being chartered so as to store unsold unrefined crude, so precipitous had been the collapse in the oil price caused by the sudden shutdown in China.

China also alienated many abroad by not admitting there was a problem until it was forced to as things had spiralled out of control. It refused to share vital data about what it knew and cooperate with efforts to understand the disease at a critical point at which it might have been contained. Much as the USSR's secrecy about Chernobyl badly undermined that country's standing, COVID-19's outbreak severely damaged confidence in the PRC. Trust had been critical to economic openness, and its breakdown was a component in the collapse of faith in economic integration.

COVID-19's pathogenic advantage was the speed with which it could be transmitted between people. The latency period, that is the time between the virus successfully lodging itself in a person and the point at which symptoms appear, was several days, in keeping with the flu and other similar diseases. However, hosts could pass the virus on during that period. And it was spread through the air and not, as initially thought, through surface contact. This provided ample opportunity for the disease to spread quickly through a population as people went about daily life unaware that they were sick and circulating the virus. And with international flights, it could move rapidly over great distances. The webs of connectivity that are the lifeblood of globalization – air travel, seaborne goods travel, the networks of finance and capital – are also vectors of vulnerability. COVID-19 moved rapidly down those channels. All the initial outbreaks outside China, in Italy, South Korea and Japan, had close connections with Chinese industry and trade.

Through March and April 2020, countries around the world implemented lockdowns to try to contain the spread of the disease within their jurisdictions while also putting in place strict limits on international movement. Trump issued a ban on travellers from China in February that year; he then banned travel from Europe in March, although exempting people from Ireland and the UK. Around the world, schools and universities began to close, shifting teaching to online modes where possible. By the middle of April 2020, more than a billion children were no longer at school. Across the world, from the rich economies of the West to the emerging powers of Nigeria, Indonesia and India, general lockdowns were imposed. Japan's government, resigned to its fate, reluctantly postponed the Summer Olympics that Tokyo had been due to host.

In the space of a few short months, cities and nations around the world found themselves copying China's policy of freezing populations in place, halting economic and social activity and implementing track and trace programmes. Liberal democracies that had, in February, looked at Wuhan and other Chinese cities with disbelief, found themselves issuing stay-at-home orders, policing curfews and closing their borders. The consequence of COVID-19 was an astonishing shutdown of the global economy. Unemployment rates shot up to unimaginable levels in the US as troubled firms dumped employees as quickly as they could. Developed economies experienced their worst contraction since 1945 and, in some cases, it was even more dire than the Great Depression, as activity collapsed and governments foundered in the face of a challenge that had last been seen in 1919 (Tooze, 2021). It was clear that a pandemic would be devastating for the global economy, given how intertwined far-flung societies had become.

As governments scrambled to work out how to test, trace and quarantine, as well as ramp up medical capacity, they also had to figure out how to respond to economic activity falling off a cliff (Agarwal, He, Yeung, 2020). The simultaneous and almost universal nature of the shutdown exacerbated problems. The previous major crisis, the financial collapse of 2007–08, while vast, was experienced unevenly around the world, with the bulk of the problems located in the North Atlantic economies. This time, not a single country of scale and significance was without economic carnage.

The experience of 2007–08 gave policy makers something of a guidebook for managing the COVID-19-enforced shutdown. It had revealed that even in an age when faith in markets was strong, in extremis, only states could correct the failings of economies (Tooze, 2018). Then governments bailed out banks, nationalized mortgage creditors and provided cash to stimulate economic growth. Financial meltdown was avoided in 2008, but the recovery was extremely slow, with many countries taking years to return to pre-crisis levels of economic prosperity (Taylor and Baily, 2014). By some measures the worst affected European economies had lost so much that it would take nearly a decade to get back to where they had been in 2008.

As governments took the steps to bring society to a halt to try to contain COVID-19's spread, they had to come up with a way of ensuring they did not trigger a wider economic collapse. But it was not just the state-forced closures with which they had to grapple. As the scale of the pandemic's reach, the speed of its spread and the complete absence of any medical means to control the disease became recognized, publics around the world acted spontaneously, unprompted by government edicts, to cut back dramatically on spending (Tooze, 2021). Household expenditure dropped precipitously even before national lockdowns were put in place. This was as true in the UK, where household discretionary spending nearly halved, as it was in India. Perhaps the most emblematic statistic of this moment was the 26 March

2020 release of the weekly US unemployment figures, which revealed 3.3 million had been added to the numbers of the unemployed. This compares with around 600,000 in the worst week of the GFC. More than 1 per cent of the population of the world's largest economy had lost their jobs in a week. The situation was just staggering. There was a good reason for people to be careful with their cash.

Economic vulnerability

Governments had to deal with the shock to the system created by the decision to close so many aspects of the economy as well as remediate the effects of citizens taking prudent steps with their money in the face of a global crisis. And they had to do it in a way that would make sure that recovery would be faster than before. No government wanted to have the kind of anaemic response to the crisis as that with which the North Atlantic economies had struggled after 2008.

In the face of what was an immense public health catastrophe and an economic unravelling, which in financial terms was becoming particularly dangerous with the breakdown of stock markets, money markets and interbank lending in March, governments had to be extremely creative. They also had to break with long-held orthodoxies of just what it was that the state should and should not do with markets. The most significant player was the US and, led by Federal Reserve Bank Chair Jerome Powell and Treasury Secretary Steve Mnuchin, Washington took steps that, in any other circumstance, would have been almost impossible to imagine a Republican administration undertaking (Lee, 2021). This included issuing massive credit lines to provide backstops to money and bond markets, state and city governments and even individual firms, something the Federal Reserve had previously shied away from entirely. This was followed by a gargantuan fiscal stimulus bill in late March that included direct cash payments to Americans, tax cuts and additional funding to a wide range of government departments that amounted to US$2.2 trillion, around 10 per cent of the US' GDP, a fiscal injection into the economy of a scale that had never occurred in US history.

Countries around the world followed suit, partly prompted by Washington but also by the more immediate realization of the dire need to put cash and services into the hands of citizens. While different countries tailored their actions to specific circumstances and what they thought they could afford, the scale of economic stimulus and government intervention was unprecedented, as were the creative ways of sustaining an economic pulse. Many governments provided cash payments, tax cuts, suspension of loan payments and debt forgiveness. Some introduced moratoriums on evictions; many provided job furlough programmes or direct payments to subsidize employment (Andreosso-O'Callaghan, Sohn and Moon, 2021). As the pandemic played out, these massive programmes of job protection, cash payments, eviction prevention and loan holidays proved to be highly effective (Salmon, 2023). Crucially, it showed the worth and efficacy of economic policies that were unimaginable even months before and from which many of the governments who put them in place would have previously run a great distance. COVID-19 illustrated in the most visible way imaginable that the economy could be subordinated to political imperatives and that old orthodoxies could be turned swiftly on their heads.

The pandemic showed that the state remained fundamental to the terms of social and economic life. While often hidebound by inertia, vested interests and faith in ideology, it can move swiftly and with creativity in times of crisis. COVID-19 also exposed just how vulnerable states and societies were to the fragilities of globalization. A mutation at the microbial level had triggered an unimaginable seizing up of the global economy. Scholars had long argued that a zoonotic disease could emerge for which there was no resistance and no vaccine, and it could spread rapidly through the dense populations of modern metropolises and globally via intercontinental travel (Khan and Patrick, 2016).

Beyond the ideas of what states could and should do, COVID-19 also revealed the specific vulnerabilities of complex international supply chains. As discussed in Chapter 4, the transformation of international production had created a finely calibrated and fragile system of manufacturing and distribution. It meant that when borders were closed, workers laid off and ships repurposed or laid idle, the knock-on shocks were immense. The complexity of these networks meant that the interaction of different shocks had a compounding effect. To protect the health of workers, microchip manufacturers in Taiwan had to slow down production of pieces of technology that had become essential to just about every kind of electronic good. This, in turn, meant that manufacturers of cars, fridges or computers could not maintain their normal production levels. But those same car producers were also affected by consumers reducing consumption; the shortage of cash coming in then meant producers had to cut back their operations, reducing their orders of parts and components. Part manufacturers, limited by input access problems and staffing, also had their activities scrambled. And even if the cars could be ordered and built, strict public health regimes meant that shipping and port facilities could not operate at the normal pace. This supply chain shock exacerbated the economic consequences of COVID-19 while also showing just how finely calibrated the global economy was and, in turn, how vulnerable societies had become when things went awry.

The discontent was not just focused on broken supply chains and the frustrations of long waits for cars, games consoles or industrial appliances. States suddenly became aware of all the things they no longer produced themselves because others did so more cheaply but which they suddenly needed in bulk. The most acute example of this was PPE. Latex gloves, face masks, eye shields, aprons and the like, which were ordinarily used in a narrow context – hospitals, medical surgeries or aged care homes – almost instantly became something that everyone needed to go about even the most mundane of daily activities. And PPE – a typical example of precisely the kind of relatively simple manufactured good that globalization was so good at making very cheaply – had been left to market efficiencies. Factories in China could produce at scale, cost and quality levels that few could match. PPE was easy to transport, simple to produce and did not require much tailoring to specific markets. But the combination of supply chain meltdowns and the absence of localized capacity exposed glaringly the ways market logic and a complacency about its reliability had created a situation of acute shortage.

Pharmaceuticals were a second area where the limits of localized production were exposed. Producing medication, whether therapeutic or preventative, is an especially globalized industry. Major firms have highly complex supply chains, with some encircling the globe three times before the completed product is shipped to a final market. Although pharmaceutical firms tend to be a little less 'just in time' in their production models, they retain a higher level of inventory than most manufactured goods; nonetheless, they are subject to the same basic fragilities of globalization. As with PPE, this meant that countries' lack of independent productive capacity was laid bare by the virus. While in the early months, a vaccine appeared potentially years off, some basic therapeutic medicine and treatments were quickly identified but the supplies were limited and capacity to acquire or produce even basic drugs was highly constrained. COVID-19 showed that globalization had created shortcomings of what some called 'sovereign capability'. Countries had been content to give up the ability to make things because of the economic benefits of market-led globalization. The pandemic brutally exposed the limitations of leaving production in the hands of the market.

The sovereign capability shock also brought to the surface vulnerabilities that were not tied directly to combatting the virus.

In the early months of the pandemic the microchip industry was significantly impacted by public health measures implemented to halt COVID-19's spread. This quickly led to shortages of cars, electronic goods and consumer durables like fridges and washing machines. 'Chipmageddon', as some called it, was a reflection not just of lockdowns and social distancing requirements but also because of the extreme concentration of the microchip industry. Silicon chip microprocessors are items on which all modern electronic equipment depend. From the targeting mechanisms of nuclear missiles to a smart TV, from washing machines to the switching mechanisms managing mass public transit systems, microchips are the foundation of vast swathes of things used so much in daily life. Their rapid development from specialized and highly expensive items for military systems to commoditized mass produced goods at highly varying levels of sophistication is an emblematic tale of globalization (Miller, 2022). But it is one where production follows an unusual pattern. Instead of complex globe-encircling chains, the industry became highly concentrated into just a few countries. Taiwan, South Korea and China account for around 70 per cent of the total production of chips globally. Taiwan alone accounts for 90 per cent of the world's production of the highest performance chips, those powering AI computing and the like, which, in turn, are produced almost entirely by one firm, TSMC. The Dutch company ASML is the only firm in the world that builds the lithography equipment that is necessary to make the most advanced chips. And, of course, Taiwan is a place that the PRC regards as a rogue province and is prepared to fight a war to assert its control.

As geopolitics had been reawakened in the years leading up to the pandemic and had accelerated through the COVID-19 years, the vulnerabilities that came with globalization in high technology suddenly seemed to be a price states would no longer be willing to play. With the experience of the pandemic, it seemed downright dangerous to rely on market demand and firm profits determining what gets made and where.

The pandemic revealed the fragilities of globalization, but these were not inherently a product of the disease; they had always been there. They were central to the whole edifice. Insurance companies, logistic managers, analysts and scholars had all been aware of the many ways in which complexity and risk were built into globalization's foundations. German sociologist Ulrich Beck had made his name in the 1990s by writing about just how important risk was to modern globalized societies (Beck, 1999). And countries across the world had developed pandemic plans to prepare for what researchers said repeatedly was inevitable. The only uncertainty was when and under what circumstances a global disaster would occur. Yet when faced with the mix of economic benefit that markets created, the political difficulty of arguing against the orthodoxies of the day and the reality that the broader global circumstances that had been so conducive to globalization had been in place for a long time, it is not surprising that societies the world over were left exposed. Despite all that knowledge when the tsunami of COVID-19 crashed, they were extraordinarily ill-prepared.

Before February 2020 the balance of economic and political factors was tipped decisively in favour of markets. COVID-19 had scrambled the global economy. It became clear that factory settings could not be restored as the pandemic had broken the intellectual and policy grip of liberal market principles that had held such a dominant position among the advanced economies.

Questioning globalization and China

Going into COVID-19, doubts about globalization's benefits and risks had started to become politically visible in many countries. The pandemic exposed many of these problems and showed them to be intolerable, at least under certain circumstances. It is important to underline that Asian states' problems stemmed from the extent to which they depended on the openness of the developed economies as they themselves had retained varying levels of protection for their home economies. The focus was on the benefits to be had from tapping into the markets created by the economic openness of the developed world. Agreements like AFTA had helped drive some intermediate connectivity but the main focus was on making things that would contribute to or be finished goods sold to the wider world. Nowhere was this more evident than in China. However, in Beijing, even before the crisis emerged in Wuhan, concerns about dependence on globalization were beginning to emerge, but the opaque nature of PRC policy decision-making, especially so under Xi Jinping, meant that it was difficult for outside observers to see.

This changed towards the end of 2020. At that point, the PRC seemed to be out of the worst of the COVID-19 crisis. While the democratic world was foundering, authoritarian China's brutal lockdowns and colossal tracking, testing and quarantine systems had evidently beaten back the virus without the need for an effective vaccine. The PRC government began to discuss publicly the need to develop what Xi Jinping called a 'dual circulation' economy (Lin and Wang, 2022). Scholars in China had used the term 'international circulation' to describe the export-focused plan for growth that had been central to the 'reform and opening up' programme. Xi's articulation of 'dual circulation' was in the main about turning away from the overwhelming focus on external markets for success and instead emphasizing the need to promote domestic markets and consumption. The two 'circulations' were firstly reducing the reliance on external sources of investment, consumption and know-how, and secondly increasing the role played by domestic factors in driving growth.

While the most immediate priority was to improve Chinese consumption and investment, the longer-run emphasis was about developing home-grown technology and industrial techniques. Just as Western powers had seen the pandemic expose their dependence on foreign countries, China was also aware of how much it too depended on others. US technology and consumption was, potentially, a dagger that could be held against China's throat. Officials in the PRC had, for some time, sought to rebalance the country's economy. Where in the past this was about moving away from capital-intensive investment – the building of highways, bridges, ports and towns – to drive growth and instead looking to domestic consumption to be the economic locomotive (Day and Simon, 2016), now the PRC was looking to reduce its exposure to the global economy, or, more precisely, to develop measures to reduce its dependence on others. This was no return to Maoist autarky, but it was also not just a technocratic refinement of the economic model. The CPC wanted to be able to control the country's supply lines and markets.

Just as the pandemic years accentuated the problems with globalization, they also accelerated competition between the US and China. Rivalry between the two countries had been building for years, the Obama administration's pivot and the response by a wary China made clear geopolitical competition was on its way back to Asia. Donald Trump's first administration had focused more directly on overt competition in its security policy and had turned the tariff screws on Chinese exports. But even into the early weeks of the COVID-19 crisis Trump held the door open to the PRC, tweeting, one felt, almost for his own reassurance, that his 'friend' Xi Jinping had things under control. When it became clear that this was not the case and that the pandemic was undercutting the central planks of Trump's bid for re-election, he began to see the virus and its consequences as a personal attack. The administration further turned up the temperature of its rhetoric and anti-China policies (Feng, 2021).

While other countries in Asia and around the world chose to present their policies in more measured terms than the 45th US president, the COVID-19 years led to a hardening of attitudes about the challenge China presented in many corners of the world. Although the pandemic was not itself a geopolitical issue, the mistrust, poor communication and inability of major powers to collaborate to understand and combat the disease was both a function of distrust and, in turn, a force driving a vicious cycle. China's secrecy and stonewalling were a particular problem. Most were not as diplomatically clumsy as the Australian foreign minister, who called for an international investigation into the origins of COVID-19 in April 2020 and one not run by the WHO because of suspicions that China would use its influence in that body to nobble any proper scrutiny. Australia had failed to develop an international coalition to support its case and felt the wrath of an angry China, which imposed a slew of tariffs and regulatory costs on many of the country's key exports to the PRC (Wilkins, 2020). Yet the call from Canberra, however clumsily handled, resonated with many around the world and China's bullying response further reinforced the sense that the PRC was a vindicative and insecure major power.

Geopolitics had slowly been coming to the surface, in a similar way to the growing doubts about globalization. But it was not until the COVID-19 pandemic that it took such a dominant role. The uncertainties of just how to compete with a critical trading partner had been overtaken by overt security concerns. While it did not mean an instantaneous return to a world of discrete economic blocs of the kind seen in the Cold War, it did signal that political and security concerns about China had overtaken the sense of economic opportunity of trade and investment that had previously been so central. In the 2016 election, Trump had said he would force firms to move out of China and bring jobs back to the US. That looked like so much fanciful bluster on the campaign trail. By 2020, firms were exiting the PRC, reshoring was becoming real and, while Trump could not take all the credit, the days of economic concerns having equal or greater say than political and security ones were gone. If anyone had any doubts about the direction world politics had taken, Vladimir Putin's decision to launch a full-scale invasion of Ukraine in February 2022 cemented the sense that the world had entered a new era, one defined by significantly heightened geopolitical risk.

Remaking globalization

The particular way in which globalization worked in the period from 1989 through to the start of the COVID-19 pandemic was the crucial factor in creating an integrated Asian strategic system. The pandemic years upended the economic applecart. The finely calibrated supply chains that were such a central part of the old ways of doing things were scrambled. The political consensus supporting open markets and that favoured efficiency and low prices over security and stability broke down. And that coincided with the acceleration of great power competition in Asia serving to reinforce the imperative to remake globalization in different ways, ways that are more resilient to shock and which serve larger geopolitical as well as nationalist imperatives. The COVID-19 years saw the global economy shut down and then, as it was re-started, critical aspects of it have changed: confidence in markets is reduced, states are no longer prepared to live with vulnerabilities that market efficiency creates, openness to foreign trade has been replaced with a nationalist desire to control access and a sense of geopolitical insecurity is pervasive. The global economy is being reconstituted in the light of these changes.

Political elites the world over recognized that they had power over markets and a social licence to act in ways that broke with the conventional wisdom of the previous decades. How will they respond to this environment? How will a reconstructed globalization function? How will the different choices made in capitals around the world interact with one another? What effect will the rewiring of globalization have on the world's most populous region?

The challenge in trying to make sense of the historical and social significance of events that are in motion lies in discerning the significant from the mundane. Developments that grab headlines one day prove, in time, to be of marginal significance; achieving the necessary perspective is challenging. Equally, the reconstitution of something as large and complex as globalization will take many years. Crises and war can destroy things very swiftly. Reconstruction and renovation take much longer. Yet there is an imperative to make sense of the direction in which events are moving; we cannot simply wait for history to produce a verdict. More importantly, choices made now as we reconfigure critical components of national and international infrastructure, redraw policy settings and make investments for the future, will determine the path down which we travel. There is a necessity to grapple with the absence of perspective that comes from analysing contemporary events and uncertainty as to how exactly things will end.

It is not just the question of scale, perspective and the complexity of the global economy that makes this a difficult task. The loose way in which terms are used and the overlapping ideas that analysts, political figures and policy makers use to refer to the mix of motives that lie behind these efforts can hinder attempts to make sense of what is going on. Observers have used terms such as economic statecraft or geoeconomics to describe the link between political ends and market mechanisms; while they have appeal, neither is especially precise nor do they shed much light on the dynamics at work. The former generally refers to the use of specific economic policies to achieve narrowly defined foreign policy goals, such as the application of sanctions to force a targeted state to act. The latter is much broader, referring to a wide range of ways in which states use economic policy or broader economic activity to advance strategic goals.

While scholars have pointed out that the incipient rivalry between the US and China prompted a renewed interest in geoeconomics (Blackwill and Harris, 2016), the ideas neither captured the commanding heights of political thinking nor did they have much bearing on the general patterns of trade and investment in the global economy prior to 2020. In the years following the declaration of the COVID-19 pandemic by the WHO, a range of factors prompted interventions by states in the working of global markets. These have collectively begun to have a tangible impact on trade and investment patterns and have started to play a major role in policy and political debate. This dynamic has been supercharged by the second Trump administration's radical transformation of trade and tariff policy that is fundamentally reconfiguring the basic rules of the road in international trade, which will have significant knock-on consequences for the world. However, the chaotic nature of the policy process in Washington and the uncertain overarching logic of the administration make discerning how the policy settings will end up very difficult.

As the global economy is being remade, where states seek to influence market forces and reshape the patterns of production and distribution, one can identify five broad but distinct political prompts driving state action. The first and most significant, at least in terms of catalysing action, was the pandemic itself. It exposed vulnerabilities created by globalization's highly complex supply chains. States want to reduce those vulnerabilities to tolerable levels. This is a reaction to the snarling up of the workings of the economy previously described as well as the way that it revealed the lack of domestic capacity to provide things that were needed to combat a large-scale public health crisis. The second is the desire to reduce geopolitical vulnerability and advance security goals. Scholars had long pointed out that economic interdependence provides both mutual benefits but also interlocking vulnerabilities (Keohane and Nye, 2011). The revival of great power competition gave rise to a growing sense that the major powers did not want to be beholden to market forces in areas of critical importance, most obviously in high-end computing, microprocessors, AI and other potentially decisive technologies. But it is also visible in more traditional manufacturing, such as ship-building, in which the US moved, within a generation, from being one of the world's major players to effectively having no commercial ship-building capacity (Thompson 2021). A third prompt is to correct a market failure, a more conventional motive for political intervention. The nature of the climate crisis – where long-term costs of economic activity are invisible to market participants, thus providing no incentive to manage or control them – is a textbook example of the limits of markets. To rectify this, states are moving to try to reconfigure market activity to drive behaviour that reduces the risks of acute climate change, and that supports adaptation or ameliorates the impacts of change already in play. A fourth factor is the political desire to restructure economies to rectify what were perceived to be shortcomings created by globalization. Perhaps the most visible example of this was the hollowing out of cities and towns in developed economies as firms moved factories and plants overseas. In response, states are trying to rebuild manufacturing in advanced economies, not just to see off geopolitical risk but to try to reweave the social fabric of their societies. Finally, the economic response to COVID-19 created an unexpected burst of inflation and states intervened to try to remove or at least reduce this pernicious economic force that many neoliberal economists had presumed they had slain in the 1980s.

These five related but distinct motives created a wide array of policies in many countries. These efforts to advance specific goals via economic means are reconfiguring how globalization will function in the coming decades. From the return of industrial policy to sanctions, from defending 'critical' areas of a domestic economy to rebuilding a manufacturing base, advanced and developing economies are all, to varying degrees, trying to recast market and firm behaviour to advance their goals. While there is a huge number and wide variety of policy initiatives at work, one can identify a clear set of categories of activity emerging among the welter of programmes and policies.

The first category of activities are attempts to defend certain sectors or industries from being owned by opponents or actors deemed to be hostile. This is about ensuring that vulnerable areas of an economy, such as its power grid or water sanitation systems, are protected. But it also includes concerns about what foreign firms might do with knowledge, information or critical technologies. The US Congress efforts to ban the Chinese-listed firm Bytedance from owning the popular TikTok app is a high-profile example of the latter (Shephardson, 2024). While there has been some concern about the role of the app in spreading disinformation and promoting PRC propaganda, the bigger concerns relate to what the company might do with the vast quantities of data it has on American citizens. Prompted by Washington's ban, other countries are also considering taking similar steps to reduce the perceived risks of PRC ownership of the software and data.

A second set of activities are efforts to build economic capacity. The aim here is for states to develop a domestic ability to undertake specific types of production and other economic activity that they had never been able to do or which had been 'offshored' by firms taking advantage of global markets. Until the pandemic the dependence of many countries on cheap PPE or global pharmaceutical production was a price worth paying, and the risks of supply shocks were seen as minimal or at least manageable. Now, across the developed and developing world one can identify efforts to correct this circumstance and ensure a level of 'sovereign capability' in key areas, such as pharmaceuticals, advanced electronics and critical minerals.

A third group of policies involves what can be described as economic engineering. The current period has seen states taking ambitious and costly steps to build or reconstruct industries or economic capacity. This includes efforts to bring back manufacturing and other processes that are thought to be of social as well as economic value (Lawrence, 2024). But it is not just American or British efforts to reinvigorate areas that were socially decimated by production facilities moving abroad and the automation of factories, it also includes efforts to promote technology and production to assist with the transition away from carbon intensive economies. In some ways, the policies of tariffs, taxes, subsidies and tax incentives that the Biden Administration created to drive investment in green technologies mirrored the efforts of emerging economies trying to develop their own fledgeling industries. But the striking fact is that states that had hitherto been content to let market logic and firm efficiency calculations generate things such as photovoltaic panels or high-quality low cost manufactured goods, now perceive the need to intervene in market processes to engineer domestically focused outcomes because they fear becoming dependent on China for this technology.

The fourth category is a set of policy tools that is familiar in that these tools are mechanisms with which to compete with or coerce a targeted state. The aim here is to use economic leverage to force a target to change its behaviour or degrade its capacity. Economic sanctions are the most common form this leverage takes, and these have been increasingly used in the decades after the Cold War (Martin, 2021). But this group also includes efforts to weaken a country's economic growth in general as well as specific policies to degrade, undermine or even destroy a firm or a sector. The US has, in recent years, explicitly sought to damage the Chinese telecommunications firm Huawei's capacity to operate. It initially blacklisted the company in 2019, preventing US businesses from exporting parts to the PRC-owned telco without a licence. Then it tightened further the company's ability to buy semiconductors and refused to approve any licences at all. The effort is intended to damage the company's ability to operate and is motivated both by specific anxieties US policy makers have about the firm being used to threaten US security directly, as well as concerns that, as a globally significant firm, Huawei has provided the PRC with an opportunity to expand its broader influence around the world. American efforts to deprive Chinese firms' access to very high performance semiconductors are also a direct attempt to choke that country's ability to develop AI and other frontier technologies, although the success of DeepSeek's AI technology has shown that these efforts have had limited success.

The final way in which states are asserting their influence is in efforts to align the interests of other countries. Here, they provide loans, grants, trade concessions, infrastructure funding and other economic benefits to bind states into their orbit. The BRI was one of the early signs of the ways in which China sought to use its economic scale and capacity to reconfigure the international environment through the provision of financing and capacity to improve economic connectivity across Asia (Clarke, Sussex and Bisley, 2020). The aim of the Marshall Plan, which the US provided to post-1945 Europe, was not just to improve the economic prospects of post-war Western Europe, but also to bind those states to Washington's vision of the global economy at a time when communism had strong appeal. Beijing today equally wants to provide international public goods that draw states towards it and keep their interests aligned. The US and its partners, such as Japan, Australia and the EU, have started to develop a range of mechanisms to compete with China. The revival of the Quad mechanism, an initiative bringing together Japan, the US, Australia and India, has focused also on collaborating in societal resilience through infrastructure and other elements that can help advance larger political goals. In the post-pandemic world, we are witnessing a peculiar competition about infrastructure financing and standard harmonization as the arena in which geopolitical competition is being played out.

What next?

The pandemic years have changed the political and policy ideas about why and how economic globalization should be managed. The power and purpose of the state to drive social and political outcomes has been reasserted. The pandemic years showed that markets can be tamed and harnessed. They also revealed acutely the vulnerabilities of interdependence. The years also coincided with an acceleration of efforts to combat climate change, with many governments seeking to use the means of rebuilding their economies after the shutdown along lines better suited to the climate crisis. Together, this has led many analysts to conclude that the neoliberal economic era has come to an end (Gerstle, 2022). Geopolitical contestation had been heating up for some time, but COVID-19 revealed the scale of the rivalry and accentuated the competitive dynamics. Between 2020 and 2022, the balance between states and markets tipped much more firmly in the direction of the state. And as the COVID-19 years recede from view, and as states grapple with the pandemic's legacy – inflation, lost growth and productivity – as well as the rising tide of geopolitics, globalization is being recast. But the process of that reconfiguration is, much like its initial emergence and evolution, not a planned or carefully structured process but is instead emerging as the result of the interaction between the differing policy settings, political interventions and the animal spirits of firms and markets.

To begin thinking about how globalization might develop it is necessary to identify the constituent elements of the global economy and how these might be influenced by this new, more politicized environment. The most significant dimensions of globalization are trade flows and the indicator that most analysts have used to provide the clearest proxy for globalization is trade as a proportion of GDP. As discussed earlier, one of the salient features of the pre-COVID-19 period of economic integration was the centring of global supply chains in the productive process, which gave rise to a large proportion of trade occurring in intermediate goods, the components and parts that comprise the finished good. The question of how globalization may fare is not just a matter of whether or to what extent trade as a share of global GDP returns to pre-2020 levels but whether there is a change to the models of supply chain interaction. Before, the drivers of firm behaviour were purely about price and quality – Apple opted to assemble its iPhone in the way it did for no reason other than that it could produce the highest quality product at a price which could provide a level of profitability with which the firm was content. Changes to how supply chains operate will come from the imposition of rules, regulations and incentives that shift those considerations either by changing prices or by more blunt forms of political intervention. The challenge is that those chains are impossibly complex and, consequently, it is very difficult to determine just how politicization will shape the final character. The second Trump administration's trade policies are, for all their chaos and confusion, clearly an example of bludgeoning firms to change their ways. Even a company as large and influential as Apple is looking to reconfigure its production processes in response as it tries to produce phones for the US market in India and the US.

It is already clear that in some sectors these changes will be significant – Washington's interventions in the semi-conductor supply business are perhaps the most visible example – what is much less clear cut is how widespread this sort of intervention will become, particularly given the sheer complexity of so much production. While the US and its allies might be content to pay higher prices for certain things by forcing China out of some productive chains, other less developed countries may be less likely to do so. Australia and the UK can afford to ban Huawei and ZTE, countries like Thailand and Peru cannot. Finally, the question of just which sectors will experience the kind of political intervention seen to date is critical to what globalization will look like in the coming years. For example, the Biden administration's Inflation Reduction Act had an extensive array of incentives to develop America's electric vehicle productive capacity. But the way the incentives were designed limited the ability of many firms in allied countries from benefitting. Even though the rules were intended to exclude PRC firms, the complexity of the inputs into batteries and other sophisticated components meant that electric vehicles (EVs) from places like South Korea were not able to qualify. This shows the difficulty the state has when trying to get markets to work towards political ends. The second Trump administration has begun to further complicate things with a crudely mercantilist understanding of trade, threatening to scramble things yet further, although quite where this will end up and what logic, if any, is at play remains entirely unclear.

The rewiring of globalization is a large-scale process unfolding as this book is being written. It is impossible to know quite how things will develop or what balance will be struck between state rules and market operations. Political forces now have a much stronger position than before but even the most hawkish forces recognize that markets should continue to have a role to play. Even the fiercest critic of 'globalism' or most anxious national security planner does not argue for a kind of autarky or full-blown retreat from the powerful forces of international investment, trade and exchange. There is considerable variety of opinion about just how far states should open themselves up to others, what states should try to do for themselves and what price they are prepared to pay to achieve their ambitions. Equally, some states will be more content to give markets their head while others, as they did before COVID-19, will seek to regulate or control firm behaviour, capital flows and market operations.

Market-led globalization worked miracles in many parts of Asia. The 'reform and opening up' period in the PRC created an astonishing period of economic growth and expansion. And, for a time, it looked as if the cycles of great power competition had ended. Asia's major powers had worked out how to get along and their shared interest in growth had created what some thought would be a golden straitjacket, limiting the prospects for hostility and belligerence.

The optimism of the early 2000s proved illusory. The growing wealth and influence of Asia's powers emboldened them to think in more ambitious terms, with China in particular chaffing against a regional dispensation that, Beijing perceived, favoured Washington. Equally, countries around the world became aware of the limitations and vulnerabilities that were the price to be paid for globalization's golden touch. The reconstruction of globalization in the shadow of the pandemic and return of geopolitics will dramatically reshape the region. While the functioning of the global economy is vital – and the balance of economic and political forces shaping its contours critical – the way it intersects with the other tectonic forces in Asia will be determinative. Those forces, geopolitical competition and Asia's risk multipliers, are the subject of Chapters 6 to 8.

6

Geopolitics and the Great Powers

The early chapters of this book showed how modern Asia was made; drawn together by the emergence of a China-centred regional economy and the growing sense of insecurity from region-wide forces, most especially military competition. In Chapters 6 and 7 I explore the dynamics of the geopolitical competition for Asia's future. This chapter examines the contest in the region among the great powers that has started. The three most important countries for Asia – the US, India and China – have different visions for the future, both in terms of what the region's power balance looks like and what respective part the major powers are to play in these futures. While these visions are unevenly expressed, they are on an incompatible trajectory. This chapter begins by explaining what I mean by geopolitics. It is a somewhat arcane term that has begun to be used widely but loosely, so it is helpful to specify exactly what I mean. Then it explores the structure of regional geopolitics and the ambitions of the great powers. The subsequent chapter examines the wide range of subregional stresses and flashpoints, looking at the zones of friction where competition is most likely to boil over into outright conflict.

Asia has many long-standing crisis points – most obviously Taiwan, the Korean Peninsula and the Sino-Indian border – and while the risks of war have been ever-present, these have been managed effectively through shrewd diplomacy and benefitted from a stable overarching strategic setting of American primacy. The anxieties and ambitions of Asia's most powerful states have unsettled things significantly and the risks of war are increasing. The ultimate risk, an exchange of nuclear weapons, has become more likely than at any time since the USSR's collapse. This possibility is likely to rise inexorably over the coming years. The long Asian peace still holds but its grip is much more tenuous, and the dangers of conflict are rising by the day.

Geopolitics and its return

Geopolitics is a peculiar word. It is loosely bandied around in much contemporary commentary. For our purposes it is necessary to provide some sharpness of definition and concept. The idea of geopolitics emerged in the late 19th century as an effort to make sense of the way in which the hard reality of geography shaped and constrained the grand strategic ambitions of empires. Pioneering scholars Halford Makinder in Britain and Alfred Mahan in the US set out competing assessments of how best to overcome the challenges of geography for national strategy. Makinder focused on land and argued that global power would be focused on the Eurasian landmass, which he described as 'the world island' (Makinder, 2022), while Mahan argued that the ability to exert control over maritime spaces was the crucial determinant of success (Mahan, 1987). The hallmarks of this early scholarship were a focus on the way physical features, such as mountain ranges, plains and maritime choke points, and the ability to move through and around these features, shaped the patterns of military advantage and vulnerability (Gray and Sloan, 2014).

Over time the term's use has expanded considerably. Outside of academic circles it is rarely used in the original sense. Often, it describes a rough and ready power-politics or is used by commentators describing a multitude of forces that are shaping international affairs. Some scholars take a broad view, seeing geopolitics as the 'grand chessboard' on which the game of international relations is played, where states seek to survive and thrive (Brzezinski, 1997). Here, I use the term to refer to the political and strategic competition for influence between states. It is a contest in which military and security matters are of the highest priority; while other aspects of national power are linked, they are subordinated to that competition. Specifically, I use the term to refer to state competition to shape Asia's balance of power and the mechanisms to manage that strategic balance. Ultimately, geopolitics is about the long-term positioning of national power in a competitive international environment, and it entails the prioritization of national security and military concerns over other areas of statecraft.

During the long Asian peace geopolitics was essentially absent from the region. In the early 2000s, scholars and analysts could have been forgiven their optimism about the region's prospects. Those who study international affairs tend to be gloomy in their prognostications, all too aware of the tendency to conflict and discord that seems to be their domain's perennial condition. But Asia appeared to have cracked the code. If the Cold War's first decades had been extraordinarily violent, from the late 1970s onward, war was almost entirely absent (Kivimaki, 2014). The critical turning point that pushed geopolitics off the policy table was the grand bargain struck between the US and China brokered at the famous meeting between Nixon and Mao in 1972.

The American president had made his name as a hard-nosed anti-communist and the image of Nixon cutting a deal with Mao, the leader of the world's largest communist party, was jarring. Nonetheless, the two struck a bargain of global significance. The US recognized the PRC and turned its diplomatic back on Taiwan, which had previously been seen as 'China' by the US and which had occupied the China seat at the UN and other international bodies. In return, the PRC would stop supporting revolutionary movements and accept the geopolitical dispensation of the post-1945 world (Goh, 2005). While the immediate imperative for the bargain was short term, both wanted to pressurize the USSR. The US also saw the deal as a way to manage the country's exit from Vietnam and, for its part, China desperately wanted a more settled international environment. The deal fundamentally changed Asia; without great power competition and ideological rivalry to provide oxygen to fuel conflict, major wars disappeared.

The absence of geopolitics also meant that states could worry less about events beyond their borders and spend more time and resources on domestic matters. Even in the late 1970s, economic development and effective state governance was the exception and not the rule across most of the Asian region. Without having to spend substantial amounts of money on international wrangling and being able to take advantage of the public goods created by US dominance, countries were able to build more effective domestic mechanisms to take advantage of the opportunities created by a globalizing world economy, something many of them did extremely well (Kim, 1995).

The great powers had worked out how to get along, the balance of power was settled – centred around US dominance and its acceptance by all the key players – and states could focus on the business of domestic welfare and governance. The region had its share of crises – such as the flashpoints of Taiwan, the DPRK's nuclear ambitions and the PRC–India border – but these were contained by the stability of the region and the consensus that existed about the larger questions of power, influence and rules. Even if an ambitious Asian power wanted to contest the US Navy it would have been folly to do so, given the gap that existed between the US and everyone else at that time. Most critically, this stability proved enormously beneficial to Asian societies and none more so than China. Its economic success would not have been possible had geopolitics remained. So why has Asia allowed it back out of the vault into which it seemed to have been banished?

At the time the grand bargain was struck, the PRC was impoverished and just emerging from the trauma of the Cultural Revolution. Four decades later it had become a huge economy, the most important in the region by some margin and the second most important in the world. But it is not just China's sheer wealth that matters, it is what the PRC has opted to do with that prosperity. Beijing has undertaken a dramatic and remarkably successful programme of military modernization (Cordesman, Hess and Yarosh, 2013). At the turn of the 21st century, China was a conscript-based military that, while large, was badly equipped, poorly trained and focused almost entirely on domestic defence. It had virtually no capacity to project power beyond its own territory and immediate approaches. Now it is a highly professional fighting force with a substantial inventory of high-quality equipment. Its navy has more ships than the US, it has more than 1,000 fourth generation or better fighter jets, dwarfing all others in Asia bar the US, and it has a strategic nuclear arsenal that is rapidly expanding in number, range and precision (IISS, 2024, 675–88). China's ability to contest American naval supremacy is real. While it remains vulnerable to American submarines, which continue to provide the US with significant advantages due their range, stealth and firepower, the days when one could discount Chinese military power are gone.

The PRC's military modernization has been in train for decades. But the real transformation in the region's strategic setting has been caused by the ambition the country has exhibited since Xi Jinping assumed leadership of the CPC. Following the launch of the economic reforms in the 1970s, Chinese foreign policy had been cautious, deliberately low-profile and risk averse. The dictum attributed to Deng Xiaoping, that the country should 'bide its time and hide its power', neatly encapsulated the desire to keep a low profile, not frighten the neighbours and avoid taking risks. This shaped China's international policy until the early 2000s (Harris, 2014). A shift in China's approach began to be seen even before Xi assumed power with the assertive and risky approaches it began to take towards the contested maritime claims in the South and East China Seas from around 2009. This included harassing vessels exploring for oil, pestering Philippines fishing fleets and even using water cannons on an American navy ship, the USNS Impeccable in 2009 (Cardoso, 2009).

Once Xi assumed the party leadership, he swiftly made clear that he was a different CPC leader. He turned his back on the collective leadership model adopted after Mao and began to present a much more assertive and ambitious face to the region. The contours of Xi's foreign policy and its ambition emerged incrementally, often presented in vague and unclear terms, which, deliberately or not, had the effect of obscuring the extent to which the country wanted to reconfigure its international environment.

Over time, it became clear from the language of speeches and formal policy statements, as well as from the country's actions, that Xi's China perceived the prevailing international order as one that was 'made in the USA' to serve the values and interests of Washington as well as its allies and partners. This sense has its origins in the foundations of the post-1945 order. When that was being constructed, the PRC either did not exist or was excluded from the planning and policy process. But it is also a reflection of a more recent sense that the system's structures, rules and values are, in China's estimation, inimical to those of the Party-state. While in a basic sense this has always been part of the CPC's thinking about the world, it did not become an explicit foreign policy ambition until the Xi Jinping era, a product both of his broader outlook as well as the fact that it is only very recently that the country has been in a position to do something of that scale.

The US has been Asia's most important power for decades. The strategy on which it settled following the normalization of relations with China proved to be particularly effective and durable. There was a stable strategic balance centred on US primacy. American power was organized through alliances that gave Washington a platform into a region from which it was separated by an ocean, and it also helped settle regional nerves. China's rise and Beijing's ambitious turn is perceived by Washington as a threat to its interest in retaining stability in Asia. As a result, the US has determined that it will seek to retain the existing order in the face of China's increasingly explicit challenge (White House 2022).

Initially, policy makers in Washington thought that Beijing had simply misunderstood its interest in an order centred on US primacy – after all China had benefitted more than any other from the decades of US dominance – and that a mix of engagement and containment would nudge the PRC in the right direction (Khalilzad, 1999; Davis, 2025). Somewhat belatedly, Washington came to see that Beijing viewed things differently and that policy adjustments would be needed to defend American interests as a new and more confrontational era beckoned (Campbell, 2016).

The unsettled military balance is a critical factor in the return of geopolitics. But it is not just the story of two tigers on a mountain. Aspirant great power India, regional powers like Japan, Indonesia and Australia, and many other dynamic and ambitious states are responding to the disturbed strategic equilibrium. Across the board, military expenditure is rising dramatically, prompted by the uncertainty that great power competition inherently creates (IISS, 2024). But it is also increasing for classical security dilemma reasons (Booth and Wheeler, 2008). The idea of the security dilemma relates to the inherent inability to know what other countries want to do with their defence forces. The fact that you can never know just what your neighbour wants to do with its submarines or missiles means that when others acquire war fighting equipment you must ask whether these might make you vulnerable and, if so, what you will have to do to mitigate those risks. These sentiments had largely been absent during the four decades following Sino–American normalization but their return has created a dynamic which, although some way off a full-blown arms race, is marked by competition that is becoming increasingly militarized.

Finally, Asia's many regional institutions have failed in their various efforts to restrain geopolitics. As briefly discussed in Chapter 5, Asian states had established a wide range of regional institutions in the 1990s and 2000s (Gill and Green, 2009). Many of these explicitly sought to provide a forum for dialogue and cooperation among the region's key powers, in part motivated by a desire to forestall the return of geopolitics. This effort did not succeed. As the 21st century wore on, the regional mechanisms that had been established to promote a sense of common cause became a place where growing friction and competition was being played out. For example, at the 2012 EAS' Foreign Ministers' Meeting in Cambodia, the dispute over the South China Sea derailed the discussion, creating a widely discussed undiplomatic stoush between China and the US (Kassim, 2012). These multilateral mechanisms proved inadequate to the task of shaping and restraining great power behaviour.

Competition between Asia's states had been slowly building in the 21st century's second decade. China's wealth and the ambition with which Xi Jinping had paired it had been met by Washington's determination to resist efforts to change the regional status quo. But the grip of this contestation was ultimately weakened by the importance placed on market-led globalization. After the pandemic years markets' abilities to dampen geopolitics appear to be much more limited.

The structure of Asia's new geopolitics

While geopolitics will be critical to the region's future, the challenge lies in discerning the dynamics of that competition, the ideas that will structure how contestation plays out and the differing role that states play within this drama. There is also a temptation to view the complexity of geopolitics as essentially the sum of Sino–American rivalry. But there are also a wide range of players that will individually and collectively shape how the competition plays out. States like Indonesia, South Korea, Australia and Vietnam, among others, as well as groupings like ASEAN, have agency and their choices will help determine the region's geopolitical future.

States can be categorized by the role that they play. The most significant of these have historically been described as great powers (Bisley, 2012). And while the term 'great power' feels like it is from another era, I will use it here in part because of the way in which geopolitics marks something of a return to more dangerous times, but also because there are a small number of states that have a disproportionate influence in the world due to their concentration of power and ambition. Asia is where they meet and their interests clash.

Great powers are those states that have significant region-wide interests, they have the means to advance those interests and to defend them from challenge for a considerable period. Crucially, they are recognized by others as having this standing and are also expected to provide stability and support to others. There are a limited number of states that are able or even have the potential to fulfil those three criteria. At present, China and the US are in that category. While Russia's nuclear weapons, energy endowments and geography provide some elements of great power status, it is not now and unlikely over the coming decades to become one. India is not yet a great power (Karnad, 2015). Although it is of sufficient scale and has region-wide interests, presently it does not have the capacity to advance or defend those against others without significant external support.

Europe's concert system, established after the Napoleonic Wars, showed that if great powers can work out how to manage their relations, they can stabilize international relations over a considerable expanse and duration. The system managed crises to ensure they did not spiral into larger, continent-wide problems (Holbraad, 1971). In contrast, when great powers compete over strategic and economic interests, or about rules and norms and values, regional and global systems can be extraordinarily turbulent.

The second group of states are allies of the great powers. Allies improve their own position by the support they receive from their senior partner while in turn the senior partner has states that can provide benefits ranging from political and diplomatic support, intelligence material through to geographic advantages of bases from which to project force into distant parts of the world. The category includes formal allies, states that have substantive mutual security obligations, as well as partners who have less legalistic commitments. These might be a mutual defence pact with specific obligations, such as the North Atlantic Treaty's Chapter V obligations to treat an attack on one member as if it were an attack on all. But they can also include more ambiguous commitments, such as the requirement of the Australia, New Zealand and the United States Security Treaty (ANZUS) that the parties 'consult' if something of significance were to occur in the Western Pacific.

While formal alliances have a legal standing and stated set of expectations, the impact that they have is a function of politics not legalism (Walt, 1990). Their influence depends less on the precise wording of treaty clauses and much more on the shared expectation that allies and others have about what steps each side would take in the event the alliance is triggered and under what circumstances. This is why one should include here partners of the great powers that do not have formal treaty commitments, but which nonetheless have a set of obligations that shape their strategic calculus. Israel's relationship with the US is illustrative. The two do not have a treaty but there is a strong sense of obligation towards one another. The difficulty that the Biden administration faced in its relations with Israel following the October 2023 Hamas attacks showed the challenges that even major powers come up against when there are strong sets of shared expectations, even in the absence of a formalized legal agreement.

Established in the early years of the Cold War, the US has had a system of alliances which has provided Washington with a group of partners in the region for many decades (see Table 6.1 for the strategic alignment of Asian states). Australia, Japan, South Korea, the Philippines and Taiwan are on the US side of the ledger. Singapore is also aligned to the US, although it seeks to ensure that it has freedom of manoeuvre in its

Table 6.1: Strategic alignment of Asia's states

US: partners and allies	China: partners and allies	Swing states	Swing states tilting towards the US
Australia	DPRK	Bangladesh	Philippines
Japan	Myanmar	Brunei	Vietnam
Singapore	Pakistan	Cambodia	
South Korea	Russia	India	
Taiwan		Indonesia	
		Kazakhstan	
		Kyrgyzstan	
		Laos	
		Malaysia	
		Nepal	
		Sri Lanka	
		Tajikistan	
		Turkmenistan	
		Uzbekistan	

Note: This table provides a stylized depiction of the different kinds of affinities of states in relation to the US and China as Asia's two great powers. Bhutan is not listed as it has a foreign policy alignment with India. The purpose of this table is to illustrate that there is considerable strategic fluidity in Asia and that the US advantage, while real, is less strong than it may appear.

foreign policy dealings. While its formal policy is not to have alliances with anyone, Vietnam has moved towards Washington, although it retains a degree of ambiguity about the extent of its commitments. Pakistan has been a US partner, especially through the last decades of the Cold War and during the Afghanistan intervention. But since 2005, as the US has more directly engaged with India, Pakistan has found itself more distant from Washington, reverting to its Cold War posture of being aligned to the PRC. China is often misrepresented as having no allies or partners. It does and, while they are much more limited in number, they should not be discounted. These are North Korea, Russia and Myanmar. China also has ties to Pakistan.

The states that are not bound to a great power have historically been categorized as 'swing states'. These states have security interests that are not firmly tied, and they can thus move between the great powers or can try to find some space that is equidistant between them. This term may be a little dated now as the complex economic ties of globalization constrain the freedom of manoeuvre states can enjoy as well. The term remains useful as a label to describe states that are not tightly linked to any one great power. To be so described they need to have the capacity to move, both in terms of the diversity of interests and in the practical political and economic terms required to undertake that kind of statecraft. Some swing states will find the ability to change affiliations relatively easy, while others may have the potential to shift but the move would be costly and difficult to achieve.

Based on patterns of foreign policy behaviour at present the uncommitted swing states include Thailand, Malaysia, Laos, Cambodia, Bangladesh, Sri Lanka and the five central Asian former Soviet republics Kazakhstan, Kyrgyzstan, Tajikistan, Turkmenistan and Uzbekistan. The most significant, in scale and potential, is India. While the US has some distinct advantages with the durability and extent of its alliances, since the creation of the 'no limits partnership' with Russia, China has extended the range and scale of its reach. But it is the number of states that can find space between the two that is perhaps most striking if one views the region from a properly continental perspective. While states are the most important figures, institutions also have a role to play in influencing states, whether by coordinating policy to advance shared goals, helping members leverage military capabilities to see off a challenge or degrading a targeted state's strength. There are two broad categories of institutions currently in the region. The first are inclusive bodies that seek to advance a cooperative agenda. These aim to moderate geopolitical forces or at the very least corral that competition and provide guardrails within which it can operate. The institutions that are centred around ASEAN, the EAS, ARF and ADMM+ are the most important of these entities. The second group are entities that are exclusive in that they are not open to all and where states gather to help each other advance shared goals in the competition for influence. Here we see some new entities, the Quad and the Australia, United Kingdom and United States pact (AUKUS) prime among them, as well as the SCO, through which China aims to secure its interest in the Central Asian hinterlands (Bisley, 2024).

Traditionally, great powers managed spheres of influence. These were zones recognized by all where one power dominated and that were accepted by the other powers. They were kept free from competition and were an important source of stability. In stable systems great powers manage their spheres of influence and ensure the careful oversight of the points of friction where their interests collide. But if other powers wanted to disrupt or contest a sphere it was hugely destabilizing, with the risks of conflict and even continent-wide war rising significantly in those circumstances.

As Asia's states jostle either to defend the status quo or to contest it, the idea of spheres of influence as places where the major powers can consolidate their international ambitions and secure their partners has some intuitive appeal. Yet the complex interweaving of interests that globalization has created as well as the scale and diversity of the continent's geography means that it is unclear whether Asia's current or potential great powers could deploy modes of 19th century statecraft today. Also, Asia's geopolitics is shaped by the reality that the dominant military of the past few decades is a non-resident power, one which depends on long-range force projection and its alliance relationships to advance its ambitions.

In the recent past, Asia's strategic balance was maintained by American military dominance. That situation no longer persists. But Asia has neither a set of spheres of influence nor a settled strategic landscape. Instead, one can distinguish between Asia's zones of military control and its zones of contestation. The former are areas where one state has military dominance and is not challenged or contested. The latter, as the name implies, are where no one power dominates and are subject to competition to create a new status quo. These are numerous, growing in risk and where Asia's geopolitics is most challenging. While there are some overlapping networks of collaboration, such as the trade facilitation programmes of APEC and ASEAN's dialogue programmes, these are sparse and have a limited grip on state policy.

The zones of competition need to be distinguished between the maritime and continental. The region's most distinctive geographic fact is its expansive and interconnected maritime domain. The waters of the Indian Ocean and the Western Pacific – recognized in marine biology as an integrated environmental space for species and thus evolutionary processes – are in practical terms indistinguishable. This is part of the prompt for many countries to adopt the idea of the Indo–Pacific to understand Asia's strategic geography (Medcalf, 2020). The geography of the region has created what is, in effect, a long interconnected coastal area, called by some a 'long littoral' (McDevitt, 2013). Before watercraft were developed that could withstand oceanic voyages, traders, missionaries and adventurers moved along the coastlines, making their way from India to modern-day Southeast Asia and up to China. Today, the connectivity that the sea provides is critical to the economic wellbeing of the region. It remains by some margin the most efficient way to move goods and commodities internationally. The seas are also home to extensive fisheries and hydrocarbons and other valuable commodities can be found in the seabed. It is also the location of many disputed claims that are escalating tensions, most notably in the East and South China Seas and, of course, Taiwan.

The sea itself is also a place of strategic significance. By its nature, it cannot be hardened or secured in the way land features can be. Since 1942 the US Navy was able to operate across the entirety of the Western Pacific and Indian Ocean region with impunity. That is no longer the case. Washington has made it clear that it wants to retain its naval supremacy. China has also made it clear that it seeks to increase its freedom of manoeuvre in the Western Pacific and beyond. In time, it can be expected that India's ambition to increase the control of what it perceives to be its own critical maritime space means that the maritime domain will be the zone the most subject to competition (Tarling and Chen, 2017). Presently, the Western Pacific is contested. The Indian Ocean is a more settled strategic space, however, that cannot be expected to remain the case over the longer run.

The contested maritime space dominates the strategic thinking of the US and many of its allies. This is part of the reason why the idea of the Indo–Pacific has such a grip on their imagination, it also echoes the maritime focus of the early imperialists' understanding of Asia. Yet the continental dimensions of the region are also significant. These give China some key advantages, including being able to use the vast spaces of its landmass for military advantage – known as 'strategic depth' – and to develop ways to broaden its access points by land. Equally, there are land zones that are or could be subject to contestation. China has long seen its thousands of kilometre-long borderlands as a source of vulnerability and anxiety. It is in open dispute with India over large swathes of their border, including in India's Northeast and Northwest. There have been numerous military exchanges between the two countries over these territories, including in 2001, 2008, 2017 and 2019, and while they are unlikely to escalate rapidly into major war, they are nonetheless another front of contestation in a complex regional strategic setting.

Maritime and continental zones provide different challenges and opportunities. The sea is ultimately much less structured with contestation about who can control which bodies of water and what can be done within those seas. This is a competition that is both about military matters – the projection of power, deterrence and coercion to control the sea – as well about the rules and practices related to what can be done by vessels in specified waters and what resource extraction can occur from within and under the seas. Land, in contrast, provides some difficult areas of vulnerability – the extreme altitude of the Sino–India border helps moderate but also prolongs the dispute – but also opportunities for resilience, strategic advantage and connectivity.

As geopolitics becomes more prominent, states across the region are increasing their military power. The PLA's modernization has produced a vast naval force. China's navy can project military might further from home than ever before; it has modernized and expanded its strategic missile fleet and has developed an impressive array of next-generation weapons, such as hypersonic missiles (Fravel, 2019). This, combined with a clear ambition to change its immediate environment, increases geopolitical risk.

Elsewhere in the region states are ramping up military spending, acquiring next-generation fighter jets, attack submarines, missile systems and broader war fighting capabilities. But to the traditional tools of military power Asia's geopolitics has added a range of new dimensions. One of the most prominent examples is what scholars and analysts have called 'grey zone' tactics. This describes efforts to use coercive means to advance objectives but in ways that fall short of conventional war. It is 'grey' in the sense that it occupies a space between war and peace (Mazarr, 2015), and it is undertaken by non-military forces, such as private security groups, maritime militias or coast guards. Such methods seek to avoid causing casualties in a deliberate effort to keep the stakes low, but they are organized and coordinated for a larger political purpose. Russia is thought to have pioneered this with the use of militias in Georgia in 2008 and Ukraine in 2014. China has frequently deployed such tactics to advance its goals in the East and South China Seas, and in the waters around Taiwan.

Grey zone tactics are challenging to combat because no one incident is of sufficient importance to justify the use of force. It also makes conventional deterrence dysfunctional as it makes the setting of red lines, whereby states make clear their expectations and signal when they will act, almost impossible. Clearly indicating areas and conduct beyond which any steps will result in extreme sanction normally makes managing sensitive and contested areas less complex. With the messy ambiguity of grey zone tactics setting and defending lines of acceptable conduct is very difficult, making accidents and unintended escalation more likely.

A further novel feature of Asia's geopolitics is in the world of development and infrastructure. As a large region with vast populations seeking to improve their circumstances, it needs significant investment in infrastructure, both physical and digital. The region's great powers see this as a way of expanding their influence in the narrow sense of aligning the interests of those on the receiving end of infrastructure investment as well as buttressing their preferred standards and lines of economic interest over the longer term. The jostling for influence and security competition is playing out in traditional military terms, in grey zones and also in the aspirational world of development policy and infrastructure improvements.

The final location of geopolitical wrangling is in the new domains of the digital age. There are two ways in which the digital frontier is a critical component of Asia's new geopolitics. First, it is a terrain of coercive interaction where state actors and their proxies seek to use the connectivity of cyberspace to exert pressure on their opponents or to gain an intelligence edge. This may entail hacking into critical infrastructure to cause havoc as part of a conventional military attack or espionage into military or government systems. According to reporting, the cyber domain is the place where the contest is at its most active and heated. The second area is the contest for technological superiority in high technology, such as AI, quantum computing and super-advanced microprocessors. The challenge here is to ensure that the opponent does not steal a march in key areas so as to be able to leverage that in the broader geopolitical competition. This area is seen as especially significant because things like AI and quantum computers have the potential to provide a decisive edge in the contest. That belief may be mistaken but it has led to both sides seeing high technology areas that were, in the globalization era, a place for private firms to make advances on their own terms, now seen as a vital national security interest. This is why the US has been so keen to attempt to damage Huawei and ZTE and to choke off China's access to the highest capability microprocessors.

Great power ambition

The ambitions and anxieties of the region's great powers are critical to determining the region's future. It is necessarily difficult to state with a high level of precision just what the US, China and India want from the region over the longer term. In part, this is an inherent problem of forecasting; ultimately, the future is contingent, and interests can shift over time, particularly in response to the actions of others. But it is also because there are competing views within each of the major powers. The domestic political and bureaucratic contest can be quite visible, as it is in the US and, to a degree, in India, but it is decidedly opaque in the PRC. That said, there are clear indicators at present about the trajectory of ambition in each of the three, reasonably strong domestic foundations for those policies and major deviations from the paths on which they are on would be costly and difficult to achieve. The sketches that follow provide an assessment of the main strategic ambitions of the two contemporary great powers. India is also considered as it has the potential as well as ambition to be a global heavyweight and its choices will be critical to the region's future.

China

While the PRC has long had an ambition to create an international environment that is more conducive to its interests, until relatively recently it has not had the wherewithal to do much about it. Also, the way the Party-state thinks about its international interests has evolved. Although some have argued that the country has a long-term master plan to unseat American power (Pillsbury, 2015), the reality is that China's goals recognize that US power is not going to disappear altogether. That said, the scale of change to the environment they seek is significant and will be costly and risky to achieve.

There are four broad aspects of Asia's international environment that China wants to change over the short to medium term. Since the 1940s the US Navy has been maritime Asia's dominant force. During the Cold War, the US fought two major wars, neither of which were decisive victories but, by the 1980s, it had devised a strategy and disposition of military force that worked to maintain its overall ambitions of strategic dominance. This approach was accepted by almost all states in the region. The Sino–American grand bargain was critical to the success of this, but it has become clear from what Chinese leaders say and in their actions that the CPC leadership no longer accepts the terms of that deal.

Put simply, China wants to restructure Asia's strategic balance in ways that favour Beijing and reduce, if not remove entirely, Washington's ability to exercise regional strategic dominance. While this goal is clear, precisely what steps China will take, over what time frame and what risks it is prepared to take to achieve that goal are not obvious nor are they likely to be a settled matter in Beijing. The opacity of elite politics and strategic thinking in Beijing is remarkable. Close observers agree that there are divergent views within Zhongnanhai – the CPC leadership compound in Beijing – about such matters, understandable given the risks that this ambition represents. But it is clear that there is a consensus supporting the basic ambition that the PRC controls its maritime approaches, this is a circumstance in which they have not been for most of the time of the PRC's existence.

China also wants to be able to project power beyond its immediate littoral and approaches, and to defend the significant interest it has in the movement of goods and commodities at some distance from its borders. Given how important the transhipment of goods and energy are to the country's economic wellbeing, these aims are understandable. Equally, the Party-state's internal legitimacy claims centre on the reclamation of the Chinese nation from the depredations of foreign powers in its 'century of shame and humiliation'. Those foreign powers all approached the country from the sea, and China wants to ensure that it will never again be vulnerable to that kind of pressure. Finally, and most obviously, China wants to be able to advance and defend its core interests, including its claims over Taiwan, as well as the South and East China Seas (Ju, 2015). If these various components of its military strategy are achieved, Asia's balance of power will experience a dramatic reconstitution.

Beyond the broader question of the region's strategic balance, Beijing has indicated that it sees aspects of Asia's current cartography as in need of revision, at least in several critical areas. In August 2023, the PRC's Ministry of Natural Resources issued a new 'standard national map', which illustrates these claims. This entails the disputed borders with Russia, India and Pakistan, which are all to be resolved in China's favour. Taiwan is 'repatriated' and its maritime claims in the East and South China Sea are made good.

The CPC regards Taiwan's de facto independence as the unfinished business of China's Civil War and it will not countenance formal recognition of Taiwan's standing. For most of the post-1978 reform era, Beijing has been content to play a long game, expecting that the gravitational pull of economic and political interests would inevitably drag the island towards the PRC. In his 2019 new year's speech, Xi Jinping signalled that the standing of Taiwan would not be left to later generations. While some read this as indicating a dramatic foreshortening of China's ambitions, the remarks were typically imprecise; he showed that Taiwan was a higher priority than before but did not give any specific timelines. China has significantly increased its harassment of Taiwanese military vessels and aircraft as well as fishing vessels in the Taiwan Strait and regularly undertakes military exercises in and around the island; at times these have been major operations. The most famous of these was an exercise that effectively surrounded the island following the 2022 visit of US Speaker of the House of Representatives Nancy Pelosi.

Taiwan's status has long been a red line issue for China's leaders. It is something for which it is prepared to pay a high price and take significant risks because of its symbolic importance to the CPC's ambition to redeem China's greatness. To have the PRC standard fly over the island is a critical national interest and one whose priority has increased in recent years. But it seems highly unlikely that there are imminent plans for invasion, given the costs and risks it would represent.

China also wants to make good on its claims to the Diaoyu/Senkaku and that Tokyo currently administers. It also has extensive and ambiguous claims in the South China Sea, where its famous 'dashed line map' (see Figure 6.1) implies that almost the totality of that sea belongs to Beijing, although China has never explicitly spelled out precisely what its claim entails geographically or administratively (Zhenhuan, 2023).

Figure 6.1: Map of the South China Sea, with the nine-dashed line

Source: iStock/PeterHermesFurian

Were these ambitions in Taiwan and the East and South China Seas to be realized, the region's strategic setting would be significantly changed. And it is not just the loss of sovereignty of an advanced democratic nation and a symbolic victory that would be of consequence. China's military capability would be significantly strengthened with Taiwan as well as the East and South China Seas disputes resolved in its favour. The US and its allies would find the maritime spaces of the Western Pacific more difficult to control and China's ability to project force would be strengthened.

China's next international ambition is to recast the physical and digital infrastructure of the region in ways that advantage the PRC. This is firstly about providing physical connectivity across the region that will improve the ability of goods, commodities and energy to move across Asia, but it has a specific emphasis on improving the number of ways in which those things can move in and out of China. The PRC's prosperity has depended in recent decades almost entirely on goods and commodities moving through its eastern seaboard ports. While the US perceived China's growth to be either positive or at least benign, this vulnerability was something with which Beijing could live. Now that the US appears to China's elites to be intent on keeping the country down, it wants to reduce this vulnerability by improving its own military capabilities as well as developing infrastructure that allows more diverse ways in which goods can move, both by land and by sea. This connectivity would also economically benefit the sending countries and those in Asia's peripheries, which, in turn, would help China.

The PRC also seeks to advance the region's digital infrastructure. A dramatic improvement in this domain would greatly benefit Chinese telecommunications firms like Huawei and ZTE but it would also provide benefits to emerging Asian economies that would align those countries' interests to those of Beijing. The BRI was launched in 2013 and, for around a decade, was the rhetorical and policy centrepiece of that effort

(IISS, 2022). It was the central articulation of this larger goal of reducing PRC vulnerability, improving connectivity across Asia and aligning the interests of Asia's states with those of the PRC. Since the COVID-19 years, the BRI has become a somewhat lower priority, but the underlying infrastructure ambition remains.

China is also keen to recast the region's institutional architecture. While it is a participant in ASEAN-centred mechanisms, it seeks to develop a set of entities that is free from the Southeast Asian club's influence. Equally, it sees several of the other bodies as antithetical to its interests, such as the SLD and the range of minilateral structures that the US and its partners have been so enthusiastic about in recent years. It has established a range of initiatives, including the SCO and the AIIB, and has sought to breathe life into the CICA, as well as establishing 'Track 1.5' initiatives, like the Xiangshan Forum and Boao World Development Forum. It recognizes that multilateralism is critical to managing a complex and globalized international environment and that it needs to buttress its broader ambitions with effective institutional mechanisms. The ambition has come to be described by Beijing as its desire to create a 'community of common destiny' in the Asian region.

The final change to the international environment that Beijing seeks is one that is not just limited to the region. China wants to push back on the expansive set of liberal values that has become an increasingly significant component of the UN-centred system. Ideas such as humanitarian intervention and liberally inspired rights systems, including those related to minorities, human rights or gender rights, are seen as a threat to PRC sovereignty and, indeed, to the operating system of international politics. Beijing is keen to advance what might be described as a return to the more classical ideas of sovereignty and non-interference that are at the heart of the UN system, but which have become eroded by the expansion of conceptions of rights and the international legal instruments and jurisprudence that advance and protect those rights. Beijing sees these systems that put the state and the individual in tension as problematic, both to the narrow interests of the Party-state as well as to the ideas that govern the broader international system (Rolland, 2020). When China and Russia's partnership formally launched in February 2022, it was accompanied by a statement whose language makes their joint motivations clear but also that they see these ideas as a direct threat to the stable functioning of the international order (Kremlin, 2022).

Beyond this 'back to the future' vision for the operating principles of international order, the PRC has also launched three initiatives to make a world that is more aligned to China's interests (Godehart, 2024). The Global Development Initiative (GDI) is an effort to put the right to economic development as a critical component of international order. Contrasting with the idea of an indivisible set of individual rights, the GDI underscores the importance of achieving a basic level of economic development as more important than political and civil rights. It is also an effort for the PRC to position itself as the leader of the developing world. The Global Security Initiative (GSI) was introduced at the Boao Forum in 2022 and represents an attempt to grapple with a more complex security environment and a way of advocating for different conceptions of security that weaken the influence of the US and its allies. The Global Civilization Initiative (GCI) is perhaps the most prosaic of these which promotes an inclusive approach to world order. The GCI is a sophisticated way of positioning China's preference to focus on the traditional understanding of sovereignty associated with the UN's founding. The idea of toleration and inclusiveness is ultimately about ensuring a system which allows a wide variety of domestic political systems, and which does not prioritize democracy or liberalism. The initiative is about creating what might be described as a more 'tolerant' international order than the liberal one which, China argues, imposes Western values across the system as a whole.

Under Xi, China has developed a set of reasonably clear and ambitious long-term objectives for its international policy. Xi has spoken repeatedly about how he perceives the period as one of opportunity but also risk. The Marxist understanding of history infuses his thinking (Rudd, 2024). This is the belief that history moves in a particular direction and that those who can discern these trends and position themselves appropriately will have the advantage. This sense of being on the right side of history was accelerated by the damage the Western economies suffered in the GFC and was reinforced, at least initially, by Beijing's response to the COVID-19 pandemic. This has moderated somewhat but the Party-state leadership sees the coming decades as a period of dramatic change, both for China and the world more broadly. As such, while the leadership has set the country on an ambitious path and it has clearly taken on riskier behaviour, such as its military harassment of opponents in the East and South China Seas, these remain relatively contained and while heightened, the overall risk appetite remains low. So far, casualties have been avoided in its many efforts to put pressure on its opponents. There is no evidence that the country is prepared to make a radical push to achieve its goals in the short to medium term, nor that it is willing to sanction the kinds of risks to social order and regime legitimacy that a war-led change to the region's setting would likely create.

This relates to one final facet of China's internal constitution that is relevant to its longer-term international ambitions. The PRC is a remarkably anxious great power. It is deeply concerned about internal social order and spends disproportionate time, resources and energy battling perceived threats to domestic stability. The structure of authoritarian political systems and the lack of an explicit consent to rule makes party elites often exhibit high levels of concern about domestic unrest. Since the easing of pandemic restrictions, China has faced the most significant economic headwinds of the reform period. In 2024 and 2025 the real estate crisis put a strong brake on an economy that had not fully recovered from the COVID-19 turbulence. It is experiencing deflation; its growth model, one predicated on massive investment in physical capital, appears unsustainable, and it is trying but not yet succeeding in efforts to move from a focus on export markets to drive prosperity to internal consumption. This is difficult and, during times of deflation, it is especially hard. It is also trying to become less dependent on foreign investment and intellectual property from abroad. Together this has created an extremely challenging policy context that is likely to further fuel the already extant anxiety. The question many have is whether an anxious and uncertain China is one that is likely to take more risks internationally as a response to these fears or whether it is likely to have a moderating impact on its behaviour. To put it more simply: does a China facing internal crisis see in international conflict a way to fend off those challenges or do those difficulties make it step back from its ambitious and assertive behaviour? It is impossible to know but both possibilities must be factored into any consideration of how the region's geopolitics might develop.

The PRC is setting out to reconfigure Asia to suit its interests and it does so with a sense of both opportunity and risk. It perceives that the balance of power is fluid, and that the US is weaker than it has been in decades. However, the mood in China has darkened since the COVID-19 pandemic. Beijing has become more convinced that the US is undertaking a concerted effort to constrain the PRC and damage its interests. This began with the Obama pivot, which elites believed was designed to contain Chinese influence in Asia. This sense was heightened in the first Trump administration, where sanctions, tariffs and China-bashing more generally became the norm. The Biden administration maintained virtually all aspects of the Trump approach to the PRC, indeed, Biden implemented policies much more aggressively than Trump did in some areas, such as blacklisting firms, introducing costly regulations about doing business with and investing in China and actively seeking to weaken PRC firms in key technology areas. The actions of the second Trump administration, especially the swingeing tariffs introduced in April 2025, simply reinforce Beijing's views that the US will not tolerate China achieving its full potential. In sum, Beijing sees the risks and vulnerability of the current era increasing. These are leading to a heightening of its emphasis on security and military modernization and underscoring the paranoid tendency in its international outlook.

China's no limits partnership with Russia, forged just prior to Moscow's invasion of Ukraine, was established precisely because it saw the US and Western powers as a direct threat. And in Washington's response to the Ukraine invasion, it sees confirmation of the US and the West's hostile intent. PRC officials refer frequently to a 'Cold War mindset' to describe this circumstance, a term that is often dismissed as tiresome rhetoric by Western scholars and analysts. The reality, however, is that despite its wealth, diplomatic influence and its growing power, China retains a deeply insecure outlook on the world and on its region in particular. While some critics argue that the West is threatened by a China that wants to make the world safe for authoritarianism, the more immediate and real challenge is that China wants to make itself feel more secure in a world that it perceives is dominated by powers that are out to hem it in and roll back its success. Consequently, since Xi Jinping took power, it has started to compete directly with the US, not just to advance its interests in Asia but to shape the economic, political and diplomatic rules of the road in the region. This underlying setting is unlikely to change for so long as Xi is in power.

United States

The US strategy in Asia has been stable for decades: Asia must be kept free from a dominant power that is hostile to Washington's interests. It took a generation for the US to work out the most effective way of implementing this strategy during the Cold

War. This was made possible by the normalization of relations with Beijing and the subsequent focus on maritime power and alliance collaboration that was devised in the 1980s. Between the early 1980s and 2020, US strategy proved remarkably effective and was widely supported in the region (Green, 2017). So far, that basic goal and the means to achieve it appear to remain in place, even as the second Trump administration's highly chaotic policy process may make things obscure.

Central to the efficacy of US strategy and regional stability was a relatively weak and internally focused China which was content to accept a subordinate role in the region. Even as China's economic acceleration produced a substantial increase in the country's wealth and capacity in the late 1990s and early 2000s, the US did not take seriously the potential challenge that a resurgent PRC could present. It seemed as if planners in Washington could not imagine that China could ever reach a level from which it could challenge the US.

American primacy was an arrangement that not only suited Washington's ambitions and global strategy but one that was welcomed by most in the region. It meant that Asian states did not have to spend as much on their defence and that they need not fear their neighbours. Japan's vicious imperialism remained in living memory and fears of a return of that impulse were politically charged, especially in China and South Korea. With US dominance, the cork was kept in the bottle of Japan's ambition, as Asian elites have memorably described things. And China benefitted enormously from a stable region.

But as the PRC became more powerful it sought to have a military footprint more in line with its demographic scale and shape its international environment in ways more conducive to its interests. Washington opted not to significantly adjust its policy. In the face of one of the most dramatic increases in wealth and influence in human history, the US essentially maintained things largely as they had been since the 1980s. Washington wants to retain the old order, that is the basic power balance centred on its dominance and the rules of the road which manages the system. It expects that China can and should be content with that set of arrangements even as Beijing has made clear that American power in Asia makes it insecure.

The Obama administration's pivot to Asia was the first formal recognition that Washington needed to reconfigure at least some aspects of its regional policy in the face of China's epochal transformation. Evocative speeches from President Obama to the Australian Parliament in 2011 and Secretary of State Clinton to the East–West Centre in Hawaii made clear that the US had recognized changes were in train, but the substance of US policy was tweaked, it was not dramatically recast. There was no significant increase in resources, deployment of forces or meaningful policy action to match the rhetorical commitment. Notwithstanding some of the hyperbole from PRC-based commentators and some interesting innovations, such as the Trans-Pacific Partnership trade agreement, as noted in Chapter 4, the policy was underwhelming (Turner and Parmar, 2020). It failed to reassure allies and did not deter China's growing confidence and assertiveness.

The first Trump administration continued the emphasis on Asia that Obama's pivot had put in place but put its foot on the geopolitical accelerator as it increasingly viewed Beijing as a direct challenge to US interests. Initially, Trump thought that he could work out a way to improve ties through a positive personal relationship with Xi. Following that ill-fated effort, the administration began to pressurize China primarily through tariffs. Once the COVID-19 pandemic began to undercut his domestic political support, in 2020, Trump unleashed the China hawks in his administration, broadening out economic coercion considerably. The Biden administration retained that focus, opting also to stick with the Indo–Pacific description of the zone of contestation that Trump had taken up in 2017. It upped the ante in contesting PRC influence and pushed even further than Trump in areas of perceived PRC advantage.

In the first six months of Trump's second administration, the precise contours of its Asia policy remained under-articulated. During the election campaign and, indeed, early months in power, there appeared to be competing views around Trump about how the US should organize its international policy. Some argued for a kind of isolationism, while others argued for focusing more directly on Asia and, in particular, pushing back on China. But in both the actions of its diplomats and military and in the speeches and visits to the region by senior officials it is clear that Trump seems likely to continue where he left off in 2020. The US will remain focused on Asia and will continue to try to roll back Chinese power in the region. The signalling so far is that the administration will try to do this in Reaganite terms, that is, that the US will achieve 'peace through strength'. It appears likely that the US will continue to present a full spectrum programme of pressure on the PRC. The only question at the time of writing is just how far they are willing to go.

When faced with the dramatic increase in power and ambition from China, Washington could have chosen to recast the grand bargain that was reached in the 1970s. The US could have opted to cede some of its influence, reduce the costs that it pays and provide space for PRC influence. At various points Trump and some of his advisors have flirted with that idea, but appear to have chosen against this path. It has done so for reasons of principle and strategy. The idea of the CPC writing the international rules of the road for Asia is unpalatable to democratic powers and it is a choice that would have high domestic political costs. Also, for the US to give up power to China would signal a huge shift in its global strategy and without obvious benefits to the US beyond a short-term cost savings.

Put simply, American strategy is to retain the basic strategic balance and rules of the road in Asia that have underpinned the past four decades. In recognition of the challenge that an authoritarian and ambitious China represents under the Biden administration it sought to frame that goal as a 'Free and Open Indo–Pacific' while Trump's mantra is 'peace through strength'. However styled, the US goal is clear. First, it seeks to ensure a stable and favourable balance of power over the medium and longer run. The strategic balance it seeks is one in which the US retains its position of primacy, not a balanced equilibrium with China. The second is to retain the legal rules of the road as they have existed over the past few decades. That is a regional order in which disputes are resolved by the prevailing practice and values of international law as understood by the US. Force, whether by formal militaries or grey zone tactics, is used only as the very last resort and as a means to protect the strategic balance and rules of the road. The one area where there is some difference between Trump and his predecessors relates to the economy. In the past there was a desire to ensure that the region's economy was open, market-oriented and organized by the international rule of law. Under Trump, there is less concern about the rules and a much greater emphasis on ensuring that the US benefits and that China suffers.

There have been a number of shifts in the policy means to achieve these goals. The US has broadened out its alliances and partnerships, most obviously engaging with India and deepening ties with traditional allies, such as Japan, Australia and the Philippines. It has also agreed to expand access to critical military technologies that it had previously been unwilling to allow. The most high-profile example of this is the sharing of nuclear-powered submarine technology through the AUKUS agreement. While Washington's decision to share nuclear technology shocked many, the reality of these initiatives is that they are moves that are ultimately at the margins of the region's strategic balance.

There are several uncertainties about the durability and efficacy of US ambitions. Since 2016 domestic politics has put major caveats on the US commitment to an open economic order. The illiberal approach to trade policy is the most evident and problematic example of this. US strategy in the past was supported by the alignment of economic and military interests – the US was the biggest market for export-focused economies and a close security partner of many Asian states. As China has become a more important trade and investment partner of many in the region, Washington needs to work harder to ensure that the political and economic interests of states in Asia are aligned with American goals. The most obvious way to do this is to allow access to its large and dynamic market. Yet domestic politics makes this impossible. Liberal trade settings are not coming back, and this will hinder Washington's ability to advance its broader agenda, especially as for most Asian economies China has become a more important economic partner than the US.

It is also unclear how long US strategy will remain as it is. The Biden administration opted to retain a surprising degree of continuity with its predecessor, which, except for the illiberal approach to trade, was largely in keeping with the longer-run trends in US foreign policy. At the point of writing, it looks likely that there will also be continuity between Biden and Trump's second term. But there are influential voices in and around the administration that argue for a quite different approach, that is one where the US plays a much smaller role on the global stage. These advisers think that Washington should refrain from shaping power balances in Asia or elsewhere but instead focus much more effort and resources on US society and its immediate approaches. This group appears to be strongly influenced by a kind of 'spheres of influence' approach to the global balance. Europe is one sphere that can look after itself; either the EU will get its act together or Russia will prevail, and it appears Trump is not bothered especially one way or the other. China may be given its head in Asia while the US focuses on the Western Hemisphere – a foreign policy that might be described as an 'Americas First' strategy. One thing that is clear from Trump's approach to politics is that he thrives on and indeed encourages chaos and turbulence so while it remains unlikely, a shift towards this kind of small global role cannot be entirely discounted.

India

The prospects of the world's largest democracy becoming a great power in Asia are real, even if they are some decades from being realized (Karnad, 2015). India has the right demographic attributes: it is one of two countries in the world with a population above a billion and, unlike the other, China, its age distribution is favourable, with its numbers projected to grow for at least another generation, if not more. It has enjoyed good economic growth rates in recent years, and its extensive set of interests and ambitions provide it with the key components of national power that are necessary to achieve great power status. This ambition is the first component of India's longer-term strategy. Delhi seeks to be a state at the top table, with the military and economic weight to advance and defend its interests across Asia. Prime Minister Modi, while somewhat politically chastened by the election outcome in 2024, remains the dominant political figure of the past few decades and his Bharatiya Janata Party (BJP) is likely to retain considerable influence even after the charismatic leader passes on the baton of power. Crucially, the ambition is supported by senior bureaucrats, analysts and the wider business community. But India's most immediate challenge is ensuring that its domestic economic growth continues to the point where it can begin to make good on these ambitions and is recognized by the region and, indeed, the world as a power of the first rank.

At this point, India's inability to defend its regional and global interests due to the shortcomings of its power base mean that it cannot currently be considered a great power. However, it is important to consider what it would do in the plausible event that it achieves its aims of attaining that stature. There are three elements that I will consider in this assessment of India's great power ambitions: its preferred strategic setting; the nature of the region's map; and what rules of the road it would like to see prevail. Scholars of world politics like to distinguish between status quo and revisionist powers, that is, countries that are content with things as they are and those that want things to change. The US is a classically-styled status quo power and China is for most a revisionist power (Chan et al, 2021). What does India want?

For decades, India has been the dominant force in South Asia, although this is more by dint of its sheer scale than its ability to convert its heft into preferred policy outcomes. Its longer-term ambition is for India to dominate South Asia and the Indian Ocean region. In some respects, its maritime aim is for its navy to have the level of dominance that the US has enjoyed in the Western Pacific in the ocean which takes its name from the country. This means hemming China in and limiting its ability to influence matters in the South Asian region. This is both about ensuring that its border disputes are not resolved in Beijing's favour but also about seeing off China's desire to dominate Asia's balance of power and establish China-centred modes of operation. This has been critical to the US, and its partners and allies, which helps explain why they have significantly increased their ties in recent years (Hall, 2014). Balancing PRC influence requires scale and reach that means Washington needs India to buttress its strategy and its alliance networks. But that should not be confused with India becoming a long-term partner or ally, nor should anyone assume that there is an inevitable convergence of strategic interests between the New Delhi and Washington.

For the concerns of this book, India's most significant ambition is to become one of the poles of a properly multipolar Asian strategic environment. If this were to occur it would entail the existence of a multipolar global order. This would mean a region in which US and Chinese power is equidistant from India and Russia. This necessarily means that the US' relative influence in the region would be significantly reduced over the longer term but China's standing would also have shifted downward in relative terms. This ambition has become evident in the way in which New Delhi has responded very differently to Russia's 2022 invasion of Ukraine. Equally, Modi has taken a more self-confident approach towards Beijing than his predecessors, who were extremely cautious about taking steps that might unsettle the bilateral relationship. Nonetheless, India's economic links to China and its disputed border mean that it has and is likely for the foreseeable future to take a complex approach to Beijing. Washington and others in its camp must not expect complete adherence to its preferences or approach due to shared concerns about PRC regional influence. There is no unified anti-China bloc on which the US and its allies can depend over the longer term. Equally, while India has the determination to step out as a major power, its success in recent years has been hamstrung by insufficient resources, some clumsy and ineffective policy delivery as well as institutional and ideological constraints.

For this ambition to be possible, however, India must achieve sustained levels of economic growth over a considerable period. While its economy has been expanding rapidly, it has been the fastest growing large economy in the world for a number of years, but it remains a long way behind Asia's great powers. Its per capita GDP is around US$2,500, so it is not yet a middle-income country. India will need to have per capita GDP that is in the US$15,000 to US$20,000 mark to be able to operate in a way that would allow it to achieve that multipolar goal. The distance it must travel to achieve that remains considerable and is at least a generation away.

If India's aims for the region's strategic setting are significant – a world where US primacy is reduced, and India and China are in the same strategic bracket is a very different world than the present – then its preferred strategic cartography is less revisionist. Most obviously, Delhi wants the disputed borders with Pakistan and China resolved in line with its preferences, while in the maritime domain it wants the dispensation of disputed areas to be advantageous to India. Most immediately, that means making sure that China's capacity to project force into the Indian Ocean is limited if not repelled. In the Western Pacific, its preference is for Taiwan to maintain its current standing, that the South China Sea does not become a de facto Chinese lake and that China remains stitched in behind the first island chain.

India does not seek the kind of rolling back of the liberal dimensions of the international rules that Beijing seeks but, even though it is a democracy of some standing, its attitude to the international rules of the road is likely to be pragmatic and driven most directly by its ambition to achieve a multipolar global order. It will be committed to the rule of law, multilateral institutions and public good provision but the content of those rules, organizations and norms will be tempered by the desire to reconfigure the basic structure of influence globally. In one sense, this ambition can be considered redistributive in that it aims for more states to have a say in the workings and determinations of the regional and global order.

Conclusion

In the years leading up to the COVID-19 pandemic, geopolitical competition had become visible. The growing ambitions of Asia's major powers were made possible by the economic dynamism of integrated Asia. But the risks and challenges of that competition, while real before 2020, operated within a larger framework shaped by globalization and the sustained political consensus supporting open markets, free trade and the benefits of economic integration. After COVID-19, geopolitics has been cut free from the fetters of market-led globalization. In this context the logic of military competition has a much freer rein. This is a world in which the ambitions of Asia's current and emerging great powers are ultimately divergent. While Beijing's and Washington's aims are starkly opposed and the two are locked into what is likely to be a generational struggle, India has its own vision and one that is not entirely compatible with that of either China or the US. Great power competition is here to stay; it has been turbocharged by the pandemic and is set to retain its place as a dominant force in the region's international relations. The places where the interests of the great powers clash are substantial; their visions for the region are different and ultimately irreconcilable, at least as they are currently configured. The region faces challenges on two scales. The first relates to the immediate clashes of interest that exist and whose temperature is rising. The second relates to the longer-term question of just what kind of region Asia will have; which vision will prevail and what price will be paid for that to be achieved? Chapter 7 will focus on the shorter-term flashpoints and the remainder of the book considers the longer-term issues.

7

Flashpoints and Zones of Contestation

Asia's geopolitical competition is of global significance most obviously because of the protagonists' scale – a war between the US and China would be catastrophic for billions around the world. But the contest has an added and immediate salience because of the vast number and geographic range of flashpoints where long-running tensions have an already high temperature. As discussed in Chapters 2 and 3, the legacies of imperialism and Cold War have left a slew of complex security challenges across Asia. From the Korean Peninsula to the glaciers of Kashmir, disputes over borders, sovereignty claims and territorial rights have been points of risk for decades. These have waxed and waned in volatility and intensity; however, in the post-pandemic years, they have become turbocharged by a geopolitical environment in which the logic of strategic competition dominates. No longer do economic ties bind the region as tightly as they did, indeed, some of the lines of contestation derive from the sense of vulnerability that economic interdependence has created. In this chapter I will examine the four zones of contestation, organized by geography and the existing flashpoints, where the heated geopolitical environment could boil over into conflict.

Northeast Asia

This is Asia's most volatile quadrant and, paradoxically, its most economically interdependent. The trade and investment links across China, Taiwan, South Korea and Japan are vibrant, mutually beneficial and of considerable depth and duration. In some ways it is a microcosm of Asia as a whole. China is the most important component, but it does not dominate. Japanese and Korean firms benefit from the PRC's cheaper-yet-sophisticated production facilities while China benefits from capital investment and technological know-how. Yet Northeast Asia is beset with rivalry, historically charged and nationalist-fuelled resentments and is, in many ways, the front line of the contest for Asia's future as well as home to complex disputes that are the most likely to tip the region into war.

Northeast Asia's current fault lines have a long history. Taiwan's standing has been a source of regional insecurity since the formation of the PRC in 1949 (see Figure 7.1). Crises have erupted in almost every decade since then as Beijing has sought to make good on its ambition to exert sovereignty over the island. Xi Jinping has increased the rhetorical temperature and has upped the tempo, scale and frequency of incursions in and around the Taiwan Strait. Beyond the ambitions of most Taiwanese not to become part of the PRC and the Party–state's insistence that the island is theirs, the Taiwan issue has several other dimensions that give the flashpoint added salience. Were the island to become part of the PRC it would have significant consequences for Asia's strategic balance. The PRC would have a major footprint from which to project power, gather intelligence and work to further transform Asia's balance of power. The island would give Beijing's submarine fleet a much greater capacity to operate across the Western Pacific. Presently, the US Navy's nuclear-powered fleet can tie the People's Liberation Army–Navy (PLAN) down through its command of strategic choke points. With Taiwan under PRC rule, the balance of

Figure 7.1: Map of the Taiwan Strait

Source: iStock/PeterHermesFurian

naval power could shift dramatically. Equally, the ability to use the island to improve the PRC's intelligence gathering capacity and provide informational advantage would also strengthen its hand. While possession of the island would not automatically provide Beijing with regional hegemony, it would substantially strengthen its position. From a narrowly military point of view, Taiwan is of immense consequence in the competition to reshape Asia's strategic balance.

Any conflict over Taiwan's standing would also be a test of US resolve and that of its partners and allies. The US has guaranteed the island's security for decades and while Washington has a formal posture of strategic ambiguity, there is no doubt that if China starts or is perceived to start any conflict, the US is expected to defend Taiwan. The problem is whether the US would or would not respond. The most immediate question is Washington's stomach for a fight, particularly one which could easily pass the nuclear threshold. Would the US be able, politically, to sustain support for Taiwan? Given the difficulties that Washington has faced in maintaining its much-needed backing for Ukraine this cannot be assumed, particularly given the support for the neo-isolationist positions of the Republican party that has been reshaped by the America-first instincts of Trump. The extraordinary scenes in February 2025, when the US president seemed to be parroting Russian talking points and cutting Ukraine loose, has already badly shaken confidence. Trump has shown a distaste for foreign wars, and it is all too easy to imagine a US led by Trump or someone cut from similar cloth being unwilling to fight. If Washington does not defend the democratic republic, then there is also the higher order question that would raise about all the other guarantees the US provides to its allies in Asia and beyond that would be called into doubt. This would be hugely destabilizing, given how important these guarantees are to so many in the region. Taiwan is not just a place where PRC nationalist ambition meets its desire to recast Asia's military balance, it is also a place that could serve as a political tipping point of American strategic credibility.

But Taiwan is not the only place in Northeast Asia where the risk of great power conflict is real. The divided Korean Peninsula (see Figure 7.2) remains one of the most militarized parts of the planet. For most of the first part of this century, North Korea's nuclear ambitions and the expansion of its missile fleet have been the primary drivers of risk and instability. In 2002, North Korea began enriching uranium in what proved to be a destabilizing and ultimately successful gambit to acquire a nuclear weapon.

Figure 7.2: Map of the Korean Peninsula

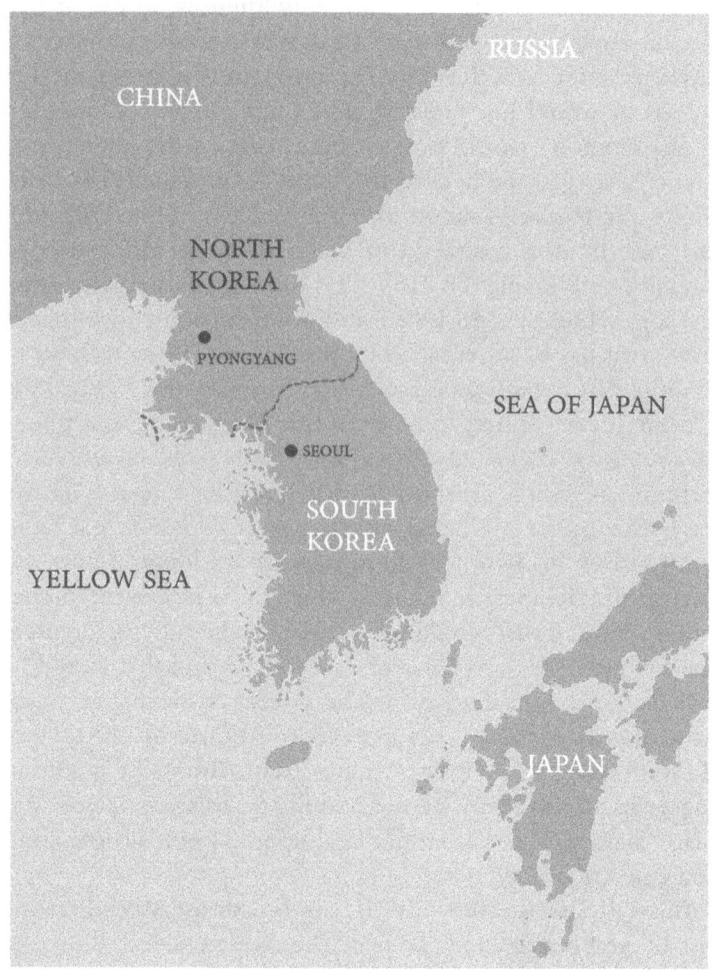

Source: iStock/Barks_japan

It has also significantly expanded its missile fleet in terms of its range, number and stockpile. While the Korean War was never formally finalized, an uneasy equilibrium was established. At several points in the past two decades some kind of breakthrough seemed possible, one that promised a more peaceful setting for the peninsula, whether in the form of a unified Korea or a settlement between the two. A lasting peace on the Korean Peninsula appeared to be within reach.

That is now a distant memory. In January 2024, North Korea's leader declared that unification was now impossible and that the South was the country's principal enemy. In October of that year the DPRK changed its constitution to reflect this new determination (Ng, 2024). Where in the past Pyongyang saw the US as its greatest threat, now it was South Korea that was deemed the existential challenge. While not necessarily increasing the prospects of imminent conflict, the move has increased the complexity of the geopolitical jostling in the region. South Korea is a treaty ally of the US and Washington has a significant military presence in the ROK, giving the peninsula an added dimension as a front for great power contestation. The DPRK and China are also allies and ones that evocatively describe their relationship as being as close as 'lips and teeth'. Tensions between the two Korean republics have immense risk. The densely populated Seoul Metropolitan Area is around 60 km from the border with the North. The demarcation line between the two is one of the most militarized places in the world and conflict could escalate at a very rapid pace. And given the alliance relationships of the two Koreas, tensions are overlaid with the risks of larger conflict.

The Korean Peninsula also plays a significant role in Asia's overarching geopolitical balance. China sees the North's existence as important, because it acts as a buffer keeping a US ally at arm's length. Were the two Korea's to reconcile their differences the South would dominate any political and economic settlement that followed and would bring a US ally to

Beijing's border. Equally, in the event of some kind of conflict in relation to Taiwan, North Korea's missile fleet and other weapon systems could be deployed to support Beijing, tie down US forces and complicate allied operations.

The East China Sea disputes, where China claims sovereignty over a series of islands to the northeast of Taiwan, which Japan administers, are a further point of tension and risk (see Figure 7.3). Although they lack the extremely high stakes of either Taiwan or Korea – either in terms of population, strategic advantage or nationalist symbolism – they remain a potential trigger point for major conflict.

The Senkaku/Diaoyu were ceded to Japan in the 1895 Treaty of Shimonoseki, the agreement which concluded the Sino–Japanese

Figure 7.3: East China Sea

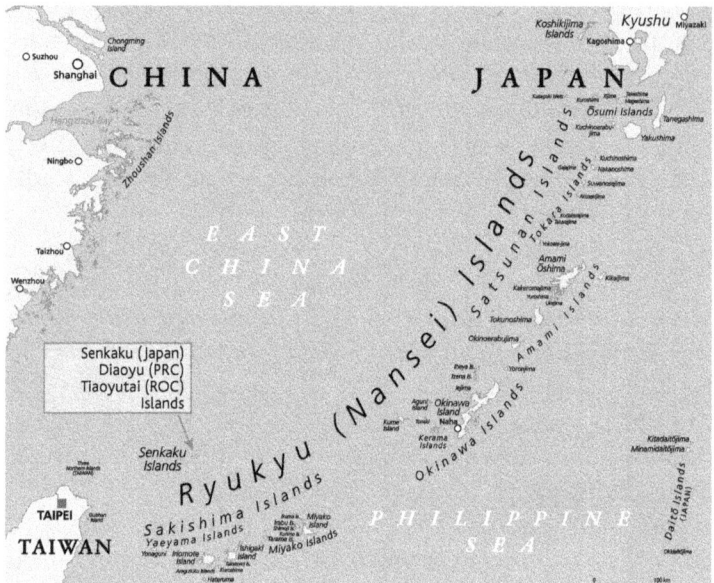

Source: Wikimedia Commons (reproduced under CC-BY-SA 3.0 license)

War that had waged since 1894. Colonial era agreements, which were forced on vanquished or colonized peoples, are now regarded as largely anachronistic. The uncertainty that surrounds the treaty's standing in international law led Washington to take a position of some ambiguity about whether the islands would be covered by the security guarantees that the US has provided Japan since the 1960s. Since 2010, the islands have become a growing source of friction between the two countries. That year marked an increase in Chinese fishing fleets entering Japanese waters, including the incident described in Chapter 1. In 2012, tensions increased again as the islands, which had been privately owned, were acquired by the government that wanted to prevent nationalist firebrand Ishihara Shintaro taking possession. Following this, in 2014, Prime Minister Abe Shinzo was able to convince President Obama to confirm that the islands are covered by the US–Japan mutual security treaty. As a result, the disputed islands have, like Taiwan and Korea, been drawn into the larger dynamics of Sino–American rivalry.

There are a range of issues at stake in the islands. As with Taiwan, there is a basic question of sovereignty and, while not quite the totemic issue of that island, the tiny archipelago retains the ability to inflame nationalist sentiment on both sides. The islands also have some strategic significance for basing, radar and intelligence facilities were China to gain hold of them, although most security analysts and scholars tend to think this would be a relatively minor advantage in terms of the larger strategic balance. There are thought to be hydrocarbon reserves near the islands, but it is not at all clear how big the fields might be, nor is their economic viability. The inclusion of the islands in the remit of the US–Japan alliance is perhaps their most significant dimension. They are now both a test of resolve for US alliance credibility and a part of the larger vector of competition between the US and China.

Friction in and around the islands between the Japanese Coast Guard and various Chinese paramilitary forces has increased dramatically since 2010. Prior to that time there were virtually no incidents of illegal fishing, paramilitary or military incursions by Chinese vessels and aircraft near the islands. By 2013, there were nearly 250 per annum within 12–24 nautical miles of the islands and, since 2021, there have been around 330 incidents close to the islands each year (Chen et al, 2024). This pattern has continued in 2025. The sheer number of incidents, the difficulty of managing them and risks of accidents leading to escalation means that the islands are a genuine flashpoint. But the less febrile atmosphere around them as well as the slightly lower stakes means that the danger of things spiralling out of control is lower than with Taiwan or the Korean Peninsula.

Defence spending in Northeast Asia has increased significantly. This has been driven due to the escalating tensions between the various parties as well as the way in which the flashpoints have become part of the dynamics of Sino–American contestation. Some scholars argue that there is an incipient arms race in this corner of the region, which is also heightening risk and levels of tension (Ball et al, 2021). Also, Northeast Asia lacks any dedicated security institutions or structures to help manage the many crisis points. The Six Party Talks that were established in 2003 to try to corral North Korea's nuclear ambitions at one point looked as if they might be developed into a broader security institution, but this petered out as the talks were ultimately abandoned.

Northeast Asia is the front line of the contest for dominance in Asia. It is a place where conflict is most likely, where positions are most entrenched and where, if one is looking for ways in which a new grand bargain among Asia's major powers might be struck to create a more stable setting, one finds the least support. The prospects of a managed and durable system of strategic stability and peace are low.

Southeast Asia

If Asia's Northeast is the zone where major conflict is most likely, with battle lines drawn, and reasonably well-known

FLASHPOINTS AND ZONES OF CONTESTATION

Figure 7.4: Political map of Southeast Asia

Source: iStock/PeterHermesFurian

points of risk, in Southeast Asia (see Figure 7.4) major power ambitions collide, but they do so in a place that is home to strong-willed and diplomatically adroit middle ranking powers. It is a place where faiths and cultures intersect and have blended for thousands of years – visible to this day in Southeast Asia's architecture, religions and cuisine – and this legacy is significant once again as great power competition returns.

During the Cold War, Southeast Asia began to be transformed. Until then it was a place of economic underdevelopment, its societies having been exploited by colonial powers for decades and, in some places, centuries. The successor states began to climb the development ladder, and it is now home to some of the world's most affluent populations. But it was conflict-ridden in the first three decades after World War II. The Indochina Wars were devastating to Vietnam, Laos and Cambodia and a stark reminder of the costs that smaller states pay if they get caught in large-scale geopolitical and ideological collisions.

ASEAN was established in 1967 to support the state- and nation-building projects of Singapore, Thailand, Indonesia, Malaysia and the Philippines. The group wanted to put their intramural conflicts behind them for good and work together to wall off their corner of the world from Cold War machinations. They were remarkably successful at this. Once Sino–American rapprochement was achieved, they were able to capitalize on broader regional stability and the creation of the Asian economy to take considerable economic strides. But as geopolitics returns, Southeast Asia faces an extremely challenging future. The most obvious risk is that the nations become collateral damage in a new era of great power competition.

While the region lacks the supercharged flashpoints of Northeast Asia, it is home to a complex maritime dispute in the South China Sea (Storey, 2017). The body of water is vital for shipping and naval operations; it is home to considerable hydrocarbon reserves as well as fisheries. Six countries (China, Vietnam, Philippines, Brunei, Malaysia and Taiwan) have a set of overlapping claims about some or all aspects of the waters. These have increased salience now because of the heightened strategic competition, as well as the demands for energy and protein. China's claim is both expansive and nebulous. The government has released a map of the sea with a dashed line encompassing it almost in its entirety. But Beijing has deliberately not set out what exactly the line means or what precise claims it is making. In practice it treats the sea as if it were its own territorial waters, reclaiming 2,000 acres of land across a set of islands, reefs and atolls. Its militarized coast guard has undertaken numerous aggressive acts against fellow claimants over many years, most significantly against the Philippines and Vietnam. It operates a local government administration, as if the islands were just another part of China. Vietnam also makes a sweeping and imprecise claim over what it calls the East Vietnam Sea, while Malaysia, Brunei and the Philippines stake smaller claims. The dispute is both narrow – whose flag appears over which features, who can exploit the resources in and under the sea – but also expansive. These broader ranging elements relate to what navies and other vessels can do in these waters, as well as the larger question of how these sorts of disputes are resolved.

While there is considerable complexity – the number of parties, the varying nature of their different claims and the range of issues involved – there are three main dimensions to the dispute. The first is in essence about sovereignty. That is, it is a dispute over which country exercises sovereignty where in the seas and what rights flow from those claims. The most important dimension relates to who can exploit the fisheries and hydrocarbon reserves that are in and under the sea. The second layer relates to maritime boundaries. The United Nations Convention on the Law of the Sea (UNCLOS), the relevant body of international law, does not have a clear way of resolving differing claims about where maritime boundaries should be drawn if states that disagree will not consent to have the dispute resolved. This is a problem in the South China Sea, as the map illustrates (see Figure 7.5), there are wildly diverging views about where precisely boundaries should be drawn. These are of particular significance in relation to who can exploit the resources in and under the water column.

The third dimension of the dispute is the most abstract but is perhaps the most significant. It relates to the nature of jurisdiction; what is and is not allowed to be undertaken in waters over which a country has control. The principal issue

Figure 7.5: Territorial claims in the South China Sea

―― China and Taiwan ----- Malaysia ―·―·― Vietnam ········ Brunei ― ― Philippines

Source: iStock/PeterHermesFurian

relates to freedom of navigation, which is clearly permitted in a country's EEZ under international law but which many of the claimants do not allow. Then there is the question of just what freedom of navigation entails. The international consensus is that free navigation means what it says: vessels can do what they please as long as they are not interfering with the economic dimensions of the maritime area. But several of the South China Sea's claimants think ships in their EEZ should have some limits imposed on their actions. For example, Malaysia requires prior permission for military exercises being undertaken, while China argues that they should not occur at all. Finally, the South China Sea dispute is, in a sense, a macro level argument, that is, it is a dispute about dispute settlement in an era of changing power balances and shifting economic interests.

The dispute also throws into relief the problems facing Southeast Asia's premier institution, ASEAN. The grouping has positioned itself as the key player grappling with the issue. It has overseen a drawn-out series of negotiations to establish a 'code of conduct' to which all can sign up as its way of sorting out the problem. Yet its ten members, some claimants, have different interests at stake and, as such, no code has been reached, and most observers believe that if one is forthcoming it will be so diluted that it will have little practical impact on the dispute itself. The Philippines sought a ruling on China's claims at an arbitral tribunal hearing of the Permanent Court of Arbitration that it said were in violation of UNCLOS in 2016. The ruling strongly favoured the plaintiff but, apart from some posturing and rhetoric, it has not shifted China's behaviour or that of other claimants.

ASEAN has been a critical player in and beyond Southeast Asia. It was crucial to forging a sense of common cause among the member states during the Cold War and has been credited with fostering the idea of Southeast Asia as a distinctive place in the world. Yet today the organization faces very significant problems. The ossification of the core ASEAN grouping as well as its offshoots is palpable. The Southeast Asian club struggled with the COVID-19 pandemic. Like many multilateral bodies, the institution found that its many years of dialogue, information sharing and trust building proved to be of little value as a public health crisis, for which cooperative bodies should have been ideally placed to manage, were impotent in the face of national responses that were unilateral, uncoordinated and overlaid with mistrust. Equally, the institution has struggled for relevance in the face of heightened great power competition. This reflects both the relative heft of the major powers in comparison to the grouping, but also the diverging interests of the ten member states, which do not share a common set of economic and military ties to the US and China.

The diversity of political systems within the members – which ranges from an absolutist monarchy (Brunei) through Leninist authoritarianism (Vietnam) to a vibrant democracy (Indonesia) – further complicates the institution's ability to find common ground. But it is also part of a longer-run trend in which many ASEAN members no longer see their interests through the prism of 'ASEAN centrality'. This was a critical component for the organization, in which the grouping was the centrepiece of each member's foreign policy. Many, particularly the more affluent members, see themselves playing on a larger international stage and, while they will not desert ASEAN in any formal sense, the importance of solidarity with the grouping has clearly declined and the significance of pursuing their own interests has increased. ASEAN also suffers from a lack of leadership. Historically, Indonesia has played a crucial role behind the scenes yet under President Joko Widodo that ebbed, and his successor President Prabowo Subianto shows little sign of rekindling interest in the grouping, while neither Vietnam nor the Philippines, the region's other two major players, seem willing or able to contribute on this front.

One of the more telling features of the institutional problems facing Southeast Asia can be found in ASEAN's multilateral security structures. ASEAN established several broad-based mechanisms that were intended to bring a wide range of critical players together to discuss shared issues of security concern, to build confidence and even take some concrete diplomatic and military steps to advance those goals (Bisley, 2009). The ARF, the EAS and ADMM+ are expansive security bodies that are cooperative in their mode of operation and inclusive of a wide range of participants. The ARF has 27 members, while the EAS and ADMM+ each have the same 18 members (the

ASEAN ten, as well as Japan, China, South Korea, Russia, the US, India, Australia and New Zealand). Yet those bodies have become notable for their entirely bland discussions that have little impact on the policy choices that their members make. Indeed, even though they were established to improve communication and dampen down competition, at times, their meetings have become the place where great power rivalry is played out. Rather than ameliorating the contest for influence and shaping the preferences of all the players, as intended, these bodies are at times unwittingly exacerbating these trends.

While Southeast Asia has plenty of institutional structures, the countries in the region themselves have relatively weak military capabilities and show no signs of changing this any time soon (IISS, 2024). In part this is due to size and wealth – many are still developing economies, such as Laos, Cambodia and even Vietnam – and some are simply too small to be able to project much power no matter how wealthy they become, such as Singapore and Brunei. The countries have also shown little interest in or aptitude for defence coordination. Even though Southeast Asia has several platforms through which this could be pursued, little of substance has been achieved. This means that, as geopolitics tightens its grip and as the dynamics of competition become increasingly militarized, the ability of Southeast Asian states to advance their interests collectively is likely to be limited.

The gap in wealth and might between the countries of Southeast Asia and the great powers is such that, alongside the decline of ASEAN's capacity to generate a sense of common cause, one might assume that the region will lack agency and must ride the waves of geopolitical contestation as well as it can. Yet, one of the striking features of Southeast Asian states has been their ability to generate political space for themselves and to exercise some modicum of influence on the major powers as well as the workings of the region's order that is out of proportion to their size and wealth. Indeed, as strategic competition has begun to become more evident, Southeast Asian states have swiftly responded to the growing interest of third parties in the region. Japan is a major source of development assistance, as is China. The US, Australia, India, the UK and France have all significantly increased their interest in the zone, and Southeast Asian states have been adept at strengthening ties to these countries, primarily through bilateral mechanisms. This trend, alongside the longer-run practice whereby ASEAN sought to bind the interests of its members and enmesh the major powers in its institutions and way of doing things, has led some to think that, rather than a place that will be an arena of contestation, Southeast Asia may be a bulwark against competition (Parks, 2023). The many cross-cutting ties that these countries have, their shrewd statecraft and the numerous institutional frameworks have the potential, from this perspective, to create a multipolar zone in which competition is dampened, if not reduced entirely by a complex diplomatic and economic latticework.

Present trends, including institutional decay, internal division and great powers 'wedging' ASEAN states, indicate that this assessment appears to be a little too optimistic. Nonetheless, it should not be ignored, and any forecast of the region's future must recognize that the lesser powers have influence; they are not just supplicants to the great powers nor are they powerless corks bobbing on an ocean of geopolitical competition. And how the domestic interests of the Southeast Asian states intersect with ASEAN dynamics and the larger patterns of contestation will determine how this area fares and how, in turn, it influences the larger Asian region. Most importantly, if the region's economy continues to be politicized and trade opportunities diminish, Southeast Asia is also likely to face economic constraints over the longer term.

South Asia

The most significant flashpoints in South Asia (for a map see Figure 7.6) have historically related to India–Pakistan rivalry

Figure 7.6: United Nations map of South Asia

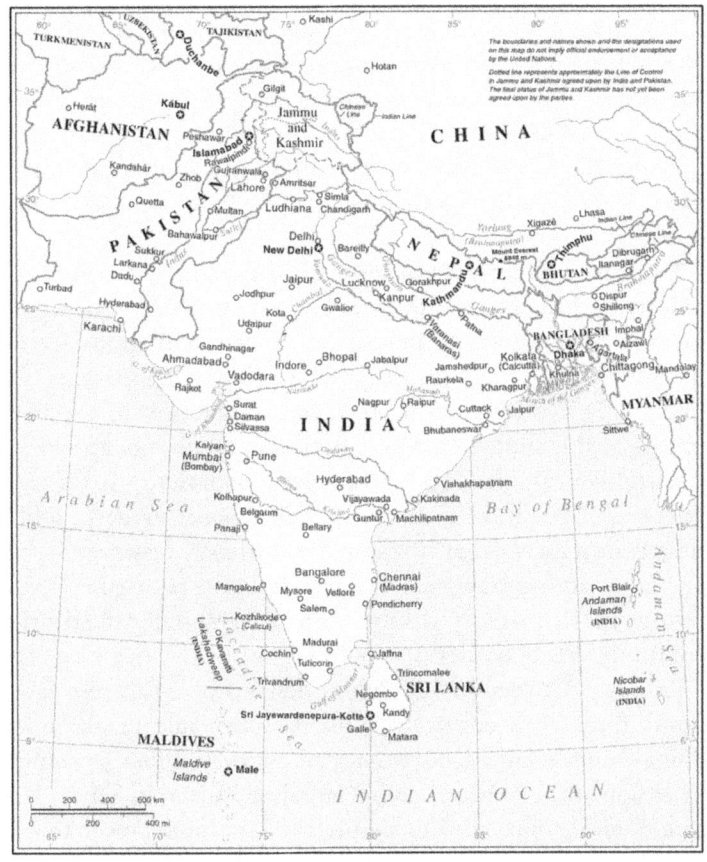

Source: United Nations

and the disputed border between China and India. The tensions between Delhi and Islamabad have been further complicated by the two countries both developing nuclear weapons in the late 1990s. The extensive border between China and India is disputed due to the uncertainty over lines drawn by the British in the 19th century. This entails territory known as Aksai Chin, which is administered by the PRC but claimed by India, and Arunachal Pradesh, which is recognized by most countries as part of India, but which Beijing claims belongs to China. Aksai Chin sits in the Northeast Corner of Kashmir, while Arunachal Pradesh is located between Bhutan and Myanmar in India's northeast. Both areas of border disputation are at extremely high altitude in very difficult terrain. The dispute boiled over into outright conflict in October 1962 when China and India fought for a month.

While the disputed border has two main locations, the underlying issue is that the two countries disagree as to where the line between them should be drawn, with both seeing the other's claim as an illegitimate product of colonialism (see Figure 7.7). The first location in the west relates to precisely where the line should be drawn between the disputed province of Kashmir and China. The second point of dispute is in the east, where China claims the entirety of Arunachal Pradesh, while India believes its border is where it is currently observed to be. The new national standard map, which China released in 2023, displays its claim most clearly, with both disputed territories behind the PRC border.

Tensions between Asia's two largest powers have escalated significantly in recent years. This has been due primarily to China's reinforcement and improvement of its military position on its side of the border; this has largely occurred in Tibet. The strengthening of its posture has included stationing more troops and improving the physical infrastructure of the borderlands through building roads, bridges and other facilities. This has led to a series of confrontations in recent years, including in 2017 in Doklam, where Indian troops supporting Bhutan pushed back PLA efforts to build a road in Bhutanese territory, and in 2020–21 in Ladakh and a skirmish near Sikkim. India's military is acutely aware of its defeat in the 1962 conflict as well as of the material advantages that the PLA generally has and is thus sensitive to what may appear to be minor changes

Figure 7.7: Disputed territories of India

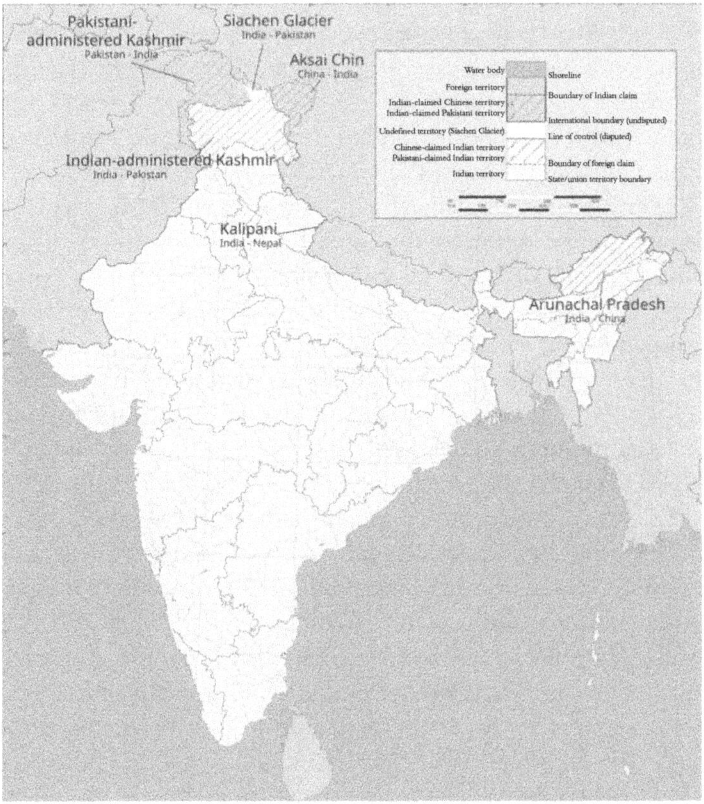

Source: Planemad/Wikimedia Commons (reproduced under CC-BY-SA 3.0 license)

to circumstances on the ground. The two countries are aware of the risks of escalation and have sought diplomatic and political efforts to improve communications and the broader relationship, although these have had relatively limited success to date (Thapliyal, 2024).

If one aspect of Sino–Indian rivalry dates back to the colonial era and the way the borders between the new republics were drawn in the 1940s, China's maritime ambitions are a new point of friction (Basrur, Mukherjee and Paul, 2019). As the PRC's military power has grown and its interest in the security of sea lanes has increased, the PLAN has expanded its capacity to project power beyond its littoral waters. It has established a military base in Djibouti and has shown interest in establishing several more in the Indian Ocean. The Indian Navy is presently a superior force in that ocean, but the long-term concerns about Chinese ambition and intentions have prompted further enhancements of the Indian military. While it is likely to be some time before a naval arms race or other acute strategic competition plays itself out, the Indian Ocean is now a zone of contestation in Sino–Indian rivalry where in the past the military wrangling was essentially only in in the vertiginous peaks of the high Himalayas.

The US and India have historically had a difficult relationship. India was non-aligned for much of the Cold War and tilted towards the USSR in that conflict's final decades. When India tested its nuclear weapon capability in 1998, thumbing its nose at international opinion and particularly at Washington, the relationship reached a nadir. In less than a decade, however, the US began to actively engage the South Asian giant. This was the direct result of the recognition by both democracies of the shared interest that they had in limiting PRC influence (Hall, 2014). President Obama made India a particular focus of his pivot, visiting the country twice, the only time a sitting US president has, so far, done that. India is the critical fourth pillar of the Quad arrangement and Washington sees it as a vital component in its efforts to contain China and underpin its preferred order. For many strategic analysts in the US, and among its allies, the combination of the PRC's scale and the inherent advantage of its geography means that without Indian alignment any effort to contain the PRC in military terms is unlikely to succeed. The shared concerns about PRC power and influence have been the prime driver of US and Western engagement, although the appeal of its growing middle class consumer market has also been a motive force.

The problem that the US faces is that the alignment of interests is strong in the short term, but over the longer run the two countries have divergent ambitions. Presently, they agree that they do not want the PRC to be Asia's pre-eminent power. However, beyond the absence of Chinese domination, the world's two biggest democracies have quite different visions for the region and the respective roles that each would play in that future order. As discussed in Chapter 6, Delhi's preference is for a multipolar regional and global order, one which entails a significant relative reduction in US power and an increase in the power and influence of India. And while it is a democracy of considerable standing, making it for some a 'like-minded' partner of the US and the West, the illiberal trends that have grown more prominent over recent years also mean that the domestic political values cannot be taken for granted as a means through which the interests of the US, its allies and India can be secured over the longer run. While this has largely been the product of Narendra Modi's government, the underlying support for this illiberal streak among the BJP and its continuing ability to generate electoral support for this trend means illiberalism is likely to remain. Overall, the current alignment between Washington and Delhi rests on foundations of ultimately limited duration.

India–Pakistan rivalry continues to influence the region, but it is becoming increasingly less significant (Hiro, 2015). The lingering point of friction remains their competing claims over Jammu and Kashmir. While the risks of conflagration remain and the military exchanges in May 2025 related to Kashmir are a reminder of these risks, compared with the scale of China–India competition, as a relative component of long-term geopolitical risk, it is less significant than in the past. The two have fought multiple conflicts and, while most scholars tend to agree that the acquisition of nuclear weapons by the two countries has acted as a moderating force, as well as the sudden clash in 2025, they have experienced acute crises in 2001–02, 2008, 2016 and 2019. Pakistan has always been a much smaller economy and military power than India and in recent years the gap between the two has widened markedly as India's economy has grown for a sustained period while its neighbour has struggled. Pakistan was able to benefit from its ties to the US, due mainly to American interests in Afghanistan after the 2001 intervention. But as Washington's interest in that country has declined and as it has engaged India as part of its larger regional strategy, Pakistan has been marginalized. Islamabad has sought to cultivate ties with China and has benefitted from some BRI projects, but these are unlikely to be sufficient to counteract India's growing weight. While Indo–Pakistan rivalry will continue to be tense and difficult to manage, it is likely to play a less significant role in Asia's future geopolitics and seems to be one of those rare regional flashpoints that is becoming less rather than more volatile.

The other security concerns of the region have almost entirely been those that follow from weak state governance, such as rebellions, uprisings, terrorism and transnational crime. Inter-state jockeying for influence and advantage was limited in part because of the dominance of India and in part because of the limited capacity of South Asia's states. As geopolitics returns to the broader region, those two points of focus remain central, but they have been further complicated. While Sri Lanka and Bangladesh, Nepal and Bhutan have clear stakes in the larger disputes for Asia's strategic balance, they are not major protagonists in this competition, mostly operating a level below East Asia's middle ranking powers, such as South Korea or Australia.

Central Asia

For most Western scholars Asia's geopolitics is almost entirely a maritime question, with perhaps the solitary exception of a recognition of the Sino–Indian border dispute. But a complete assessment of the region must include the not-inconsiderable continental components. Central Asia has always been important to Asia's economic, strategic and cultural dynamics. It was a vital crossroads linking the great civilizations of Europe and Asia along the routes that were, before long-distance maritime transport was possible, the only means of communication. It was also a key component of the Timurid Empire and was the heart of Chinggis Khan's vast domain, the most expansive empire that Asia has ever seen.

In the first part of the 20th century, Central Asia was incorporated into the USSR and, as Moscow settled on a nominally federated model for governing its extraordinary expanse, the lands were formed into five republics in the early years of Bolshevik rule. As the USSR began to break apart in 1990–91, the old administrative boundaries morphed into international borders, with the five stepping onto the global stage as independent republics (see Figure 7.8). Kazakhstan is the largest geographically, Uzbekistan is the most populous, these as well as Turkmenistan and Kyrgyzstan are ethnically Turkic while the fifth, Tajikistan, has ties to the Persian-speaking peoples. As happened in many corners of the world where empires ruled, the lines drawn by the imperial power cut across those of the ethnic and tribal groups who inhabited the area and divided critical lands and waterways. The most notable of these is the Fergana Valley, whose riparian systems are vital to the societies and economies of much of the region. The valley is primarily in eastern Uzbekistan but runs through Kyrgyzstan and Tajikistan. While Soviet rule prevailed, this was not a major problem due to the nominal nature of the Soviet republics' sovereignty. As part of the USSR, the central Asian states were oriented towards Moscow, both literally and figuratively. Their economies were organized by the dictates of the central planners in the USSR, and the infrastructure was designed to serve the needs of the Soviet Union and not the peoples of the republics.

Figure 7.8: Political map of Central Asia

Source: iStock/PeterHermesFurian

After the initial chaos of the Soviet collapse, Central Asia was transformed by the discovery of major hydrocarbon reserves in the Caspian Sea basin. This gave the region not just hugely improved economic prospects but also geostrategic significance. Equally, as a zone of independent countries of some geographic heft abutting China, Iran and Afghanistan, Central Asia's geopolitical significance was slowly recognized, particularly as Vladimir Putin began to move Russia away from its pro-Western leanings in the early 2000s. America's 2001 invasion of Afghanistan after the 9/11 terror attacks gave Washington a direct presence in the region, with the construction of military installations in several republics. China's formation of the SCO as well as Russia's careful cultivation of the republics were part of an effort to limit Washington's influence. Over time, the US withdrew, and Central Asia once again became a place where

Russian geopolitical influence predominated. Yet by 2010, China's interest in the region had grown substantially, evident in the many infrastructure and development programmes that they were supporting (Patnaik, 2016).

While external powers are of great importance, the autonomy and capacity of the states themselves must not be overlooked. They are acutely aware of their relative puniness compared with their neighbours and have long memories of imperial domination. They have been quite successful at cultivating relations with the three most powerful states as well as with India, Pakistan, Turkey, the EU and the Gulf states, with Saudi Arabia a notable presence. Riyadh has been particularly active as part of its strategy to reduce Iranian influence and to become the greater Middle East's most significant power. The lack of coordination and, at times, rivalry between Russia and China has provided Central Asian states the opportunity to leverage Moscow's and Beijing's interests to their advantage. The series of high-profile summits of recent years are illustrative of the way the five are cultivating key third-party relations. These include an annual China–Central Asia summit first held in 2023, a US–Central Asia summit hosted by President Biden in 2024 and the Central Asia–Gulf Cooperation Council (GCC) Summit of 2023.

The Russian invasion of Ukraine has been beneficial to the region as traders looking to move goods and commodities who want to avoid Russia have rerouted trade through Central Asia. Equally, those seeking to sell goods to Russia but wanting to avoid the ire of Western sanctions are also choosing to channel their goods through the region. This has helped with the longer-run aim of diversifying their economies as well as improving the diplomatic gambits in which, like Southeast Asian states, they wish to avoid picking sides and to be able to take advantage of multiple lines of geopolitical interest in their corner of the world.

The Sino–Russian alignment may be a major challenge to that ambition. The partnership is styled by Moscow and Beijing as having no limits and is a direct effort to advance their shared interests to reduce Western power and influence. It is reasonable to expect much better coordination on their respective approaches to Central Asia. Geopolitically, the relationship between the two countries provides not just a more united front in their shared aim to undermine Western interests and push back on liberal values, but it also means they do not need to spend time and resources managing their borderlands, which have historically been unstable and the source of friction and conflict. Central Asia has in the past been a point of competition between the two major powers and it has the potential to be a literal and figurative wedge between them in the future. We should expect that Beijing and Moscow are likely to better coordinate their activity in Central Asia.

Beyond this, China's interests in Central Asia are threefold. First, it wants political stability and secure borderlands next to its southwestern periphery. Second, Beijing seeks to ensure that the five Central Asian republics are geopolitically aligned with Beijing. Third, it has economic interests in accessing energy and improved physical connectivity through the region to diversify the routes through which goods, commodities and energy can move in and out of the PRC. These three goals have in the past been most directly advanced through the BRI infrastructure programme (IISS, 2022). By providing major infrastructure loans, investment and capacity, Beijing hopes to improve this movement. In turn, the economic development that would occur because of better infrastructure would promote political stability and security and, in turn, the recipient countries would be keen to support China's larger ambitions. For its part, Russia also wants to see a stable Central Asia that is not a source of transnational insecurity. Those fears have in the past focused on terrorism and the narcotics trade. But Moscow would prefer that its historical dominance of the zone continues in the 21st century. Moscow's ambition is that Central Asia is safely corralled within a Russian sphere of influence. Its most immediate priority is to reduce, if not remove entirely any Western influence but over the longer run Moscow would clearly prefer that Central Asia were a place where it is the predominant power and not a zone where it shares influence with or is subordinate to Chinese interests. However, the reality of power differentials as well as Moscow's invasion of Ukraine and consequent dependence on China mean it is likely to have to learn to live with sharing influence with Beijing, at least over the next five to ten years.

For some time, Washington has seen Central Asia as a place where both China and Russia can be pressurized. However, its primary focus on the region was as part of the long-running 'war on terrorism' that dominated US foreign policy after 2001. As terrorism was emphasized less, Central Asia dropped down Washington's priority list, even as it recognized the potential the region had to divide Beijing and Moscow. As geopolitical competition has become the dominant focal point of US strategy, China and Russia have become more aligned. It follows that the US is likely to find renewed interest in Central Asia. It is a zone that has in the past been open for competition and one must assume that it is a place where Washington and the Western powers will continue to probe for opportunities.

Through the 19th century up until the Russian Revolution, Central Asia was home to the 'Great Game', a label given to the imperial machinations to control Central Asia. The term described not just the scale of what the competitors thought they might gain were they to 'win', it also conveyed the difficulty of the contest. The nature of the terrain, its location far from the seaboard and the immense challenges of communication meant that it was an extraordinarily difficult place to do the hard business of geopolitics. Many analysts see in the jockeying for influence in recent years and the potential for future great power contestation a parallel with that period (Raby, 2024). Tempting though that may be there are many differences between the current period and the high point of European inter-imperial competition. The most important is the sovereign status and independent capacities of the Central Asian states. They are adept at managing relations with a wide range of powers while also maintaining positive ties to their two powerful neighbours.

The future of Central Asia's geopolitics is not as a passive venue for major power contestation. Rather, it will be a function of the interplay of the intra-Central Asia relations, great power machinations and the complex web of third-party relationships. And while Central Asia has been successful at avoiding outright war since the Soviet collapse, there remain considerable security tensions within the region, notably in relation to water access, both for energy and for consumption, as well as for use in agriculture and other production. Narcotic smuggling and inter-state tensions, most particularly between Tajikistan and Kyrgyzstan, also remain a significant long-term challenge.

While Central Asia lacks some of the economic dynamism of Southeast Asia, it is, in geopolitical terms, the continental obverse of that corner of Asia. The parallels between the two subregions are striking. Both are frontal zones of great power competition. Both have an array of institutional structures that seek to shape and contain security tensions, but which fall short. And both comprise a set of relatively small states that are skilled at a complex diplomatic choreography to advance their interests in the face of or, indeed, through shrewd harnessing of geopolitical competition in ways that can be paradoxically stabilizing.

Conclusion

The extent of Asia's zones of contestation is considerable. From the high Himalayas to the South China Sea, from the Korean Peninsula to the deserts of Rajasthan, the flashpoints are numerous, dangerous and increasingly complex. Most importantly, the growing geopolitical competition is putting more pressure on these already volatile areas. Each of the flashpoints has an internal dynamic that often goes back decades and even centuries but that is now overlaid with the larger competitive dynamic. Each is seen not just in its own right as a fight about territory or jurisdictional claims but also as part of a struggle for Asia's future. This makes managing the flashpoints harder and the risks of miscalculation greater.

At this point in time more zones of contestation are maritime than continental, but those land-based spheres remain a challenge with significant long-term consequences. And it is in the heightened sense of risk and tension in the flashpoints that we see the loosening grip of shared economic interests. The extensive commercial ties between Taiwan and the PRC will in no way act as a brake on conflict or as a prompt to cooperation and, as tensions rise, it appears that the economic dimensions have a lower and lower salience. Equally, the Asian strategic imagination described in Chapter 4 is increasingly visible in the dynamics of these contests as they are seen as linked, not necessarily in a fundamental way, but in the manner in which they are connected by the larger sense of contestation for Asia's future.

Finally, the increase of tension and the sense that some scholars identify of the risks that they may prompt a slide into a more generalized regional crisis (Taylor, 2018) show us how difficult it will be to reestablish a strategic equilibrium. Asia's long peace rested on a strategic balance or, more correctly, on US dominance and its widespread acceptance. To achieve a more peaceful future, the region must restore a military equilibrium, but the cases discussed in this chapter indicate the direction of travel is very firmly moving away from such a state of affairs. More worryingly, major forces that cut across the region are likely to further exacerbate this trend, and it is to those that we turn in Chapter 8.

8

Sources of Risk and Volatility

In the early years after World War II, Asia was seen by outsiders as a place of endemic poverty, where conflict and popular revolts were as common as the diseases and malnutrition that accompanied its destitution and maladministration. Asia's modern affluence is, from that perspective, astounding. A quarter of the way into the 21st century, it is the most dynamic zone in the global economy, at the cutting edge in manufacturing, high technology production as well as a leader in infrastructure, telecommunications, digital payment systems and a host of other areas. Few could deny the flash of Shanghai's skyline, the glitz of Mumbai's mansions or the engineering marvels of Japan's and China's extensive highspeed train networks. But as Chapters 6 and 7 have reminded us, Asia is one of the riskiest places on the planet, with a slew of hotspots, many of which could escalate into major conflict and even nuclear war.

When assessing the history and prospects of regions and continents, there is a temptation to focus on large-scale macro factors and distinctly international matters: which countries have the superior military forces, what do comparative GDP growth rates look like, what does that ambitious new power actually want? Yet there are critical aspects that are operating within and across states and societies that are vital to understand the current state of the region as well as its future. In this chapter

SOURCES OF RISK AND VOLATILITY

I explore three major forces that exist across Asia and which, when they interact with the region's geopolitics and economic development, have the potential to act as dangerous multipliers of risk. These are powerful cross-cutting forces that can drive a crisis into a conflict with terrifying speed. They can act not only as accelerants, but also as forces that increase the consequences of events spiralling out of control and can themselves act as further sources of friction and contestation.

Nationalism is one of the most powerful social and political forces of the modern era (Hutchison, 2017). It has been a central component of Asia's politics across the 20th century. The harnessing of the national idea was key to the success of liberation movements and the legitimation strategies of democratic and authoritarian states, although the form and function of nationalism varies greatly across the region. During globalization's expansionary phase, nationalism appeared to recede in significance, at least at the international level, but it has returned with a vehemence and visibility that is counter to what many expected at the turn of the millennium. The second force is the division between liberal ideas and the forces of illiberalism. A generation ago, liberalism was on the march across Asia, democratization was casting out the old autocrats, human rights were being expanded and open markets were embraced. Today, illiberalism is ascendant and how that battle of ideas unfolds both within and between countries will be vital to Asia's future.

The final force is perhaps the greatest challenge of all, that is the social, political and human consequences of a changing climate. Asia has always been a place of significant climatic diversity and widespread natural disasters. The typhoons of the Western Pacific, the monsoons of the Indian Ocean, the volcanoes and earthquakes in Indonesia and Japan, the Bay of Bengal's floods and the droughts of South Asia and the Central Asian steppes all have powerful effects, and their human consequences are often extensive precisely because of the populations' size and density of inhabitation. How changes to the climate will impact the region matters not only in relation to natural disasters but also because of the way it will transform the natural systems that are vital to human existence. From the waters of the Tibetan plateau to the fisheries of the South China Sea, climate change will have a dramatic impact on Asia's future.

Nationalism

Nationalism has played a major role in in the domestic and international politics of modern Asian states and societies (Leiffer, 2000). The idea of nationalism is simple: a particular group of people with a shared sense of identity and a defined territory ought to be independent of others. At first glance it appears to be a perennial of the human condition. But in the bundling together of territory and a group of people, the way in which that group of people understands its identity and the political assertion of independence, it is a distinctly modern creation. In the pre-modern period, in Asia and in Europe, political authority was linked to kinship, conquest and divine intervention. There was no uniform set of principles or practices. China's Communist Party likes to style itself as the direct heir of an uninterrupted sense of Chinese nationhood going back thousands of years, the casting back of contemporary ways of doing things on the Ming or Chin dynasties gets the practice of imperial Chinese authority and the way Chinese imperial subjects identified themselves entirely wrong (Li, 2018).

Scholars have shown the ways in which nationalism emerged alongside the development of modern society marked by industrialization, the expansion of the global capitalist economy and the liberal revolution in North Atlantic politics (Anderson, 2006; Smith, 1998). European imperial powers brought these ideas, which transcended their place of origin and found fertile soil in Asia. In some cases, Asian elites consumed the ideas in

Europe having travelled there for education or work. Ho Chi Minh's experience in France was emblematic of this (Duiker, 2012). But others in India, Indonesia and elsewhere saw in the idea of nationalism an argument that could be used against the Europeans who dominated their lives. The long and rich civilizations of Indochina and the South Asian subcontinent had a great deal on which they could call to mobilize the idea of a group with a shared past. The struggle against colonialism gave a real point of unity for groups that had previously lived separate but related lives. That people from Hanoi or Jakarta would be prepared to die for the belief in a nation that was imagined in their minds and that did not yet exist was evidence of nationalism's powerful, but protean force.

In the post-World War II period Asian societies threw off colonialism and embraced independent statehood. Nationalism had been central to those struggles, and it remained a significant part of the postcolonial state-building project once independence had been won. While nationalism was a critical component of state building, the role that nationalism played in that process – what might be described as the form and function of nationalism – varied considerably and not just for the obvious reason that each state was calling on its own cultures, languages, traditions and histories (Sidel, 2012). There were three sets of factors that shaped nationalism and its varieties in Asia.

The first was how the new state related to the empire that had preceded it. Most of the states in Asia are built out of what had been administrative units of the empires. Vietnam, Laos and Cambodia were part of French Indochina and, for a brief period, Vietnamese nationalism looked as if it would be constituted as an Indochinese nationalism, but that ebbed away (Goscha, 1995). Malaysia, Myanmar, Brunei and Singapore were parts of the British Empire, as were India and Pakistan. Indonesia was created out of the various elements of the Dutch East Indies and the Philippines had long been a colony of Spain, but its independence came from the US, whose brief experiment with the old-world practice of colonialism ended abruptly after Japan's defeat. The Koreas and Taiwan had been part of the Japanese Empire. Japan and China here are the outliers as they were imperial powers that had, in the case of the PRC, experienced a social revolution overturning the foundations of the old order and reconstituting just about all aspects of the system barring the borders and ethnic dominance of the Han. Japan was a defeated empire, that which it had seized had been stripped away, it was occupied and had a new political order forced upon it. While the basic geographic and cultural order remained, the political and social fabric of society and thus the idea of nationhood had to be fundamentally recast. Consequently, there is a significant difference in the form and function of Chinese nationalism as cast by the CPC from that deployed by Indonesian elites. Some forms of nationalism present themselves as embodying an essential national characteristic from a primordial past, such as Thailand or Vietnam, while others are more self-consciously trying to forge a civic identity out of an obviously diverse population, such as Indonesia or India.

A second key factor shaping the dynamic of nationalism is the way in which the postcolonial state became part of the global economy, while the international political context was the third. In Asia, the many conflicts driven both by Cold War contestation and postcolonial struggles and rivalries added further to the way nationalism developed across the region. The demands of the Cold War order, its push and pull of conflict and ideology served to reinforce particular versions of national identity and their links to the postcolonial states.

Nationalism was a central determinant of the way Asian states and societies developed in the post-1945 period. It was the self-conscious effort to craft not only the institutions and structures of modern statehood but also the idea of the people whom those institutions would ultimately serve. In the 1990s, however, nationalism appeared to retreat from centre stage. The receding tide of Cold War competition promised a benign future in which the need to defend a particular vision of state and national identity would be less necessary. Many scholars argued that the transnational nature of so many challenges, along with the increased power and influence of international institutions, meant that nationalism's grip on populations would weaken (Hobsbawm, 1992).

Experience in Asia today illustrates that not only was nationalism not eroded by interdependence or diluted by multilateral organizations, but it retained its power as a political mobilization strategy and as a means of responding to the very global forces which some thought would lessen its grip. Across Asia nationalism is a visible and central component in all polities, although it is highly variegated in the relationship to ethnicity and religion that is evident – in some instances ethnonationalism is significant, while elsewhere its dynamics are more civic and syncretic – as well as in its centrality to the state. This in part reflects the differing types of political systems in the region. In authoritarian China, the Party–state's nationalism is central to the overall political programme of the CPC and, as such, deeply ingrained in state action, while in democratic India the competing political parties have differing ways of mobilizing nationalism. Given space constraints, this chapter is unable to examine the full spectrum of nationalism in contemporary Asia; however, there are several dominant forms that nationalism takes in the region, particularly in the largest and most significant states, and that will be our focus.

The most striking fusion in modern Asian politics is the binding of Leninism with a redemptive nationalism that lies at the centre of the CPC's political programme (Zhao, 2004). In the post-Mao period, the party moved away from an ideological and, in some ways, more conventional Marxism–Leninism as its lodestar and instead saw its purpose as focused on nationalist redemption. In the past, the party had seen the fall of Imperial China as the result of the outmoded characteristics of the old order. Consequently, the symbols, values and ideas of that period were denigrated. The party saw itself as a force for emancipation and modernity in contrast to the antiquated attributes of the imperial system. Following Mao's death, the party shifted its approach. The period from the Opium Wars in the 1840s through until the foundation of the People's Republic, was now framed as a century of 'shame and humiliation' that was inflicted on China by foreign powers. The CPC's role was to make China whole again, to ensure that it remained intact in the face of immense centrifugal forces and that it was able once again to become a world power of the highest rank. The long arc of Chinese civilization was no longer a source of Marxist embarrassment but of pride. Indeed, it became an anchor of the CPC's claim to rule: the party would enable a return to past glories and it would do so by blending market-inflected economics with a disciplined Leninist politics.

In modern mass societies, how political elites achieve legitimacy is crucial to the success of their systems of rule (Beetham, 2013). Among the range of ways this is done, from charismatic forms to the invocation of tradition, the CPC has focused most intently on performance legitimation. That is the rightness of its authority stems from its ability to achieve its nationalist redemption programme. The redemptive approach gives the party the capacity to mine an extensive past to burnish itself and its ambitions, but it also provides an obligation to deliver and to do so in all three dimensions of the programme. First, China must be made whole again. The simple story is that the empire that China created by conquest and subjugation simply was there, as an ever-present fact before the bullying foreigners turned up and tore the country to pieces. In this narrative, Taiwan remains unfinished business. Second, the party must ensure that the country remains an orderly and stable society that is intact. The scale of the territory and people, its diversity and complexity as well as the poverty in which it was mired for most of the 20th century makes this especially challenging. For outsiders wondering quite why the CPC is so extraordinarily anxious about domestic threats and disorder, it is easy to forget that social chaos, poverty and famine on a horrifying scale remain in living memory. Finally, the Party-state must deliver on its ambition, and one that is increasingly stated in public, to make China a country that sits at the pinnacle of global power.

The CPC is a Leninist party in service of a profoundly nationalist programme. This nationalism is fuelled by a sense of grievance and victimization. The nation's greatness was stolen by the imperial powers. China was excluded from the meetings where the contemporary international order was designed and built; even worse, when a Chinese voice was allowed to speak at those discussions, it belonged to the nationalist KMT. China was also excluded from all the key international institutions until the 1970s. It should not be surprising that elites in Beijing believe that the world order is one that serves the interests and values of others. While this nationalist redemption programme is not explicitly enthonationalist, the Party-state's vision of the Chinese nation implicitly links China with the Han majority ethnic group. Some have argued that authoritarian China's nationalism is inherently expansionary (Pillsbury, 2015), pointing to recent efforts to make the international environment one which better suits its interests and advances the broader opportunities of illiberal powers. While it is correct to note that, under Xi Jinping, China has sought to make the world more amenable to authoritarians, there is little evidence of an appetite for the expansionism that was the hallmark of European nationalism that fuelled empire and led to world war. The CPC's version remains firmly rooted in its domestic function and indeed its international ambitions ultimately serve those internal goals. That said, Taiwan's place in that nationalist programme – it is a red line issue for Beijing because of its significance to the CPC's claim to rule – risks major international conflict.

For China, nationalism provides a sense of purpose to the party and its more than 90 million members as it works through the structures of the state to advance those larger goals. It provides a rich and resonant means through which party rule is legitimated among the population. The coercive direction of the party is not just the whim of one-man rule. The reorientation of rivers, valleys and villages to create modern infrastructure creates a wealthier and more prosperous society; the suffering of those displaced serves the larger goals of national recovery. But it has costs and risks. The problem of a performance legitimation strategy, particularly when tied to nationalist goals, is how to grapple with failure. This is about the longer-term problems of a system of rule that may have painted a rhetorically rich purpose for itself but which it can no longer achieve.

As Xi Jinping's China faces some of the most severe economic headwinds in decades, the ability to continue to be seen to deliver will be crucial to the country's prospects. But the other problem of a particularly nationalist strategy is maintaining control of the forces that are being harnessed. The PRC has proven to be remarkably entrepreneurial in using the internet to control expression, shape larger narratives and propagate the party's line, whether on long-run matters or day to day issues and crises (Chin and Lin, 2022). Free expression and association are tightly controlled, except if the purpose of that is to march on the Japanese embassy about a crisis in the East China Sea or fulminate about US foreign policy. But the army of what have come to be known as 'netizens' has emerged almost organically as the contemporary face of vitriolic Chinese nationalism. Netizens are highly active online individuals, typically on platforms like Weibo, a leading microblogging site in China. Nationalist netizens rapidly propagate hardline positions, excoriate those who are deemed, either explicitly by the party, or more spontaneously by the netizens, to cross an imagined nationalist line. These mass impulses are powerful, but they have in some cases proved hard to control (Weiss, 2014).

Nationalism is not just the purview of the region's authoritarian powers. In contemporary India, we see a particular type of nationalism that ties a populist political style to an almost chauvinist view of the Indian nation. This can be described as a kind of populist nationalism and was key to Indian prime minister Narendra Modi's rise to power in 2014. This is not unique to India, indeed it is part of a broader trend towards populism among democratic polities worldwide (Mudde and Rovira Kaltwasser, 2017). Donald Trump was able to harness an established reputation to a crude populist message to narrowly win the 2016 US presidential election and regain the presidency in 2024, while Rodrigo Duterte's populism in the Philippines was frighteningly violent as he unleashed murderous vigilantes to try to deal with the country's narcotics problems.

Populism is an approach to politics that has several key attributes (Mudde and Rovira Kaltwasser, 2018). The most important of which bestows the title – it is a political style that describes society as divided into two groups, the 'true' people and the elites. These groups are presented by populists as in tension if not outright opposition, with the elites framed as corrupt, self-interested and possibly bought or owned by interest groups. In some cases, it might be banks or big business, labour unions or machine politics. In others, the elites are not just corrupt but are in thrall to foreign interests. Antisemitism regularly appears in populist political strategies. In contrast, 'the people' are described as pure but downtrodden, sold out or otherwise taken advantage of by the elites. Populism is also a style that is simple. The messaging is clear: society has big problems caused by elites, but the solutions are simple and emotive. Related to this, populism is often described as not being broad or sophisticated enough to be an ideology as such as it rarely has a broad ranging set of policy interests or prescriptions, focusing instead on simple messages. Populists consequently tend to locate themselves in existing political movements – the speed and breadth of the Republican Party's takeover by populism has been striking – and often couched in a larger set of ideas. In

Europe, populism has been anchored both to left-wing socialism as well as to right-wing nationalism.

In Asia, populism is tied most clearly to nationalism, most prominently in India (Ayyangar, 2024). Narendra Modi, India's most successful leader in decades, is notable for a political strategy that harnesses new digital communication techniques to advance a populist agenda that is both economic and nationalist. There is much that is remarkable about Modi's successful appeal but one of the more striking dimensions has been his ability to generate enthusiasm among those who were left behind during the rapid economic growth of the early 21st century as well as among those who have done well (Gudavarthy, 2019). His message resonates with the ambitious who had improved their lot but who wanted to do better, as well as with those who remained stuck at the bottom of the economic ladder. Critical to this success was the Hindu nationalism that his party propagated. The essence of the idea is reasonably typical of ethnonationalist programmes: that the nation belongs to a single homogeneous group. In the case of the BJP, Modi's party, the in-group is defined by its Hindu faith. This notion, known in India as Hindutva, has a longer history but Modi's political success came at the cost of the secular and pluralist idea of the Indian nation that had been central to the independence movement in the 1940s and which was advocated by the long-dominant Congress Party (Jaffrelot, 2023). In keeping with the basic message of populism, Modi presents the once-dominant Congress Party and its secularism as the corrupt elite while the excluded 'silent majority' of Hindus are the forces for which he is the avatar. As Modi's hold on power consolidated through the late 2010s, Hindu nationalism was paired with a growing authoritarianism as the thin-skinned government clamped down on media freedoms, curtailing the judiciary and closing off individual rights. It was rebuked in the 2024 elections to the Lokh Sahba, India's parliament. The BJP had looked to be cruising to a victory that might have given it the chance to rewrite the constitution but ended up losing its absolute majority. But the party remains in power and does not look to be deviating meaningfully from the tenets of nationalist populism that has given it more than a decade in office.

Japan's political system is unusual. It has been democratic since the 1940s when it had an American-authored constitution imposed on it after the war. But it has been governed for virtually all the years since 1947 by the conservative LDP (Kohno, 1997). That party has been careful to manage nationalism both within Japan and how it is perceived internationally. The place of World War II and Japan's imperialism is the critical issue. The party has within it a wide spectrum of ideas about Japan's identity, its history as well as its political and civic culture, and the roles these should play in government policy. They range from a reasonably moderate civic nationalism that attempts to draw a line at the war's end and centres the experience of the atomic attacks and Japan's 'peace constitution'. At the other end there remains a small but at times voluble group that believes Japan's past is something of which to be proud, that it has little to apologize for or about and that the country should take a more prominent and independent role in the world (McVeigh, 2004). The contests between these views are rarely visible, with the civic and pacifist visions dominant. But they occur behind the scenes. As China has become more powerful, and the complex and difficult history and territorial disputes resurface, Japan's more strident nationalism has become more evident. However, to be clear, it presently is a minor political force (Lind and Ueki, 2021), but one with considerable potential.

While nationalism is an important component of the domestic political cultures of countries across the region, and one which is more visible and, in at least some states, has overtly military dimensions, it is important to emphasize that the phenomenon remains overwhelmingly domestic in its orientation. Asia does not presently have an expansionary nationalism of the kind that prompted Nazi efforts to conquer Europe, or which fuelled Japan's annexation of vast swathes of the region in the 1930s. In both China and India nationalism has strong chauvinist dimensions and, when linked to the expansion in defence expenditure and growing military acquisitions, it adds a complicating dimension to the region's strategic contests. But it is a force that primarily serves and shapes domestic political and social life. That does not mean, however, that this more visible nationalism is isolated from the international environment. The role played by nationalism domestically has clear consequences abroad in that it shapes and constrains how political leaders manage foreign policy issues, especially crises and complex matters, such as disputed borders and territories. It can also shift the political costs and benefits of making policy choices, especially in a time of crisis. For example, if the Japanese Coast Guard were to sink a Chinese paramilitary vessel within the territorial waters of the Senkaku/Diaoyu islands, how the PRC leadership responds will be shaped decisively by nationalist calculation. The diplomatic calculus would involve considering the nationalist elements, both opportunities and risks in terms of the choices that they face, as well as how netizens might respond. This adds a level of complexity and emotion to already difficult circumstances that can inflame tensions and narrow the room for manoeuvre. Finally, digital media, such as microblogging platforms, increase the speed with which nationalist sentiment can be inflamed and make those forces much harder to grapple with. It can also increase the costs political leaders might pay if the outcome fails the nationalist test. Not only does nationalism increase the prospects that more emotional decisions will prevail, but that modern technology also compresses the available time to negotiate and decide courses of action, further increasing the risk of dangerous choices being made.

Among the ideas with which Asia's nationalism is most visibly associated in the contemporary period, the sense of victimization stands out. The recent and traumatic experiences of colonization and war make this understandable but the way in which it is activated to legitimate political authority and programmes often harvests past grievances and lays the blame directly or implicitly at the feet of outside actors. For the nationalists, the perpetrators of past grievances reside in the present. In China, it is Japan and the West and, in particular, the US that is the main target, while in India, the BJP targets Muslims and other minorities. A victimized view of the past heightens friction and can also be an accelerant when crises occur. Not only can it drive up the emotion and sense of risk in a crisis by placing national redemption as a critical or, indeed, fundamental priority of states, but it can raise the stakes in complex areas in ways that can increase the number of flashpoints and make their management much harder. The high-altitude disputed border between India and China requires careful and delicate military and diplomatic management, as do the many complex and overlapping disputes in the South China Sea. But having these viewed through the high octane and black-white dynamic of authoritarian or populist nationalism increases the risks of problems emerging, limits the ways of managing these high-stakes disputes and allows a more emotional component the scope to influence decision-making.

Finally, Asia is not immune from the return of economic nationalism. While the dynamics in the region lack the emotive dimensions of the hollowed-out industries of the advanced economies where the desire to bring back 'good manufacturing jobs' is redolent with a romanticized sense of the past, there remain strong currents that are advancing more nationalist and less market-focused economic trends. As discussed in Chapter 5, China's dual circulation economic reform is a major effort through which the PRC is seeking to become less dependent on international demand and export markets to drive growth and instead trying to have local demand become the prime driver of domestic advancement (Garcia-Herrero, 2021). While Beijing is not pursuing autarchy, it is actively cultivating a much less internationally oriented structure to its economy. India, a longtime practitioner of economic nationalism, is part of this trend, although one which is simultaneously trying to take advantage of firms trying to diversify away from China while also seeking to keep foreign competition at bay in many sectors. Despite implementing significant economic reforms, Modi's government adheres to extensive protectionism. Indonesia too has expanded protectionism and its attempts to build a mineral processing industry is a typically state-led effort. Economic nationalism is on the rise across Asia.

No assessment of Asia's current or future trajectory can ignore the important role of nationalism. While alone it is not the sole driver of the tectonic forces that will determine the region's contours, it is an accelerant in many aspects of the most contentious elements in the region. Its redemptive purpose is one of the most important reasons why the CPC is not content to live forever in America's shadow. Its sense of unfinished business regarding Taiwan, however historically questionable that may be, is the reason that the island's future is so contested and fraught with risk. Nationalism increases risks, limits the time that is available in crisis management, reduces rationality and lowers guardrails. In short, it is something that makes the task of Asia's diplomats, whose job it is to manage crises, so very difficult.

Liberal retreat

The divide between liberal and illiberal Asia is among the most significant and yet least recognized cleavages in the region. In part this is because of the tendency to focus largely on the national level. Asia has a broad spectrum of political systems resting atop highly diverse sets of cultural and social values. Unlike Cold War Europe, where there was a sharp and violently enforced line that divided the liberal democratic states from the communist powers, Asia has a sliding scale with no neat geographic delineation nor binary demarcation. Brunei is an absolutist monarchy; Indonesia and India are vast cacophonous democracies; Leninist regimes rule in China, Vietnam and Laos, while illiberal semi-democratic systems sit alongside military dictatorships. Critically, the liberal facets of the region are a relatively recent addition.

The growing contest between the US and China has brought the differences between liberal and illiberal states to the surface, particularly as the Biden administration sought to use this as an organizing feature of its regional policy. But it learned that the regional diversity made managing the broader ranging coalition of interests difficult. Although Vietnam has a significant set of clashes with the PRC, its participation in any China-balancing strategy is complicated by the gap between the liberal preferences of the US and its authoritarian political system. Asia is not a place where styling the US–China competition as one between democracy and autocracy is likely to be a winning strategy (Xiang, 2024). But beyond the complications political variation brings to the management of geopolitics, the larger global tensions between the liberal ideas at work in the contemporary order are a further vector of complication.

When the UN system was established in the 1940s, it was built on the bedrock of traditional Westphalian ideas of sovereignty. States had absolute authority over their territory and no one else could interfere with their affairs. Yet over time liberal ideas began to become a greater part of the system and began to reset aspects of the international order's operating system. Individual rights were agreed to be sacrosanct. The UN organized treaties and charters that began to eat away at the absolutism of sovereignty – states had to treat minorities, women and labour in certain ways, they could no longer use certain weapons systems and so on. By the end of the 20th century, many states tried to renovate the idea of state sovereignty so that it would no longer simply mean that a country could chart its own course in the world but that the state had an obligation to protect its people from egregious crimes. This dilution of sovereignty with liberal characteristics was and remains contested. The international order that was established in 1945 was predicated on a sense of the universal applicability of its ideas. Liberals to this day believe that their ideas are universal and see the broadening out of liberal protections as something that is good for all. This is increasingly being contested, and Asia is one of the front lines of this fight.

The division between liberal and illiberal Asia is also somewhat hidden from view because it occurs at the subnational level. In India, where the BJP government has curtailed a range of liberties, activists on both sides clash at times in violent ways. In illiberal states, like Singapore, advocacy must be more cautious and the space for activism is extremely limited, while in hardline authoritarian states, such as China, it is extraordinarily risky. But it is the dual nature of the division, at once domestic and international, and its intersection with geopolitical and global forces that makes it such a salient feature of the region and its future, yet one which, with the focus on military contestation and the reconfiguring of markets, is strangely underappreciated. The cleavage is about not just what kind of values the larger international system should serve in the region but how societies should function at home in their day-to-day realities.

The diversity of cultures, values and religions in Asia led many to argue, even relatively recently, that the continent could never cohere as Western Europe has, as there was simply not sufficient social glue to bind such an expansive place into a coherent idea. It was not just the geographic barriers of mountains and deserts, but the expansive spread of peoples matched with such diverse faiths, languages and social norms that meant it seemed impossible to come up with a centre of social gravity to create a common culture or shared sense of identity or purpose. Yet in the 1990s, there was a brief period where elites from the region, particularly from East Asia, argued that there was indeed a set of distinctive Asian values (Barr, 2002). The idea had derived from the recent success of a range of Asian economies and was contrasted with the relative decline of many Western economies that were, in the early 1990s, struggling with recession.

The most visible proponents of these ideas, including the then Malaysian prime minister Mahathir Mohammad, argued that the success of Asian societies and economies rested not just on shrewd economic policy or the miracle of the market but on the interplay of state policy with a distinctive set of purportedly Asian values. Critics argued that this advocacy was a sophisticated justification for illiberal political systems, that they were hardly distinctively Asian and that they overlooked the significant cultural and social diversity within Asia (Kim, 2016). Politically, the rug was pulled out from under the feet of the proponents of this idea by the Asian financial crisis and the devastation it caused on so many hitherto dynamic economies. But as the region began to rebuild in the late 1990s, the networks of the broader Asian economy began to emerge and Asia entered a phase of liberal expansion.

Democracy and liberalism did not become a significant part of modern Asian experience until relatively recently. Only India and Japan were part of the 'second wave' of democratization that followed the post-1945 unwinding of empires. It was not until what scholars have described as the 'third wave' of democratization in the 1990s and early 2000s that the region began to experience a wider flourishing of liberal and democratic values and institutions (Markoff, 2016). The expansion of democracy in this third wave entailed a broadening out of different aspects of democracy in many corners of the region. While many assume that democracy simply describes the electoral systems to select representative governments from an electorate, it entails a good deal more. This means that democracy is not a black or white question of whether one does or does not have it, rather, it is a multidimensional proposition. Scholars of this process have developed highly sophisticated ways of measuring the many dimensions of democracy, its expansion, consolidation and contraction (Coppedge et al, 2020). Some models measure hundreds of variables, breaking down the larger components, like free and fair elections, into their many constitutive parts. For our purposes here, it is critical to recognize the multidimensional ways in which liberal democratic ideas operate in political systems and, to simplify things, we will focus on the six main elements identified by researchers as the most significant.

The first dimension is the most evident: democracy entails a representative government formed from regularly held elections that are free from interference, fairly adjudicated and that entail a peaceful transfer of power. The second dimension is the rule of law in which impersonal systems of rules are enforced equally. They are not capricious, nor do they treat citizens differently based on their status, rank, wealth or other attributes. The third is a clearly articulated set of constitutional limits on state power. The state is ultimately constrained not by resources, capacity or the whim of elites but by well-recognized and respected boundaries. The fourth element relates to freedom and specifically the freedoms of expression and of association. These dimensions depend on the fifth, and that is the enforcement power of an independent judiciary. Democratic systems provide majorities with the capacity to monopolize power, and thus the final dimension relates to the rights and protections for minorities. Democratic systems can also be assessed by the extent to which different groups are represented in legislative and policy processes, as well as the fairness and equity of the laws and rules.

In the mid-1980s, the people power movement in the Philippines was the harbinger of an Asia that was becoming more liberal (Thompson, 2023). The mass protests that removed the long-standing autocrat Ferdinand Marcos from power were the start of a widening of democracy and liberalism across Asia (Cheng and Chu, 2018). Taiwan introduced democratic reforms in 1992 and, by 1996, the system was entirely democratic, the year in which the presidential election was held for the first time, and which presaged a crisis as the PRC tried to intimidate the island's voters. South Korea moved out of its Cold War authoritarianism and became a democratic polity through the late 1980s and 1990s. Thailand enjoyed a period free from its cyclical coups and, perhaps most remarkably, the Asian financial crisis brought about a sudden collapse of Indonesia's autocracy and the world's most populous Muslim nation became a democracy in short order. It was barely a year between the tumultuous collapse of the value of its currency in 1997 and the fall of the longstanding dictator Suharto. Democratization in Indonesia led directly to the eventual independence of Timor Leste and the creation of a new and avowedly democratic state in the region.

Even in China political space was opening in the late 1990s and early 2000s. The CPC had receded from the highly involved ways in which it had controlled people's lives previously; it tolerated a level of public discussion about at least some aspects of policy and even experimented with grassroots democracy in the early 2000s (O'Brien and Zhao, 2011). Alongside the flowering of political liberalism, economic ideas of openness found further favour driving economic integration through growing trade and investment networks.

While few in the region fully accepted the basic premise of Francis Fukuyama's famous argument that democracy had won the historical battle of ideas, at the time there did appear to be something of a liberal spirit in the regional winds. Scholars were intrigued as to why the region had begun to become more democratic (Friedman, 2019). The reasons put forward ranged from the rise of an Asian middle class that had developed a preference for liberalism to the easing of the Cold War, making the anti-communist justification for authoritarianism no longer credible in Indonesia, Thailand or the Philippines. Added to this, the failings of the economic systems that authoritarianism had overseen in Indonesia and Malaysia, which were so cruelly exposed by the financial crisis, meant that the ability to deliver economic growth was no longer a defence for the constraint of freedoms. By 2008, Freedom House, the Washington-based non-governmental organization (NGO), which maintains an index of freedom, could identify the Philippines, Thailand,

Indonesia, Timor Leste, Malaysia, Singapore, India, Japan and South Korea as either free or partly free. A generation before only three of those could be so labelled. Authoritarianism appeared to be on the wane.

Within a few years, however, the mood began to shift, and the region began to experience a sustained period of what Stanford University scholar Larry Diamond calls a 'democratic recession' (Diamond, 2015, p. 141). Just as democracy has a range of dimensions, each of which can wax and wane in strength and durability, the assessment of its decline has multiple aspects. Among the many ways in which states and societies can become less democratic and more illiberal there are three main categories (Gerschewski, 2021). The first form it takes is what some scholars call 'deconsolidation'. This entails the weakening of the core idea that democracy is the best and most legitimate type of political system. For much of the 'third wave' period, democracy had a remarkable hold on the idea of what government could or should be. Deconsolidation describes the erosion of this and weakening of support for democratic values.

The second is democratic backsliding. This refers to ways in which democratic institutions and practices are deliberately weakened but the system has yet to become autocratic. It includes limits on free expression, politicization of the judiciary or the banning of some political parties. A distinctive facet is a phenomenon that scholars have described as 'democratic decoupling' (Croissant and Haynes, 2021, p. 2). This occurs when some democratic attributes remain in place, but others are eroded. A notable example of this occurred in Thailand's 2023 general election. The electoral process was reasonably free and fair and produced a sizeable plurality for the newly created Move Forward Party. But due to machinations among the ruling elite, most especially the military, the party was prevented from forming a coalition with other anti-military groups, leading ultimately to the party being dissolved by the courts and its leader banned from politics in 2024. The electoral process was democratic in terms of process but the way in which the outcome failed to be matched by substantive political change is a shining example of democratic decoupling.

The third is autocratization in which the core institutional and functional components of liberal democracy decline very significantly. This phenomenon encompasses both the situation in which democratic systems break down and fall into autocratic practices as well as circumstances in which the more democratic aspects of authoritarian systems are weakened or destroyed. So China's closing off of political space under Xi Jinping, the dispensing of political norms around collective leadership and the removal of the experiments in grassroots democracy are all examples of the further autocratization of the PRC's political system.

Asia has experienced a wide range of all three forms of democratic recession. Myanmar's 2021 coup is an extreme example of a sudden move to autocracy and one that shook even the most hardened of regional observers due to the crudeness of the way democratic processes and principles were dispatched. In India and Indonesia, the region's two biggest democracies and the ones on whom so much hope has been placed by liberals, ruling parties have displayed major examples of backsliding. The Modi government's attacks on journalists and opposition political leaders, and its cramping of the judiciary have been extremely unsettling particularly for democratic partners. Although the BJP's poor showing in the 2024 Lok Sabha elections – where it lost its majority and had to form a coalition – appears to have chastened at least some parts of the party and limited its ability to change the constitution, as some had feared.

President Joko Widodo's presidency entailed a wide range of examples of backsliding from curtailing the powers of the anti-corruption commission, arbitrary crackdowns on free expression, and vigilantism among many others (Power and Warburton, 2020). His successor Prabowo Subianto has continued this trend, removing some of the guardrails that had been put in place to limit the military's role in society. The

Philippines similarly experienced backsliding in the form of attacks on judicial independence, free expression and, perhaps most visibly, the violence unleashed by President Duterte's encouragement of vigilantism (Thompson, 2023). In South Asia, Sri Lanka experienced severe problems under the autocratic rule of the Rajapaksas, while Bangladesh and Pakistan also remained either mired in or enjoyed only brief and spasmodic breaks from authoritarianism. The ousting of long-time Bangladesh leader Sheikh Hasina in August 2024 was a surprising bright spot in an otherwise long-term trend in which liberal ideas have receded from influence across Asia.

There are several reasons why liberal ideas are in retreat in Asia. One is the simple reality that democratic transitions are difficult to achieve, and setbacks are almost inevitable. Given the relative novelty of democratic rule, its complexity and cost, as well as the scale of many Asian societies, it should be expected that democratic decline of some kind would be likely. But beyond this basic fact, China's rise and its power of example as well as its support for illiberal forms of politics is an important contextual factor. Alongside this, one should add the decline of Washington's support for liberalism. That the leading advocate and example of democracy has its own credibility problems and its tendency to preach a sermon it does not follow has led to democratic disenchantment. Equally, the broader challenges facing Western democracies should not be ignored. Across the older democracies, problems of sclerosis, disengagement, populism and dysfunction are rife. There seems to be something wrong with the basic constitutional structures as well as the interplay with parties and representation systems that sits poorly with contemporary societies. In this sense, Asia should be seen as experiencing a regional inflection of a broader global trend.

Illustrative of this are the problems of Asia's many political parties. In democratic systems, parties play a key role in mobilizing popular coalitions of interest groups to capture legislative power and provide a social basis on which consent for rules can be achieved. In simple terms, parties get a majority, either individually or as part of a group, and this provides legitimacy for governing. Asian political parties are either deeply entrenched in ways that invite cynicism – such as the LDP in Japan or Congress in India – or they do not bother building wide-ranging coalitions of interests but instead reflect patronage networks, as they do in Indonesia. This means they provide a weaker means of channelling interest groups and are also less likely to provide the kind of guardrails against backsliding than more broad-based parties. Asia also provides a curious counterexample to a central thesis of some prominent scholars of democratization. Many scholars argued that the emergence of a middle class is not just a prerequisite for democracy but that, once it is established, that group will act as a buttress for liberal systems. Yet Asia's experience is that middle-class interests, once established, may help bring democracy into being but cannot be assumed to be willing or able to protect it. Indeed, in some cases middle-class interests have been aligned to illiberal forces and have contributed to democratic recession in Asia as in Thailand, India and Indonesia.

Table 8.1 provides a simple categorization of Asia's states, dividing them into three groups. Liberal states are those that perform well, although by no means perfectly, in all six of the domains associated with liberal democracy. There are only nine here, but notably this includes two of Asia's most populous countries, India and Indonesia. Yet four of them, including those two, have experienced sustained erosion of democratic practice recently. The rest of the region is either illiberal – that is states that provide citizens with some features of liberal democracy but fall short in significant ways – or is outright authoritarian. That Asia has only five countries that are robust democracies is on the face of it illustrative of the headwinds facing liberal ideas and democratic aspirations. That this number has declined in recent years and that the democratic spaces that had existed in

Table 8.1: Asian political systems

Liberal (5+4)	Illiberal (6)	Authoritarian (13)
Australia	Bangladesh	Bhutan
Japan	Malaysia	Brunei
Korea, Republic	Nepal	Cambodia
Taiwan	Pakistan	Kazakhstan
Timor Leste	Thailand	Korea, DPR
	Singapore	Kyrgyzstan
*India		Laos
*Indonesia		Myanmar
*Mongolia		PRC
*Philippines		Tajikistan
		Turkmenistan
		Vietnam
		Uzbekistan

Note: * = Liberal states that have experienced sustained democratic backsliding.

some authoritarian states have been closed down tells a clear story: liberal ideas are in retreat.

The liberal–illiberal division is something of a fault line in the region and one that has the potential to release energy that can be highly disruptive to states and societies. In contemporary Asia the differences in political systems and the values they represent are becoming increasingly politicized. The US and its allies have tried at times, not to great effect it should be noted, to use the defence of democracy and freedom as a means of mobilizing action to counter Chinese and Russian influence. Equally, democratic states have begun to build coalitions of what are sometimes described as 'like-minded' states to advance their shared interests, and they increasingly see the geopolitical challenge of an ambitious China as a threat, not just to crude matters of material power but also to the liberal rules of the international game. Australia has defined a stable 'rules-based order' in the region as one of its core strategic interests (Department of Defence, 2016). This is not just a rhetorical flourish as Canberra seeks partnerships that are bilateral, minilateral as well as multilateral to try to defend a broadly liberal set of regional arrangements. Novel minilateral arrangements, like the Quad and the AUKUS pact, are all among democracies and Japan and South Korea have, for the moment, managed to overcome their history of bitter acrimony to advance their shared military and political goals.

The divisions are more acute within states. This includes what might be described as the conventional push and pull of liberal activists seeking to expand democratic space and the reaction of the state and vested interests to that pressure. In Thailand, extensive youth protests have sought to achieve a more democratic political system and reduce the reach of the monarchy and business elites. In India, the Philippines and Indonesia, clamping down on free expression has prompted significant responses leading in some cases to reforms from above. These domestic lines have become heated as backsliding is contested, but to this has been added an international dimension. State forces seeking to defend their positions have begun to use what might be described as the Moscow playbook in painting liberal activists and critics as puppets in the service of foreign forces, often implied to be the US or Western interests. The contest between liberal and illiberal forces occurs actively online with social media a vector both for activism and for the dissemination of authoritarian messaging. Some actors, particularly Russia, China and North Korea, have been very adept at using social media to spread misinformation to advance an illiberal agenda. The speed with which Russian information technologists sought to portray the popular uprising against Bangladesh's autocratic leader Sheikh Hasina as orchestrated by US forces was striking.

It is to an extent obvious that the diversity of values and particularly the diverging cultural systems and political forms they take will be crucial in shaping Asia's future. Yet determining the precise manner that shape takes, the steepness or otherwise of the region's contours, is somewhat more challenging. Perhaps the most obvious immediate way is the extent to which domestic political systems become a front line in the emerging geopolitical competition. In the Cold War, a contest that was explicitly ideological, the democratic West was hardly a purist in requiring partners and allies to be democratic. Indeed, one of the major problems the US faced was managing the decidedly illiberal and unpopular regimes with which they made common cause in the larger fight with the USSR. The Shah's Iran, the kleptocratic South Vietnamese leadership of President Diem and the dictatorship in Guatemala are only the most obvious examples of the unpleasant regimes which the US supported. So there is certainly precedent for ideological differences being able to be subordinated to the realpolitik needs of the day. But even so, it makes the managing of geopolitical strategies more complex, both in terms of the basic dynamics as well as ensuring the domestic support for those strategies.

The challenge to liberal ideas in Asia is a regional front in a larger global contest. It is clear that authoritarian powers are deeply uneasy about the role, significance and power that liberalism represents. Leaders like Putin and Xi see them as a threat that must be crushed. The statement announcing the Sino–Russian partnership that was launched shortly before Russia's invasion of Ukraine in February 2022 is about a plain statement of this sentiment as can be found. The two jointly 'oppose the abuse of democratic values and interference in the internal affairs of sovereign states under the pretext of protecting democracy and human rights, and any attempts to incite divisions and confrontation in the world' (Kremlin, 2022). China wants to reduce liberal and Western influence not just in terms of the disposition of military power or the shape of the infrastructure of the region but the larger principles that structure the nature of international relations. It has the advantage in its home region and will seek to further that over time, making the 'values' front a critical site of contestation. This front is one that, it appears, the US and its fellow liberal states are less well attuned to than they might be. The second Trump administration's inward turn and its seeming desertion of liberal values is likely to exacerbate these trends. The cleavages also present sites of internal division and potential conflict that will in turn have an impact on the way those societies function and their future trajectory. A freer Asia, understood in liberal terms, is one to which many aspire, but equally it is an idea that will be fiercely contested and that battle will come at the cost of the wellbeing and development of some of the world's poorest people.

Climate change

Asia's geographic scale means that its people and societies experience a wide set of climactic conditions. From the world's highest peaks in the Himalaya range, the fertile river plains in Bangladesh and India, the deserts of Kazakhstan and Pakistan through the lush tropical forests in Sri Lanka and Indonesia, Asia's climates are diverse and often extreme. The climate that has allowed such large populations to exist for so long – Asia has been far more populous than any of the other continents for thousands of years – is notable also for regular and traumatic disasters. In the Western Pacific typhoons, the regional term for cyclonic storms created by warm ocean waters, regularly batter the archipelagos and coastal states from August until September. Earthquakes and tsunamis are a frequent occurrence as well, due to the extensive set of geological faults across the Western Pacific. And major flooding and landslides are an ever-present problem in the tropical and subtropical latitudes that include much of the region's populace. On the south side of the Himalayas, the Indian Ocean monsoon is the most critical climactic feature.

From late April to September, moisture-laden air blows from the Southwest Indian Ocean and leads to massive rainfall across South Asia. It is critical for agricultural production and fresh water supplies as well as being vital to electricity systems, due to a large focus on hydropower in the subcontinent. The monsoons can be extremely damaging when they are as expected. But slight shifts in timing, either early or late, can be devastating as can overly powerful weather systems.

The region is, not surprisingly, one which is already experiencing significant impacts of the changing climate. The number of 'super typhoons', that is storms with winds more than 240 km/h, has increased and consequently the reach and scale of the damage that they cause has also risen. As populations have grown and become more affluent the cost of the destruction created has increased significantly. Shifting rain patterns cause disruption in agriculture systems across the region. In 2023, India, a country responsible for around two-fifths of global rice exports, banned selling most types of rice abroad because of harvest shortfalls caused by unusually heavy rainfall. This was linked to higher prices, and many analysts fear that over time such circumstances may contribute to significant social disruption. Scientific modelling projects that ten of the 25 countries most likely to experience extreme increases in rainfall are in Asia, which will impact more than 2.5 billion people (Transco et al, 2024). Equally, significant portions of the region live in coastal regions that are at risk of inundation as sea levels rise. This is especially acute in the very low-lying areas in Bangladesh, Southern India, Java in Indonesia, the Mekong Delta, areas near Bangkok, much of Honshu, Japan's main island, as well as significant portions of the Chinese eastern seaboard.

The challenges of a changing climate are very significant for the region. In many cases these are problems of the present and not theoretical challenges to be faced decades in the future. It is in part because of this that the CPC in Beijing has put such a significant priority on developing green technology in its cars and power systems. That Chinese firms are at the forefront of solar technology and low-cost EVs is due in no small part to a recognition of the urgency of the problem that is lacking in many other parts of the world.

The changing climate will be an immense source of disruption within Asian states and many of the poor countries will struggle to cope as it will test their resources, as well as their administrative and governance capacities. But climate change will also interact with the larger dynamics that this book has identified in a range of critical ways. Perhaps most immediately, it is likely to increase tensions in existing flashpoints. The South China Sea is seen by many analysts as a likely place for this to occur. As discussed in Chapter 7, the complex set of disputes in this critical waterway has multiple dimensions. As climate change puts more pressure on fish stocks globally and as demand for protein increases in the region due to rising prosperity, the tension between the claimants is likely to increase. Indeed, for a country like China, the pressures on food production could well become very dramatic, given the size of its population and the limits of arable land cultivation that it faces. Other areas where a changing climate might exacerbate existing points of tension include the East China Sea as well as parts of the Indian Ocean and the disputed border between India and China.

Climate change is also likely to create new points of tension and potential conflict (Glasser et al, 2022). This has multiple dimensions although many identify water and its access and control as a likely source of contestation. Changes to the environment will shift both where water falls from the sky, the length of time it is frozen and its flow through riparian systems. Adding to that the human efforts to shape and control water, such as irrigation systems, reservoirs and hydropower, the risks are both real and obvious. Furthermore, geographic advantages that upstream states have on downstream states and the resentments this may bring provide further grist to the climate change conflict mill.

A changing climate is also almost certain to increase the instability of great power competition as the major powers will have to adjust their circumstances to the shifts in the natural environment. From energy systems to the impact of trade patterns, from the disposition of troops to the ways strategic waterways function, climate change will unsettle existing geopolitical patterns and as countries like the US, China and India adjust to manage its circumstances and advance their interests, it will redound on the competition that exists between them. The US may see, for example, in a China that is experiencing severe inundation on its eastern seaboard an opportunity to pressurize its adversary. Antarctica could easily become a source of strategic rivalry and further tension between the major powers, while the melting of the Arctic ice sheet has already created competition at the North Pole. There is also the prospect of climate adaptive technologies contributing to geopolitical rivalry. The US developed atomic weapons in short order, driven by the acute pressures of World War II and fears of others getting their hands on the destructive technology first. In a similar manner states may throw vast resources at adaptive technologies to deal with energy transition or other problems which yield 'dual use' benefits as the technology can be applied to strategic competition. While hypothetical, the scale of the challenge climate change presents and the disruption its response may generate means these prospects must be taken seriously.

But there is an important attribute of the threat a changing climate brings to the region that can be forgotten, particularly in a time of growing rivalry and fear, and that is its potential to enhance cooperation. The dramatic transformation of the planet's environmental systems caused by the intensive release of carbon and other gasses during the industrial period is an example of what international relations scholars call 'transnational problems'. These are challenges which originate from activities across multiple countries and are beyond the ability of any one country, no matter how wealthy or focused on its endeavours, to solve. It is also an immense collective action problem, meaning that dealing with it adequately requires getting many different actors with diverging interests to act in their collective long-term interest, an interest that may well be at odds with their short-term incentives.

The existential nature of the climate challenge promoting a more cooperative dynamic has more and less optimistic paths to consider. In the first scenario, the US, China, as well as the EU, work actively together to develop policies and technologies to manage a transition from carbon-intensive economic growth to something much more sustainable. This may be prompted by changes in their domestic politics – it is very difficult to see the current political systems in China and the US as allowing this to occur – or by acute crises driving the great powers to cooperate with one another. There have been examples of grand coalitions of convenience to fight a common enemy in the past, and it is possible that the immensity of climate change brings Asia's states together. A second and more realistic scenario is that the competition between the US and China, and particularly their efforts to 'win' the next generation of technology may create a dynamic that does indeed yield technologies and policies that work at scale to mitigate the effects of a changing climate. The political imperative in China is acute – it is difficult to imagine the realization of CPC ambition to make the country the most powerful and affluent on the planet without meaningful action on the climate and failure to deliver on that ambition is potentially existential for the party. Equally, the financial rewards for firms which get there first in green technology globally are almost unimaginable, thus a competition driven by the animal spirits of capitalism may well deliver.

But whether changes to the environment exacerbate existing conflicts, bring new hotspots and increase transnational insecurity or even promote cooperation of some kind, there can be no doubt that it will have a dramatic impact. A changing climate will inevitably create a more volatile Asia.

Conclusion

Nationalism, the liberal–illiberal cleavage and a changing climate are three profoundly important forces that cut across Asia, and that will interact in complex ways with the larger forces of geopolitics and globalization to shape the region's future. Each in its own way brings significant new risks to bear and collectively they have the prospects of generating a much more unstable future. Not only do these forces increase the likely causes and consequences of crises, they will also drive the disintegrative trends at work in Asia.

As we set out to make sense of what direction the region may go and as we try to craft policies and strategies to manage risk and reduce the prospects of conflict, due care must be paid to these forces that do not get the same attention as geopolitical contestation, or the question of trade patterns and high technology competition. This is in part due to the ways in which they do not map neatly onto the conventional modes of thinking about international affairs. Nationalism is usually conceived as a domestic phenomenon that only seeps into the international domain when it is particularly metastasized. Yet the significance of nationalism in Asia and its qualities make it a significant source of volatility. Equally, the battle of ideas about liberalism can be seen as largely ally-focused. But China's fears that liberal ideas will damage the CPC's rule are matched by concerns about the international system and that its efforts to advance a domestic agenda have significant international implications. The significant transformations of the natural environment are inherently transnational and challenge state managerial capacity. Because of this these forces tend not to figure in the analysis of Asia's geopolitical future. For most people in Asia the most immediate threat to their security comes from natural disasters and this source of insecurity is only likely to increase over the coming years. Yet geopolitics tends to dominate government thinking and consequently it absorbs the lion's share of government expenditure on security concerns, even as the more pressing threats to the wellbeing of Asia's peoples relates to a changing climate.

The balance of probabilities is that nationalism, illiberalism and climate change will make Asia less secure and more prone to conflict. The flashpoints across the region are likely to be more combustible, and the crises that emerge will be much harder to wrangle and prevent from spiralling out of control. And a changing climate is likely to create new flashpoints as critical facets of national systems, such as energy, water supplies and food production, are badly disrupted. Asia's future will be much more volatile, and the amplitude of the shifting risks will be pushed to greater heights by these cross-cutting forces that multiply the already significant risks facing the region.

9

Three Paths to the Future

The making of modern Asia is an epic; the continent's breadth, population and diverse cultures can boggle the mind. But it is a transformation whose speed is, if anything, even more remarkable than its scale. Within a generation independent states were created out of expansive imperial holdings. In 1946, a trader who sailed from Bombay to Rangoon, then onto Singapore and Hong Kong, would see the Union Jack fluttering on the flagpole at each harbour. Today, those are key ports of four independent states. Many countries, like Malaysia and Indonesia, never existed before. When they were established, commentators thought they were ersatz creations, likely to come apart at the seams under the pressures of nationalism and the Cold War (Tillman, 1963). But a quarter of the way through the 21st century, those states are solid members of international society, their economies are dynamic and many are important players on the global stage.

This book has shown that the way in which Asia's economies grew, through the integrative forces of market-led globalization and the emergence of value-chain models of production, created a China-centred, but not Sino-centric economy. Asia had become an integrated system, and it has been the engine for global growth for at least a decade. This prosperity has brought about a new era of competition as some emerging powers bristle against an international environment they feel limits their potential and impedes their ambitions (Auslin, 2020). The disintegrative forces of geopolitics are back.

The key driver of Asia's integration, globalization and a consensus in the developed world about economic openness has been shredded by the pandemic years and the increasing grip that nationalism has in capitals across the region. How the global economy is reconfigured, how it intersects with and is shaped by great power contestation as well as the dynamic forces described in Chapter 8 will shape Asia's future and will be of fundamental importance for the world.

The purpose of this chapter is to think systematically about what Asia's future might look like by carefully assessing how the forces discussed in this book are likely to evolve. Modern Asia was made by the way the global economy developed in tandem with the choices made in Asian capitals. This wove a web of trade and investment, binding together the states and peoples of this vast continent. It was also forged by the ambitions and fears of re-empowered countries. But just as modern Asia was coming into focus, the pandemic years scrambled everything. The global economy was upended and geopolitics was turbocharged. As the region charts its way forward, how new patterns of strategic competition and globalization are reestablished and how they interact with one another will define Asia's destiny. While nationalism, illiberalism and climate change will intersect with the economic and strategic dimensions in cross-cutting ways and sharply escalate the risks and dangers facing the region and the world.

The approach taken here draws on the practice of scenario planning that is used by firms and governments to make informed assessments about future trends (Ramirez and Wilkinson, 2016). The basic approach is to develop plausible scenarios based on a thorough analysis of the key material and social forces shaping events. A rigorous analysis of the underlying assumptions and key variables is then applied to identify the critical factors on which different scenarios depend and then a careful elaboration of the scenario occurs. Here I will draw on the preceding chapters, which have laid out the key forces shaping the region's future, and, based on this, map out three broad ways in which Asia's future may develop.

Fractured Asia is the bleakest future, in which uncontained geopolitical rivalry reinforces deglobalizing trends. These are amplified by nationalism to create a dangerously unstable and combustible world. **Rebalanced Asia** describes a future in which an uneasy strategic equilibrium holds. While political and nationalist imperatives have distorted some sectors, many elements of the region's economy have returned to pre-pandemic levels of interdependence. Finally, **Unified Asia** paints a more optimistic picture, in which geopolitical competition has been corralled and a stable and structured strategic balance prevails, allowing the many shared interests across the region to drive collaboration to tackle problems like climate change, health crises and economic inequality.

The three scenarios do not include major shocks. In part this is because assessing when and where seismic shocks might happen in international affairs is notoriously difficult. More importantly, once they are introduced, they are of such magnitude that they badly distort the scenario and thus get in the way of the primary objective of thinking through how current trends may unfold. Several of these shocks will be very briefly flagged at the end of the chapter.

A more multipolar and less Western world

During the first quarter of the 20th century the entire globe was ensnared in a set of economic structures and political systems that were of Western origin and that served Western interests. The cataclysm of World War II brought the old mode of dominance to a close. Empires were cast aside, European powers retreated to their homelands and their influence was curtailed. The creation of the UN established a structure that would ultimately dilute Western influence. By creating an institution to oversee and manage relations between states, one that treated all sovereign nations as equal, the founders levelled the international playing field. It went a long way institutionally and morally to casting imperialism from the table. But the UN system, which entailed not just the General Assembly and the Security Council, but a slew of affiliated organizations, including the financial bodies created at the Bretton Woods Conference – the International Monetary Fund (IMF) and the GATT – most immediately created an international system that entrenched Western interests and values as the global norm. As the post-1945 long economic boom unfolded, the Western dominance of the 19th century looked set to continue indefinitely, only this time with the crudeness and cruelty of imperialism replaced with the high-minded rhetoric of the UN order.

The circumstances described in this book are a central component of a larger trend in world affairs in which the West's influence is in decline. From Latin America and the Middle East to Africa, as well as Asia, non-Western states and societies are playing an ever greater role. Asia's future will be forged in a world in which the current trends of Western decline continue. British scholar Samir Puri convincingly argues that the world is being rebalanced (Puri, 2024). Where in the past the influence of the West was disproportionate to its scale, all the dimensions of global power are being reconfigured in ways that reduce the influence of the old. Power is being relocated and the instruments of influence, from culture to fashion, from security to finance, will be shaped by far more multinational forces and will take more multicultural forms (Stuenkel, 2016). In short, the broader context for the future will be a multipolar global order.

While the world will be multipolar, there will continue to be significant elements of Western influence. Perhaps the most important will be the role of the US dollar as the global reserve currency. Some, such as former IMF chief economist Ken

Rogoff, argue that the place of the US dollar is at risk (Rogoff, 2025). This seems unlikely in the short to medium term. The sheer volume of US dollar markets, the confidence in which the currency is held and the costs and risks to those other issuers of currency are far too great to bring about a change. The second Trump administration has increased some concerns in global markets, but these do not seem to be sufficient to dislodge the US dollar. The only realistic alternatives, China's renminbi or the euro, have significant problems. Their issuers are not in the position to bear the costs and risks of having large quantities of currency beyond their borders and the sheer scale of moving from their current positions to that of the US dollar makes the move literally unimaginable. Digital currencies backed by fiat currency and issued by China and Russia are likely to try to muscle in, but will continue to lack the confidence of major banks. They are also likely to be seen as politically tainted, leading most investors to be wary of participating in any of these new payment systems in any significant way. This will continue to give the US advantages in being able to manage debt, exercise economic coercion and operate more easily in the global economy.

The global financial system will continue to be strongly Western inflected, with the role of ratings agencies, bond and equity markets from the North Atlantic world continuing to reflect Western interests. But just because some of the key structural features of the global economy will continue to be as they are, one should not presume that this means Western powers can wield these entirely to their advantage. The inability of the US and its partners to use economic instruments to coerce Russia effectively since 2022 is a lesson in the limits of economic statecraft. Following Moscow's invasion of Ukraine, Russia has been subjected to the most wide-ranging economic sanctions seen in the post-Cold War period. As that war continues, Russia's economy has displayed a remarkable durability, created in part by the continuing strong global demand for hydrocarbons, of which Russia has immense reserves. Trade sanctions were intended to strangle many elements of the Russian economy, but countries are content to allow firms to reroute trade through third parties, particularly in Central Asia, as well as through Germany, Malaysia, Japan and South Korea. Critically, China has extended significant financial support as well as through trade and technology transfer.

The global economy will continue to have a Western accent, but its diversity, flexibility and porosity will underpin and reinforce a system in which power is more evenly spread than it has been for decades if not centuries. Related to this, the institutional architecture that attempts to manage the global economy will be badly fractured. The core institutions of global economic governance reflect the old North Atlantic world: the IMF, World Bank, WTO and BIS. Each of these face significant problems as the location of power shifts, while the structure and mandate of those organizations has not kept pace. Even efforts to introduce new means to grapple with a changing global order, such as the creation of the G20 in 1999, have foundered. That body, which was created after the Asian financial crisis and which seemed to grow in significance following the 2007–08 GFC, has been effectively sidelined due to sharpened geopolitical divisions. As the G20 includes both China and Russia, the US and its allies have retreated from the group reverting to a creation of the 1970s North Atlantic world, the G7, as the preferred forum through which global economic governance can be exercised. These circumstances will not change. Global institutions will increasingly be dysfunctional and, where novel efforts emerge, they will be limited in membership, like the G7 or more focused on geographic zones. This will make coordinating global responses to major economic problems, health crises or other challenges increasingly difficult.

For most of the post-Cold War period the US enjoyed an unparalleled period of military dominance (Walt, 2005). In the future, the US will remain the world's top military power.

It will continue to outspend other states, and it will remain the only country that can project significant force globally. However, the gap between the US and the rest of the world has already narrowed in terms of total spending and in military capabilities and technological sophistication (IISS, 2024). This trend will continue. The US will also face constraints on several fronts. Its practical ability to project force will be reduced because of the growth in scale and reach of opponents' militaries. For example, where in the not-too-distant past the US had almost complete freedom of manoeuvre in the air and seas in the Western Pacific and the Persian Gulf, it now faces real threats that limit where it can operate and what it can do. Missile and drone technology, such as China's DF-21 'carrier killer' missile, imposes constraints about where the US Navy can operate, adding a level of circumspection about action that did not previously exist. Also, the domestic political support for the kind of global constabulary role that Washington has grown accustomed to playing has broken down. Trump and the 'Make American Great Again'-dominated Republican Party have made considerable political mileage from disillusionment with the 'forever wars' of Iraq and Afghanistan. The scepticism among American voters about the US military being used to fight what are perceived to be other people's conflicts will remain in place. It is unlikely that either Democrats or Republicans who are interested in rebuilding the domestic foundations of American internationalism will be capable of creating sufficient political support to do so. Finally, even if the US can mobilize political backing to use substantial force abroad, its ability to achieve its preferred policy outcomes will be limited. The central problem in both Afghanistan and Iraq was a mismatch between military means and political ends. Technological advances will work to negate the ability of great powers to use their military to achieve decisive strategic results. America's military advantages will be even harder to wield to shape events in its favour.

The global multipolar order will be less militarily stable than in the past. In previous eras when multiple power centres existed, spheres of influence were effective at creating an overarching stability. As discussed earlier, the combination of a lack of acceptance of the idea of spheres of influence as well as the inability of major powers to control those areas means that option will not exist. While the second Trump administration has articulated, in its distinctively chaotic way, some support for this view, the actions of the administration to date have not shown that this has any grip on policy. Indeed, the real and visible constraints on US power are likely to create a cycle of instability as ambitious emerging powers sense opportunity and take steps to exploit this weakness. Israel's audacious attack on Iran in June 2025, openly defying American preferences, is illustrative of the kind of opportunism that will become more common. This will be compounded by the absence of any other major countervailing capabilities being in place in the medium term because all the US allies have to some degree been free riding on American security guarantees for so long.

The two wars being fought out in 2025, in Ukraine and in the Middle East, are salutary reminders of the limits of US power. It is not that Washington does not have the military wherewithal to end both conflicts, it is that the political and economic costs of doing so are intolerable to the US. Its opponents know this and are taking advantage. This trend will be more evident in the coming years. The broader military context for Asia's future is one of an unbalanced global order, where US capabilities are constrained but one in which Washington is still unable to reduce its commitment to a genuinely global role. Equally, other states will not have sufficient power to provide an effective alternative source of stability.

Global leadership will be diffuse. There will be no clear centre of influence and authority of the kind that prevailed for a generation after the Soviet collapse. In the 1990s and early 2000s, liberal internationalism, led by the US and its Western allies, was dominant. The US and other Western powers will retain influence and some leadership, not least because of the ongoing wealth and positions of structural advantage, either at the centre of global financial systems or in the institutions of influence, such as the UN Security Council. But Russia, China, Saudi Arabia, Brazil, India, Nigeria as well as institutions like the SCO, the GCC and the Southern African Development Community will become louder and more effective voices for alternative coalitions of values and interests.

Scenarios

The time frame for these future scenarios is projected at 15–20 years. While drawing up assessments of the future is an inherently fraught task, attempting to work out how things may evolve much beyond two decades is almost impossible. The time frame here takes things out to the early 2040s, and we can say with some confidence that the likely key drivers of prosperity and conflict then are visible today. Military power takes a long time to develop – the AUKUS programme aims to deliver the new submarines at the outer end of these projections. And even with technological breakthroughs like generative AI it is unlikely that over the time frame adopted here that the form of the global economy, the nature and modes of production, trade and finance will change substantively.

In developing the scenarios' geopolitical dimensions, I have focused on three elements. The first is the nature of competition: how structured and balanced is it or is the contest unstable, lacking restraint and control mechanisms? The second is the extent to which the sides can see the world from the other's perspective. This is what can be described as the levels of 'strategic empathy'? Empathy here does not imply fellow feeling or the removal of competition but instead relates to the way having an ability to see things from the other's perspective shapes levels of mistrust and, in turn, drives greater or lesser levels of stability. The third is the extent to which there are structured means to manage competition. The importance of having diplomatic mechanisms to deal with crises, improve communication and help manage the dynamics of contestation is clear. Just as such mechanisms helped deal with the Cold War's worst risks without obviating its competition, in Asia their presence or absence will be critical to shaping the nature of great power rivalry in the future.

Alongside geopolitics, Asia's future will be shaped by the structure of its economy and what shape a reconstituted globalization takes over the coming generation. When considering the economic side of things, the following issues structure the scenarios. How much political interference exists in the workings of an interdependent regional economy? How much do nationalist forces unravel or indeed destroy complex production chains and trading networks? And just what kind of role will the market and questions of efficiency play in relation to questions of security and national self-reliance? My judgement is that the kind of complete collapse of globalization that looked possible at the worst moments of the pandemic seems unlikely. The speed with which global supply chains bounced back after the COVID-19 years was remarkable. The animal spirits of capitalism will ensure that firms will continue to seek profit and advantage in as efficient a manner as they can and that this gives good reason to think that some form of reglobalization is likely to occur. What is less clear is exactly what shape that will take. The second Trump administration's announcement on 2 April 2025 shredded the last vestiges of US commitment to open markets and free trade. Political influence of some kind is here to stay. But just what the balance between states and markets will be is unclear.

The market-led globalization that prevailed in the years leading up to the pandemic was not created by careful policy design nor was it systematically planned and executed. It was an organic, unplanned and almost inadvertent creation, but one that was rooted in the neoliberal policy consensus that existed in capitals around the world. This means that, as globalization is reconstructed, we are likely to see a similar kind of interplay between deliberate political and policy choices and the more organic microeconomic considerations of firms and markets creating an overarching regional economic structure that will be some kind of mix of state and market imperatives.

The third dimension that will shape the scenarios are the risk multipliers explored in Chapter 8. How will the protean forces of nationalism, the contest around values and the slow-moving but implacable demands of a changing environment influence events? How will they interact with globalization and geopolitics? What trends will be accentuated and which ones will be damped down? Where indeed may these be controlled by the larger imperatives of states navigating a highly complex regional environment?

Before getting to the scenarios, I should deal with one other possibility that has been advocated by some scholars as the best way to manage Asia's future: the creation of a 'grand bargain' in which power is shared among Asia's great powers (White, 2009). This is the situation in which the great powers strike a diplomatic deal to establish a strategic balance and distribution of influence with which the US, China and India were content. That, in turn, would require a resolution of the territorial, sovereignty and symbolic disputes in the region. While some ambiguity might remain on issues of lower priority, it is unimaginable that a grand bargain could be struck that did not resolve the status of Taiwan as well as the border dispute between India and China. Equally, clarity about the standing of the competing claims in the South China Sea would be necessary. This would need to include a regime managing the sea lanes of communication, rules governing behaviour in EEZs and the broader maritime environment that was supported by all the major naval powers. This would almost certainly mean that Washington would have to cede a considerable amount of power and influence to both India and China in key areas across the region. It would necessarily mean that the US allies would be in a weaker position than previously and that Russia's position in Asia, as a junior partner of China, would be strengthened. To come up with a diplomatic deal that manages to bring all of the powers along with it would be a truly heroic achievement.

But just having a deal in place would not be enough. Asia's major powers would also need to devise a means to manage the arrangement over time, and to grapple with and resolve crises that emerge across the vast landmass and maritime domains over a long period. Here scholars and analysts look to the Concert system established after the Napoleonic Wars as a possible model (Holbraad, 1971). Devised at the Congress of Vienna, the Concert was intended to prevent the recurrence of the wars that had ravaged the continent since Napoleon's seizure of power in France. The Congress devised an acceptable strategic balance and created a diplomatic means of dealing with crises, ensuring that localized problems did not escalate into continent-wide war. Given the complexity, scale and diversity of the region, any durable peace system would need careful and active management by the major powers and their partners.

It is extraordinarily difficult to imagine the ambitious powers of Asia agreeing to something mutually acceptable about an issue such as Taiwan's standing. Equally, the idea of a reconstituted Concert system has a decidedly sepia tone to it. These are diplomatic strategies from a different era when inequality, not just material but of principles and rules, was the norm. The power and prestige of the bigger players gave them a louder voice as well as a more privileged formal position. Today, all are sovereign, all have formal equality and, in Asia, for many the right to rule themselves and to chart their own path remains within living memory. It was something for which they fought extremely hard and which is highly prized. There would likely be considerable hostility among Asia's middle-ranking powers, such as Indonesia, Vietnam, Japan, the Philippines and South

Korea, to any deal worked out among the major powers. This hostility would not only be one of principle or resentment about not being party to the process, but anger would emerge because the bargain would lead to the deterioration of their influence and autonomy. Japan and South Korea have for decades designed their defence and security policy on the assumption that US military power would remain dominant in Asia. Ceding ground to China would upend that planning and make them considerably worse off. ASEAN members would likewise find themselves in a place where, for decades, they fought not to be: subordinate to an international system where the great powers make the rules and the rest just must accept things.

While there is much to recommend a new grand bargain – a settled strategic environment among Asia's great powers has considerable appeal – it is extremely unlikely. Among all three of Asia's key powers the domestic political price that would be paid by making the kind of geopolitical concessions needed to strike an acceptable bargain is far too high and likely to remain so for some time. Equally, there are good arguments, both in terms of key military interests and ideologically speaking, against the US making the kind of concessions necessary for China to accept a grand bargain. Equally, it is unlikely that India would accept conceding too much ground to the PRC on interest-based grounds as well.

The possibility of a new grand bargain in Asia is very close to zero. The second Trump administration sought to reset its relations with Russia and Europe with head-snapping speed early in its term but then changed direction. While some are tempted to think this may be a precursor in Asia, the one issue that both sides of US politics can agree on is that the PRC is the country's pre-eminent threat. It is extraordinarily difficult to conceive of plausible political circumstances in which Washington and Beijing work out a grand carve-up of the region. The prospects of the US being content to allow China dominance of Asia are very unlikely, even under the decidedly unorthodox second

Trump administration. The assumption in each of the scenarios is that competition in Asia is here to stay. What is less clear is the nature of that contestation and how it might ebb and flow.

Fractured Asia

The splintering of the region that is implied by this scenario's title is created by the dominance of a highly militarized and unstructured geopolitical competition and a globalization that has been reconfigured to reflect that contestation. While it is tempting to see this as creating 'blocs' – both figurative and literal – between a US-led side and a China-led grouping, this scenario is considerably more complex than a simple replay of the Cold War's divisions. This dangerous world is one where the logic of geopolitical contestation is almost entirely unrestrained, in which some economic interdependence exists but where nationalism and geopolitics have scrambled many sectors, not only the sensitive domains of high technology. War is at its most likely here and, as during the Cold War, the threat of nuclear conflict will become a day-to-day reality in the lives of the billions who call Asia home.

For nearly four decades Asia's military environment was defined by US primacy and its acceptance by all the region's key powers. China's military modernization programme has, by 2025, cut significantly into America's lead. In this scenario, the situation has become unstable as the region has not established a new military equilibrium. The US seeks to recreate the dominance of the first years of the 21st century in the face of mounting challenges from China and Russia. Political leaders cling to the idea that the US must be able to control Asia's sea lanes, contain China's military and push back on Russian ambition, even as the costs and risks of doing so grow. By the late 2020s, Washington is spending nearly 6 per cent of GDP on defence. This has also forced the US to make decisions about its global role and Washington has opted to reduce its focus on the

Middle East and parts of Western Europe to provide the scope to try to recast Asia's military environment.

Part of the reason for this is that the ambitious, assertive and risk-taking trends of Chinese foreign policy introduced by Xi Jinping have become the mainstays of its approach over a sustained period. Notwithstanding a few years in the mid-2020s, when post-COVID-19 economic malaise prompted a more cautious disposition, once China's economy is re-energized by the leadership resetting its economic policy balance, China's caustic approach continues.

By the late 2020s it has become clear that Beijing is intent on creating its own version of military primacy in the Western Pacific, but it is not interested in extending this to the Indian Ocean region, where it projects power but does not seek dominance. The PLA regularly exerts pressure over contested areas in the East and South China Seas. It conducts frequent military exercises around Taiwan and has conducted multiple simulated blockades of the island, some of which have come close to cutting it off from some resources. The sabre-rattling has not been accompanied by efforts to manage crisis incidents as the CPC leadership perceives such structures as strengthening the legitimacy of the other parties. Beijing's planning is informed by the continued perception that the US lacks strategic resolve. This has led to increased military activity with Russia across the Western Pacific from the Strait of Malacca to the Arctic. And while Washington is more focused on Asia than previously, the combination of its incoherent global strategy, internal discord and lack of clarity over its strategic ambitions presents Beijing with what it perceives to be a generation of opportunity. The PRC has set its sights on becoming Asia's pre-eminent military power and, as the party leadership has made clear repeatedly, it aims to resolve all the outstanding disputes, particularly Taiwan, by the centenary of the People's Republic's creation in 2049.

But Fractured Asia's instability derives not just from heightened Sino–American rivalry. India's increasingly nationalistic government has responded to the growing tension and a sense of American relative weakness by increasing its distance from the US. Its growing military power is a presence in the South China Sea and its ties to Russia also subvert aspects of US strategy. Japan has responded to this setting by further increasing its own military capability. The nationalist right has long been uneasy about the dependence the country has on Washington and sees in the unstable environment a need not only to have a greater level of independent military capability but also a greater degree of autonomy. Its diplomacy is beginning to explore a 'multi-dimensional' strategy with Russia and China while ensuring that its alliance ties with Washington remain intact. Middle powers, such as South Korea, Australia and some of the ASEAN states, have also further stepped up military spending. While they continue to hold their ties to Washington tightly, they are, like Japan, beginning to develop the means to achieve higher levels of autonomy. These cross-cutting trends further enhance a sense of strategic instability that encourages ambitious risk-taking moves from emerging powers.

Fractured Asia's military setting is one of long-term instability. The modernization of Beijing's strategic nuclear missile programme, the development of its hypersonic weapons systems as well as use of autonomous platforms has created an arms race dynamic. The suspicion and ill will that exists between the key capitals has become entrenched. There is essentially no strategic empathy, with the US and China assuming the worst motives of the other. Elite opinion in the foreign policy, defence and intelligence sectors is suffused by a pervasive mistrust. This sentiment is reinforced by the political context in which leaders are punished for taking anything other than a hard and nationalistic line towards the other.

In Fractured Asia, the China-centred regional economy has been broken up by geopolitical contestation and mistrust. This has led to a significant restructuring of Asia's economy, breaking apart its integrated economic system. As the global economy is being stitched back together following the pandemic years the balance between state and market is tipped decisively in favour of the state; the global economy has come to be badly scrambled.

The fragmentation is not carefully designed and planned out, and has created a complex, messy and at points highly inefficient structure. What begins as efforts to separate high technology sectors – the US wants to isolate and weaken China's technological capabilities, but Beijing also wants to be less dependent on externally sourced technology and trading systems – rapidly spreads out across a wide range of areas. This is in part due to the sheer complexity of production chains and the important role financial institutions play in the capital-intensive business of high technology development. US legislation and executive actions become more expansive and penalties on financial institutions that have anything to do with any aspect of production that could end up in Chinese hands have led banks to dramatically reduce their exposure to almost any form of production that could wind up in China. This intersects with well-intentioned efforts to recast industries in key countries, notably efforts to decarbonize economies, that have led to high levels of political interference in the workings of many sectors such as EVs, energy systems, and transport and logistics. Even food production and distribution systems have been periodically distorted by political suspicions and strategic anxiety.

The logic of competition has created a much lumpier global economy. Initial efforts to disentangle Chinese inputs from the US market are easily evaded by routing trade through third countries or relocating factories from the PRC to Mexico or Vietnam. Washington decides to impose much more draconian measures on trade substitution that begin with the clumsy 'liberation day' tariffs on April 2025 but which, over time, have led to more targeted efforts that effectively push PRC producers out of most sectors of the US economy.

There are now multiple tracks of global production with three zones: a US-focused zone, a China-focused zone and a third zone that is global in the sense that it operates in the spaces between the other two. This has created a world economy of considerable friction, where rule compliance drives up costs, rule breaking and operating between the zones in critical areas is rife but risky. Each operates according to its own rules, with a high premium placed on security ahead of efficiency. The security of the zones has a particular emphasis, and this has created divisions in cyberspace, with each having a discrete cyber domain. Predictions of a 'splinternet' have proven to be prescient. While there is a good deal of trade in basic goods, such as commodities, even these are from time to time subject to political panics. Among the US and its allies and partners there are periodic campaigns about trading with the enemy that makes all types of international trade unpredictable, difficult and costly.

The consequences for the global economy are considerable as growth has slowed, and inflation remains a persistent problem. The geopolitical and economic context has also provided an environment that is highly conducive to the nationalism that has become a mainstay of Asia's political culture. A vast range of sectors in each economy is viewed through the lens of geopolitical competition that is magnified in intensity by the scale and reach of nationalist outrage. In Western countries this has taken on a racial dimension as well, leading to xenophobic violence at home and the narrowing of the scope for political manoeuvre afforded to elites. Equally, the changing climate has increased tensions and risks creating dangerous feedback loops. At the global level, Fractured Asia fuels and, in turn, is reinforced by a broad-ranging global instability. Russia can take advantage of this to advance its ambitions in East and Central Europe. The struggle in the Middle East between Saudi Arabia and Iran has intensified, and there are strong prospects of a nuclear breakout in that part of the world. Fractured Asia is also an increasingly illiberal space. China's growing influence and its ability to wield geoeconomic power has significantly undercut democracy and liberal rights-based norms that, by the early 2030s, are struggling badly.

In Fractured Asia, the risks of war are at their most acute. The shared interests of economic interdependence have been completely swamped by geopolitics and nationalism. The places where clashing interests and visions of regional primacy meet – the zones of contestation in the Western Pacific, the borderlands between China and India in the high Himalayas – and the complex politics of Central Asia are highly febrile. This is a bleak future for Asia's peoples. Development opportunities for the hundreds of millions who remain outside the middle class have been reduced significantly. Chauvinism and violence are rife and the prospect of systemic conflict, one that could escalate to a nuclear exchange is far too probable for comfort.

Rebalanced Asia

This scenario describes a situation in which geopolitical competition has been stabilized by a new equilibrium of military force. One of the confusing elements of the contemporary period is that many countries that favour the US-centred strategic status quo often describe it is a stable strategic balance. The reality is that the four-decade long Asian peace rested on an imbalance, one that was heavily weighted towards the US. It was a setting more accurately described as one of military primacy or, indeed, even hegemony. The situation was stable because of the sheer preponderance of US military force. Rebalanced Asia is a future in which a genuine balance of power has been established. Alongside this, even though some critical elements have been shaped by political and strategic imperatives, globalization has largely been restored, and economic dynamism remains a hallmark of the Asian economy.

At its core, Asia's geopolitical competition is a contest for military advantage between the region's great powers. The stable setting that was critical for the making of modern Asia was built on US primacy. China is no longer willing to accept that setting and seeks to reconfigure the region to better reflect its interests. The problem, as detailed in Chapter 6, is that the US is unwilling to cede the core features of the old order. In Rebalanced Asia, a stable military setting has been achieved through the reconfiguration of the critical strategic interests in the region. Up until the mid-2020s, the US has sought to try to defend its freedom of manoeuvre in the Western Pacific and the Indian Ocean region that it has enjoyed for decades. It has also sought to ensure that China is unable to achieve its ambitions to claim Taiwan, resolve the disputes in the East and South China Seas in its favour and ensure that the Korean Peninsula remains stable, with the ROK secure from DPRK adventurism.

Following a complex set of secret negotiations, in the early 2030s, the White House has begun to reveal a subtle but important shift in the US' regional focus. In the years immediately following the pandemic, Xi Jinping increases pressure in the three maritime disputes in the Western Pacific, with Taiwan as a particular focus. There are several crises around the island in 2026 and 2027, caused by accidents where PLA and Taiwanese forces clash. One incident, in which a PLA Air Force (PLAAF) jet is harassing Taiwanese reconnaissance aircraft, leads to both planes crashing, with the loss of the flight crews from both sides. The nationalist uproar in China is almost impossible to quell and the two sides approach the brink of conflict. This proves to be a catalyst for the parties to take steps to move away from the course they are on, to improve communication, build trust and manage risk. US strategic policy elites also begin to recognize the futility of trying to retain the old posture of primacy. Domestic circumstances within the US have solidified against the old liberal internationalism during Trump's second term in office. US global strategy then begins to be reconfigured to retain significant global influence but with much lower costs and risks. The secret diplomacy starts to yield results with a China that has, somewhat surprisingly, taken a more moderate posture. In a move akin to the sudden about-face following the COVID-19 lockdowns, the CPC propaganda machine rapidly changes direction to reflect this shift.

Washington has made clear that it continues to have a critical interest in Asia's strategic setting and will ensure that vital American interests are protected. But the conception of those interests among elites in the US has shifted and this has been articulated to Beijing. Where in the past the US has, albeit with some ambiguity, made clear that it saw Taiwan's status as a fundamental interest, in this scenario, this has changed. There are several points on which this shift depended. First, the diversification of semi-conductor production that the Biden administration launched and which the Trump administration eventually sustains after some chaotic early policy shifts, is successful and the criticality of its production for the US has been reduced. Taiwan has also been strongly reinforced over those years and it is now able to defend itself in the face of Chinese pressure. Third, PRC moderation, both in foreign policy tone and in its domestic politics, has reduced concerns about Beijing's risk appetite. The conditions for a more stable military environment have become possible.

Competition remains in Asia, but the tension has been moderated by some areas of cooperation, particularly related to climate change. The US and China retain different visions of the region, but they have devised a viable modus vivendi through which those competing visions can be played out. Not every development in Asia's international landscape is viewed through a zero-sum competitive prism. China's and India's borders remain unresolved, but tension here has also abated, and a crisis management process has been established. The precise areas where China and US interests clash, as well as those of its allies, remain sources of tension and require constant management. The Korean Peninsula remains a zone of considerable complexity, but the resuscitation of the long-frozen Six Party Talks process has proven to be effective in developing a formal diplomatic structure for securing stability on the peninsula. Again, this has been made possible by the more collaborative postures of the US and China and the shift in attitude from Moscow that has occurred following Vladimir Putin's death in 2028. In New Delhi, the leadership continues to develop its own independent approach to regional affairs but takes its cues from the more stable military equilibrium to keep its ambitions from unsettling the existing order. Given the continuing need to focus on domestic economic growth this is a welcome set of circumstances in India.

The reduced geopolitical tensions have been key to winding back the trends that emerged in the early post-COVID-19 years. The politicization of the economy appears as if it might completely restructure the rules of the game, Trump's election in 2024 and the chaotic foreign economic policies he adopted in the first year of his term seemed to confirm that. Yet the combination of a moderated geopolitical setting and the effectiveness of firms to advocate for their economic interests, perhaps most notably the watering down of US efforts to isolate China, has meant that the worst outcomes have been avoided. But Asia has not returned to the market-led version of globalization that prevailed before 2020. Confidence in markets has returned to some degree, although geopolitical contestation and other statist ambitions to hem in markets and firms have had a significant impact. The new hybrid setting is described by commentators as 'state-led globalization', but these efforts have been only partially successful in achieving their aims. Many firms are not willing to subordinate their interests entirely to politics while others in the US and other Western economies that have introduced these statist policies have taken advantage of the new industrial policy to become highly effective at rent-seeking and are less competitive internationally.

The 'small garden high walls' approach is focused initially on vital economic domains in high technology areas such as microprocessors, advanced computing and AI. Governments of the countries where these sectors are most significant, notably the US, China, Japan, Taiwan and South Korea, have created tightly regulated sectors. They are highly subsidized and have severe scrutiny of and interference in supply chains with governments limiting participation to identified firms from partner countries. This has created two areas of high technology development, one centred on China and one on the US. While there is some opportunistic leakage between the two, it is not significant. This has caused the pace of development to slow and neither side has been able to carve out a distinct advantage. PRC production capabilities continue to surprise, and China's ability to retain pace with the US-centred networks is a source of both irritation and puzzlement.

While some have argued that the 'gardens' of security should remain small, China's advances in a range of areas, particularly related to green technology, such as EVs and photovoltaic panels, as well as in telecommunications and transport logistics technology, have led nationalists and strategists to win the argument that China's advances require intervention. This has created distortions in production and supply chains. In some cases, this prompts rule-avoiding location hopping, such as moving assembly lines out of the PRC and into countries less subject to US pressure, while in other cases it has led to PRC firms giving up on the US market and focusing on the rest of the world, particularly growing demand from emerging markets in Africa. The inertia created by the sheer complexity of production chains and the difficulty that policing them in the way the most hawkish hope has proved hard to break, and in many areas, such as consumer durables, things return to the market-led practices of the pre-2020 era. Periodically, however, nationalist and security concerns bubble up and disrupt market practices. Tariff barriers in key sectors remain high and minor tariff and non-tariff barrier escalations occur regularly, driven both by the oscillations in security threats as well as the permutations of industry policy and attempts at domestic economic engineering in the US and other economies.

The Asian countries that have benefitted most from the internationalization of production, particularly those of Southeast Asia, find this setting tolerable. Growth is not at the pace it once was, and traders are regularly frustrated by the US-led efforts to try to use economic means to advance the contest with China. But it is a world with which they can live.

Rebalanced Asia is one in which none of the major powers are fully satisfied. Neither the US nor China can achieve their goals of regional dominance. But instead of pushing hard at their ambitions, the major powers have established a strategic equilibrium which, while at times fragile, has established an effective set of mechanisms for reducing risk and containing the worst excesses of contestation. The Asian economy continues to bind disparate parts of the region and China remains the centre of gravity. However, many economic sectors are now fragmented with geopolitical concerns and domestic interests driving the politicization of many component elements. This is a less dynamic world than existed before 2020, with growth rates lower and geopolitical risk a significant hindrance. While a manageable modus vivendi has been established, the flashpoints remain volatile, but the dynamics resemble the early 2000s more than the high tempo tensions of the mid-2020s.

Unified Asia

In this scenario geopolitical competition remains an underlying component of Asia's strategic setting, but it is at a low temperature and considered a longer-term matter. Economically speaking, the region has largely reglobalized, although some political interference is visible, particularly in high technology areas. Unified in this context does not mean the institutionalized and legalistic integration of the kind pioneered by the EU but instead refers to the way the region has reverted to the more integrated mode of operation that was in place prior to the pandemic years.

Indeed, in some areas, notably those related to climate change, there is more collaboration occurring than before.

In Unified Asia, a new strategic equilibrium has been established, one, as with Rebalanced Asia, in which military power is more evenly distributed; there is no replication of primacy. While the region's major powers are not entirely satisfied with this setting, it is a situation somewhat akin to detente during the Cold War. The great powers retain their long-term ambitions in relation to what Asia's strategic setting ought to look like, but they have opted to pursue not just stable relations but have taken steps to take some of the heat out of competition and advance some shared goals.

As this situation has settled into a longer-run pattern of relations it has led to the creation of a pluralistic and multipolar order. While the US and China remain the most significant players, the strengthened military power of India, Japan and South Korea, each of which has undertaken extensive defence modernization programmes during the unsettled period leading into the phase of balance, have a higher standing. Formal arms control agreements, particularly in relation to hypersonic weapons and the new generation of nuclear armaments, provide confidence and regular summits and diplomatic management of the strategic order ensures that the many minor crises are contained. A series of protocols have been established, such as the ASEAN-brokered Code of Conduct in the South China Sea, that work reasonably well to keep the status quo in place. The EAS been dragged out of its torpor and has become a mechanism through which policy coordination occurs. Its pan-regional membership, broad policy remit and leaders' focus have provided it with just the right elements to become a clearing house for the major issues of the day. It has become not just the region's most important annual gathering but one of the most anticipated summits in world politics. Geopolitical competition remains on Asia's international stage, but it is in the background, although the region's diplomats and political leaders are aware of the speed with which it could return and thus work assiduously to maintain a stable and generally peaceful order.

Unified Asia's regional economy has been largely reconstructed to resemble the complex international production chain model of the pre-COVID-19 years. Although the memory of supply chain shocks and sovereign capability shortfalls remains sharp in most capitals across Asia, and most particularly in Washington and Beijing, there is a policy recognition of the power of markets. The inflationary pressures of the years after the pandemic were a prompt to push efficiency back to the top of the priority list. Moreover, the US and its allies seem to have regained confidence in the ability of their firms to compete in international markets. State subsidies are no match for the benefits that come from market competition. A few high-technology areas and sectors, where there are obvious military applications, are subject to very tight scrutiny and control, but these are limited to a small number of areas. States are also closely involved in areas of market failure and focused heavily on taking steps to deal with climate change and the energy transition. But, overall, there is a virtuous cycle existing between geopolitical and economic interests in Unified Asia.

Notwithstanding this, nationalism has not disappeared and periodically erupts to unsettle regional relations. The diversity of political values remains but the stable setting has meant that an international order of pluralistic political systems does not create or feed into larger security divisions. Geopolitical friction and competition remain in place and there are occasional reversions to the dangers of the past. Despite this, the shared interests in driving economic growth and dealing with transnational problems, most particularly climate change, are at the centre of a more cooperative regional order.

Seismic shocks

None of the three scenarios entails a shock to the region's system. History reminds us that many of the critical developments that fundamentally reorder the world are unimaginable crises that seem to come out of the blue. The Asian financial crisis of 1997–98 shattered many economies in the region. It immiserated millions as the value of savings were wiped out, it led to rapid political changes and seemed to spell the end of the 'Asian miracle'. But financial crises have become an inevitable part of the global economy since the end of the Bretton Woods arrangements; they ought not be a surprise. The terrorist attacks of 9/11 were shocking in the extreme. Those who watched in real time as hijacked aircraft were used as missiles to attack symbols of American power and wealth stared on in disbelief. Yet scholars and intelligence agencies had warned for years about the rising threat of terrorism. Aircraft being used as suicide bombs was logical if frightening and had been discussed. But the likelihood of it happening was written off. The same can be said for the COVID-19 pandemic. Public health scholars and epidemiologists had made clear that it was a question of when and not if another global pandemic occurred. The problems of zoonotic diseases were well known and there had been recent precedent in the 2002 SARS outbreak and the 2012 Middle East respiratory syndrome crisis. Yet again the world was caught off guard because the probabilities were either miscalculated or not taken seriously. All the major crises that shake the system to its core are all perfectly within the realm of probability and any consideration of the region's future must at least consider events that may seem unlikely, but which could have devastating consequences.

Among the many possible shocks, there are four that are the most likely and should be factored into any long-term planning for Asia's future. The first entails the US departing from the region. Donald Trump captured the Republican Party and has dominated American politics for more than a decade. The mix of bombastic nationalism, grievance and mercantilism sits at odds with the post-1945 orthodoxy of the Republican Party and US foreign policy more generally. The forces that Trump has unleashed have reset the policy debate in the US. It is now more plausible than at any time since 1991 that the US might initiate a full-scale drawdown of its military presence. This would fundamentally transform Asia's military balance and create a period of tremendous geopolitical instability.

There is a tendency among commentators and analysts of international affairs to assume that the China of the moment is the China that will be with us forever. This led Western strategists in the 1990s to assume that the PRC would not be a country to be taken seriously in military terms. It also led many to assume that after the technocratic leadership of Jiang Zemin and Hu Jintao the subsequent leadership would follow that mould. And it is the same tendency that makes us assume that the authoritarian, nationalistic and thin-skinned China of Xi Jinping will be a system that we will have to live with for many decades to come. The PRC remains a young political system. At the time of writing, it has existed for only one year longer than the USSR. Its formative years were filled with social and economic turmoil and its political system does not have deep social roots (Overholt, 2018). A second plausible shock involves the CPC removing Xi Jinping from power and installing a new leadership that takes China away from its current assertive trajectory. Just as with the first scenario, a change in the domestic politics of one of the region's big two powers would be of immense consequence for Asia's future.

By the late 2020s, climate change is readily visible across Asia. Every summer heat records are broken across the region, cities in Southeast Asia regularly have days with temperatures exceeding 45°C. A third, all too believable shock entails a series of climate catastrophes, such as an intense drought leading to a collapse in agricultural production twinned with widespread inundation caused by a series of super typhoons in the Western Pacific. These could be devasting to millions and also prompt political extremism and hyper-nationalism.

Finally, major power war is now a plausible scenario in Asia's short- and medium-term futures (Shellbourne, 2021). The region's flashpoints are combustible, escalation risks are growing and victimized nationalism fans the flames of conflict. In this fourth shock, the regular brinkmanship and tensions over Taiwan spiral out of control and escalate to a nuclear exchange. Millions are killed in an initial nuclear blast. Can the region prevent a rapid escalation to Armageddon?

Conclusion

In developing these scenarios and briefly reflecting on some shocks, this chapter has sought to think through how the forces that made modern Asia are likely to intersect and produce complex futures. The major point that I hope to make in dramatizing these elements is to show that nothing is predetermined, that while there are some significant parameters in place, there remains a wide variation of ways in which the region's future may play out. War is not preordained. But there is a considerable amount of careful and persistent work that will be needed to ensure the more damaging futures are avoided while also building in flexibility to cope with the inevitable shocks that will seem to come out of nowhere. And it is to that work that Chapter 10 turns.

10

Securing Asia's Future

On 17 October 2024, China deployed 36 naval and coast guard vessels as well as 156 aircraft in the waters and skies around Taiwan (Hille, 2024). The exercise was intended to help prepare the PLA for combat but was also a show of force that simulated a blockade of key ports. It was the largest yet of a series of exercises that have been occurring with increasing frequency and came days after President Lai Ching-te's national day speech defending Taiwan's sovereignty (Lai, 2024). China's air force has dramatically increased its movements into the island's Air Defence Identification Zone, a self-declared space that all countries use to manage their approaches. From fewer than 20 in 2019, there were nearly 2,500 in 2024 alone. The heightened tempo frays nerves and heightens the risk of misadventure. In 2001, a PLAAF fighter clashed with an American reconnaissance aircraft, forcing the US jet to the ground. After months of tense negotiations, the matter was eventually resolved. Today, with literally thousands of sorties, the risks of something like the 2001 incident happening are growing rapidly. But now the stakes are exponentially greater than they were a quarter of a century ago. Asia is at risk not just of its many flashpoints igniting but there is the real possibility of the region sliding into a generalized crisis and a cataclysmic continent-wide war (Taylor, 2018).

The making of modern Asia into a dynamic and integrated zone – one of wealth and prosperity but also of growing geopolitical risk – was made possible because of a widespread consensus in the region about two major forces. The first was a belief in the power of markets and the value of an open and integrated global economy. Even if the price was growing inequality and increased societal vulnerability, the efficiency and prosperity that globalization created were prized and the risks of leaving a nation's fate in the hands of the market were seen as manageable. The second was the widespread acceptance of US primacy and the geopolitical dispensation that it created. Asia was the most stable it had been since the mid-19th century. The US dominated the region and, crucially, Asian states were happy to live with this fact. All benefitted from the stability that US military might had created. Across the region, states spent a good deal less on defence and security than they otherwise would have. This provided ideal circumstances to focus on domestic economic development.

Between 2020 and 2023 things changed fundamentally. Faith in markets cratered. States were no longer willing to live with globalization's vulnerabilities. The 2024 election of Donald Trump to a second term has cemented the anti-globalization sentiment in the world's most consequential economy. Exactly what tariffs, taxes and other barriers will become the standard is not clear, but there is no going back. The country that was market-led globalization's greatest avatar has turned its back on the ideas that had been central to the world economy for decades and had been critical to Asia's great integration. Geopolitical rivalry is also here to stay. It remains unclear which way Trump's foreign policy will go – will he double down on US primacy in Asia, cut back US presence or openly contest Chinese power? At present, China, the US and the nascent great power India have irreconcilable visions of the region's future. It seems all but certain that competition and instability will remain an integral aspect of Asia's future.

The current period is one of immense flux and uncertainty. The stability of the old order is gone. A new dispensation that is stable and acceptable to all the key powers seems to be beyond reach. The locus of power is fluid; the aims and aspirations of the great powers are in conflict and a grievance-fuelled nationalism suffuses many corners of the world's most populous continent. The coming decade will be decisive in determining the pattern of relations in the region. A generational period of dangerous competition and slow economic growth could be established, or, with some careful navigation, the region could be put onto a less risky and more optimistic path.

In this final chapter I will tie the various threads of the book together and then discuss how Asia's future can be better secured. This will begin with some measures that should be taken in the short term to stabilize regional relations, particularly its geopolitics. I will then turn to the constituent elements required to ensure Asia's security and prosperity over the longer term.

Asia's tragedy

In the 150 years prior to Napoleon's defeat at Waterloo, Europe was in a state of almost perpetual warfare. Wars of religion and attempts to achieve military dominance on the continent made conflict the norm and peace the exception. At the conclusion of the Napoleonic Wars, Europe's great powers carved out a diplomatic settlement at the Congress of Vienna that forged an enduring system to manage the continent's international affairs. The Concert of Europe, as the system was known, proved to be a remarkably effective diplomatic mechanism and ushered in an extended period of peace. While the Crimean War and the conflicts associated with national unification in Italy and Germany showed that the system was not infallible, these were exceptions and, importantly, they did not trigger a continent-wide war.

In comparison to the years prior to 1815, Europe's century leading to World War I was astonishingly peaceful. Some have even argued that this long tranquillity was a contributing factor to that war, as it created a complacency among diplomats and allowed pressure to build. But for thirty years Europe fell back again into its dark habits, this time the destruction was industrial in its scale, fuelled by the advances in engineering, technology and finance that created devastation of a hitherto unimaginable size.

Asia has experienced a truly astonishing century. In 1925, virtually all corners of the continent were subject to imperial rule by foreign powers. Britain, France, the US and the Netherlands controlled virtually all of South and Southeast Asia. The newly forged USSR retained the Tsarist imperial domains of Central Asia. China remained in pieces; parts of its eastern seaboard controlled by Europeans while the remainder of the nascent republic was in varying degrees of misrule and chaos, with the civil war just two years away. Japan was the exception. It had not been colonized but instead had opted to follow the European lead and build an empire of its own. At that point it controlled Korea and Taiwan and would soon begin to push into China. By 2025, imperialism was a distant memory. Independent states had been created in the furnace of the Cold War. Asia's peoples had created durable political structures and, in many cases, had embarked on economic development programmes that rewrote the textbook of capitalist growth.

Export-led industrialization had been the key to this success, supported by shrewd government policy, strong state capacity, an impressive work ethic and thrift, as well as a broader international environment in which markets were being opened, firms given their head and the animal spirits of capitalism encouraged to work their magic. The era of markets ushered in during the 1990s, where globalization was an article of faith among the developed economies, created opportunities that Asian states seized with great enthusiasm. But it was not just that globalization provided dynamism and markets, the shift towards value-chain models of production widened the range, speed and scope for firms to benefit from global markets. This led to the creation of a genuinely integrated Asian economy, one whose rates of intraregional trade approached those of the EU but which had been achieved with nowhere near the level of policy harmonization of the European institutions. This was a market-led process. But perhaps the most important component of the story of Asia's growth and emergence as a genuine region was the geopolitical stability that it enjoyed in the decades following the Sino–American rapprochement established in the 1970s.

Asia's long peace was centred on US military primacy and its acceptance by all key powers in the region. With American might maintaining a strategic balance, deterring adventurous foreign policy and keeping sea lanes open, Asia's states were able to focus much more intensely on domestic state and nation building. Geopolitical stability provided conditions for globalization's promise to deliver prosperity for so many in Asia. Inhabitants of the region had good reason to feel proud of their place in the world and their prospects. Economic development had been achieved in remarkable circumstances. Globalization-fuelled growth had turned the continent from a place of poverty to the engine room of the global economy. The world had never seen economic change at this pace or scale before. The problem of war and conflict had also been resolved. Great power competition was banished and military contestation retreated. Asia had cracked the code of international peace.

But the region's integration and economic growth served to undermine the geopolitical foundations on which it was built. As Asia's states grew wealthier and more ambitious, and as they began to adopt defence and foreign policies that matched their growing stature, the strategic balance was slowly but surely undermined. Long-term stability began to be replaced by nagging doubts and a growing sense of insecurity. This dynamic fuelled nationalism and turned up the heat across long-standing regional flashpoints, such as Taiwan, the Korean Peninsula and the Sino–Indian border dispute.

During the late 2010s Asia began to cohere as a strategic system. It was bound together by the bonds of economic interdependence and a growing strategic imagination created by the return of geopolitics. These circumstances promised a challenging but still relatively optimistic vision of Asia's future. The complex competing claims in the South China Sea and Taiwan, for example, would always be vexing to manage, but the shared economic interests of all of Asia's great powers as well as its not inconsiderable group of middle-ranking players, gave good reason to think that the worst excesses could be contained. Globalization's golden handcuffs would keep the US, China and India from pursuing policies that were too damaging to their own economic wellbeing.

The COVID-19 years shattered the integrative forces of globalization and accentuated the disintegrative pressures of geopolitics and nationalism. The economic growth of globalization fuelled geopolitics but the bonds of economic interdependence had promised to keep competition within manageable bounds. With the shuttering of market-led globalization, Asia now faces a more dangerous and less prosperous future. The global economy is experiencing the greatest reconfiguration since Nixon took the US off the gold standard in 1971. Political factors are beginning to play a much more decisive role in how globalization works, with economic nationalism and geopolitical considerations in a much more dominant position than before. The political reconstitution of global supply chains and production, prompted by the vulnerabilities exposed by the pandemic, has been accelerated by the economic policies of the second Trump administration. Tariff barriers are at their highest levels in decades, an aggrieved nationalism animates the world's biggest economy and the implications for how globalization might be reconfigured are immense. Asia can no longer depend on the opportunities of market-led globalization, at least not as it operated in the 1990s and 2000s. Globalization was a powerful force, driving growth and binding the region together. How it is reconfigured will have profound effects on levels of prosperity in the region. There remains immense promise, as there needs to be, given how many of the region's citizens remain outside the middle class, but it faces the headwinds of nationalism and geopolitical competition.

The pandemic years compounded the tragedy of Asia's long peace. The greatest period of stability in modern Asia's history has given way to a risky and dangerous future. The chances of conflict and war are much greater than before the pandemic and the direction of travel is disconcerting, to say the least. The growing militarization of the region's politics is creating a self-reinforcing loop in insecurity and instability. Lack of clarity about American policy and long-term strategy is further enhancing this uncertainty. The shrill blasts of victimized nationalism are multiplying risks. Competition is inevitable and, with the shredding of economic interdependence, new mechanisms are needed to stabilize the region. Careful statecraft will be required to ensure that the worst outcomes are avoided. The remainder of this chapter sketches out some of the ways this might occur.

Crisis management

The number of Asia's hot spots is frightening. The risks of conflict in the Korean Peninsula, Taiwan, the Himalayas and the East and South China Seas are high and rising. The prospects not just of casualties but a rapid escalation into all-out war are significant and increasing almost on a day-by-day basis. In the first instance, the region must take steps to manage these crises based on the political reality that they are not going to be resolved peacefully in the short term and that the dangers of some relatively minor crisis spiralling out of control are immense.

The complexity of the flashpoints means that there needs to be multiple layers to crisis management. Most immediately, the disputants need to establish clear lines of communication that are regularly used and maintained so that if something happens a channel of communication can be rapidly established. In the pre-digital age 'hotlines' were established that provided a physical telephone line that was kept open to be used in case of emergencies. With mobile phone coverage and internet telephony, physically making the call is not the issue, rather, it is about establishing practices in which emergency communication can happen and in which there is confidence. The Biden administration trailed publicly that it was going to establish a Cold War-style hotline with Beijing but did not implement it. Reports also showed that during various incidents in recent years officials in Beijing were unresponsive to calls that had been put through by counterparts in Washington and Tokyo.

Critics of US–China 'hotline' proposals rightly point out that two formal lines already exist (Morris and Marcrum, 2022). In 1997, the President-to-President hotline was established and the 2008 Defence Telephone Link connects the Defence ministries. Their limited use and efficacy are a salutary reminder that the utility of such mechanisms ultimately depends on political will. Japan and China established a hotline in May 2023, but it has not proven effective either, while India and China have also discussed hotlines at a high level and have introduced theatre-level communications in their borderland disputes. Just having lines of communication is clearly not enough. One of the problems evident at present is the differing views on either end of the line about the political function of communication as well as the crisis. For example, it may suit PRC interests not to respond to calls as their perception of what is occurring is not deemed to be a crisis. In responding to a call about an incident between PLA forces and Japanese aircraft or naval vessels in and around the disputed islands in the East China Sea, China senses that managing the matter gives tacit legitimacy to Japan's position. The immediate priority therefore is to use diplomatic and political means to generate a common interest in communication and a shared understanding of its purpose.

A second related task is to establish basic protocols for military forces, coast guards and others at the front line of geopolitics for handling specific crises. In many cases these exist on one or other side. Militaries train and prepare for all sorts of contingencies. Japanese Self-Defense Forces officers and Indian Army troops practice responding to interactions with their PLA counterparts and know what steps to take to try to ensure problems do not flare up. But there is a need to work towards shared protocols so that all parties to a potential clash understand a common set of steps that should be taken. Communication at the higher level is difficult to achieve, as it has been in recent years. Even in this era of instantaneous communication, relying only on high-level interactions may prove to be too slow and cumbersome to help deal with circumstances that are unfolding at sea, in the air or at very high altitude. Thus, it is critical that parties have the means to manage often tense and dangerous interactions in ways that minimize risk.

The only way in which these two important aspects can be developed is when all key parties see a shared value in communication and crisis management systems. The Cold War is a highly imperfect analogue to contemporary circumstances. But it earned its name through the successful maintenance of peace between the USSR and the US. This occurred in famous examples, such as the Berlin Blockade and the Cuban Missile Crisis, but also in the more mundane places where the two sides' militaries met, in the Pacific Ocean, the Mediterranean and the high Arctic, among others. These were made possible not because the two sides were less antagonistic than Asia's current great powers, they most assuredly were not, but because both sides recognized the need to see and accept the others' ambitions for what they were and to establish ways to manage their competition. Asia's most obvious strategic reality is that there is a not a shared understanding in the nature and structure of strategic competition and as a result no foundation exists on which to build communication channels and crisis protocols. It is the highest imperative that this is achieved.

A second broad area that can help stabilize the region's turbulent geopolitics is to establish mechanisms to build and reinforce confidence among mistrustful states. Creating what are known as 'confidence-building measures' (CBMs) as well as developing more formalized agreements to put constraints around and clarify the intentions of arms acquisitions. Part of the reason that hotlines and other communication measures are of limited utility stems from the lack of shared sense about the nature of the region's strategic environment, as well as a lack of trust and a willingness or ability to build a common understanding of the strategic facts on the ground. CBMs can provide informal but structured means of improving trust and shared understanding to build reassurance and a basic sense of confidence among Asia's great powers. Much of the discussion about how to manage the region's unstable setting focuses on the role of deterrence and credibility. The growth in military spending that is increasing countries' abilities to fight at distance from their homelands – such as Australia's submarines, China's missile fleet expansion, Japan's conversion of its helicopter carrier ships to aircraft carriers, India's aircraft carrier development programme, among others – is an effort not just to assuage security concerns in general but to increase deterrence. But strategic stability also requires reassurance to ensure that others do not respond in dangerous or destabilizing ways and create security dilemma responses or arms race dynamics.

CBMs played an important part in the Cold War in helping to reduce the risks of nuclear exchange. As the name implies, the logic of CBMs is to build mutual confidence among participants through transparency, predictability and communication. Perhaps most important for Asia's flashpoints is the way in which CBMs can be used to make clear the intent of military planning and posture and reduce insecurity concerns and fears of aggression.

Related to this, they can establish a clear baseline of normal military operations that can be used to assess changes by each side so that misperception risks are reduced. CBMs create regular communication channels and can increase the ability to interact effectively and understand the intentions and worldviews of the other sides. Finally, they can also lead to formal declarations of restraint in which states agree to take certain strategic options off the table. CBMs can be informal or codified in treaty form. The Cold War's most famous example was the Helsinki Final Act, an agreement signed by 35 countries from both sides of the Berlin Wall under the auspices of the Conference for Security and Cooperation in Europe.

There is a pressing need to build confidence in Asia, and there are a range of platforms, such as the EAS or Track 1.5 processes, such as the SLD, where these ideas could be developed. If these mechanisms are too large scale or perceived as politicized, then more localized CBMs could be developed focused on specific crisis points. However, a necessary precursor for this to occur is the establishment of some base level of shared agreement about the need for increased trust. This will need to be led by senior figures and most likely occur out of the public eye, due to the extent to which the domestic politics of the key protagonists has a strong nationalist overlay that narrows the options for manoeuvre.

Some are sceptical of whether a confident and emboldened China would be interested in such endeavours. They argue that the only way to condition PRC behaviour is through shows of strength and effective military deterrence. There is no doubt that this is a critical component of responding to a militarily ambitious Beijing. However, the costs and risks to China of conflict will be immense, and they have a strong set of interests in ensuring that competition is managed. To only pursue power politics without reassurance and communication narrows the range of options states have, strengthens a logic of contestation and does not ameliorate risk. This is not a counsel of naivety, rather it is a call to ensure that the necessary task of establishing a stable military balance requires creating a strong sense of confidence among Asia's great powers about intentions, goals and limits.

If CBMs can be established or even just a shared sense about the need to manage competition can be forged, the next step is to build arms control agreements on that foundation. The region's defence expenditure has been growing dramatically over a sustained period. More recently, these have included increases in nuclear weapons acquisition and development of next generation technology like hypersonic missiles. The track record in the Cold War was not perfect, but agreements struck between the USSR and the US helped provide transparency about just what weapon technology each side had and what they planned to do with it. They led to greater mutual understanding of intentions and, while not removing the risks of conflict, helped stabilize the strategic environment. All the major powers, and the region more generally, would benefit from the steadying impact that arms control regimes can foster.

The final element is to create institutional mechanisms or structures to maintain the diplomatic momentum of CBMs and arms control agreements. These can also be a place where dialogue can occur and where new initiatives can be tested and developed. There are a range of existing broad-ranging structures, such as the ARF and EAS, although their track record to date has been underwhelming. But experience of smaller-scale or more functionally specific entities has been more positive. If steps can be taken to create a sense of confidence and a recognition of the need to control geopolitical contestation then that can provide impetus to create and sustain a simple institutional structure.

The Six Party Talks that were established in 2003 provide one possible model for how this might occur. Established as a multistate response to North Korea's nuclear ambitions, it brought all the parties with a vital stake in that issue together – the two Koreas, the PRC, Russia, the US and Japan – to grapple with the DPRK's departure from the Nuclear Non-proliferation Treaty regime (Hur, 2018). While the talks ultimately failed to resolve the nuclear crisis, the platform was a creative piece of what would now be called minilateral diplomacy. High level envoys from each of the parties worked productively and showed that when the US and China had a shared interest in a common outcome there is a real possibility to manage broader issues. Indeed, the talks themselves included discussion about establishing an ongoing mechanism to address Northeast Asia's array of security crises. This kind of structure should be revisited as a matter of priority.

Long-term stability

Crises are the small sparks that ignite major conflagrations. Those infernos occur not out of the blue but because of years and decades of steps that create the preconditions for war. Christopher Clark's masterful account of the outbreak of World War I shows how, in his terms, Europe sleepwalked into conflict (Clark, 2012). The assassination of Archduke Franz Ferdinand was the spark, but without the mounted woodpiles of alliances and secret diplomacy, shows of strength, visions of honour and a misunderstanding of modern warfighting technology, Europe would not have been consumed.

The integration of modern Asia and its prosperity was made possible because of political and economic decisions themselves decades in the making. It took a generation and two major wars until the US worked out how to calibrate its regional strategy effectively during the Cold War. Building the foundations of a stable Asian order will be difficult, and it is pressing that the creation of a reconfigured strategic equilibrium does not cost the millions of lives lost in Korea and Indochina this time. In this remaining section, I outline key principles that will be necessary to establish a future for the region that is stable and prosperous under conditions of long-term military competition and a restructured global economy.

Striving for balance

The most remarkable facet of Asia's long peace was the acceptance of its central strategic fact: American military primacy. Hundreds of years of European history prior to 1815 showed that however ambitious, wealthy or well-equipped, achieving hegemony on that continent proved to be impossible. Asia's premodern history while often mistaken by Western strategic analysts as an unbroken period of Chinese dominance, was equally one in which hegemony was impossible. American military power was paramount across Asia, indeed across the world, in the post–Cold War era. But Washington was not hegemonic, nor did its leaders think it was so dominant. It may have overplayed its hand, such as in Iraq and Afghanistan, but American elites were acutely aware of the limits to which US power could be put.

While much about Asia's future is uncertain, the clear strategic reality is that none of the region's great powers will be able to achieve hegemony. The US will have neither the will nor capacity to recreate its old dominance. The scale of the region, the capacity of lesser powers to leverage asymmetric tactics to hinder more powerful states and the implausibility of any of the powers being able to concentrate the necessary combination of military might and political support to achieve domination means that hegemony can be ruled out. Even in the most optimistic scenarios for China's growth and prosperity this will be beyond Beijing. But it is also likely that none of the great powers will be able to achieve an Asia whose strategic environment is their preferred outcome, at least not based on the current configurations of domestic political interest and material wherewithal.

The principal problem at present is that the major powers, particularly the US and China, have incompatible visions of the future. Washington wants to retain primacy; this appears to continue to be the case in the second Trump administration, although the chaos of the policy process makes discerning its grand strategy a challenge. This is an objective that is unacceptable to China. Beijing wants to push US influence out of the Western Pacific. Both are marshalling resources, developing new military programmes and diplomatic initiatives to advance their goals, albeit in sporadic, uneven and, at times, unclear ways. Also, there are diverging views among policy elites in both capitals about what strategic ends and means ought to be. It is a complex, dynamic and long-run process.

If one assumes that the PRC and the US, as well as India and Russia, retain the basic direction of their current strategy, the region and the wider world will be best served by the creation of a long-term military equilibrium. This is a circumstance in which the distribution of military power – whether that of the individual states or that leveraged through alliances and partnerships – is such that none of the powers perceives that it can change the status quo without paying a significant price. During the long Asian peace, American military dominance was so great that even in those states who wanted change – such as Beijing's desire for Taiwan or North Korea's aims to reunify the peninsula – decision-makers knew that Washington's power made the price too high to pay. They were kept in check. The current period is uncertain because the stability that flowed from dominance has gone, and a new equilibrium has yet to be found. More worryingly, the major powers, most especially China and the US, are fixed on policies that make creating a genuine balance difficult to achieve.

Among conservative circles in the US there are discussions about how Washington can and, indeed, must vanquish China (Pottinger and Gallagher, 2024). Advocates take their cues from the USSR's defeat in the Cold War and argue for some kind of repeat of what is perceived to have been a Reagan-engineered toppling of the Soviet behemoth. Apart from misunderstanding what happened to the USSR – which was almost entirely an internal process driven by economic crisis and political sclerosis (Zubok, 2021) – such an approach will take the region into the Fractured Asia future described in Chapter 9. The US and China are indeed in competition but the strategy for that contest should not be defined by an end-state of victory, however rich-sounding the rhetoric or beguiling the historical parallels may appear. Rather, the Cold War cue should be from that contest's early days when planners, such as Kennan and Rusk, recognized the dangers of competing over every single line on the map. Instead, the priority should be on creating a military disposition that makes very clear what is unacceptable conduct and what price adversaries will have to pay if they overstep the mark. It means ensuring that there are no incentives to make a push for hegemony. Asia's war in the 1930s became a world war because Japan perceived it had no other option but to make an ultimately doomed drive to achieve dominance. Great power competition cannot be structured so that either the US, China or India feel that they have an incentive to take risks because they are cornered or because they have a sense of strategic opportunity. The only way in which this can occur is through the creation of a genuine strategic balance.

This will necessarily entail some significant challenges for all sides as none will be able to achieve their preferred outcomes. It will also require considerable improvements in communication, both in the operational sense but, more importantly, about large-scale and long-term ambitions and plans. There is a wide array of already existing mechanisms which can advance this goal, such as the ADMM+ process. There are many formal dialogues, such as Shangri-La, Xiangshan and Raisina, which have become platforms from which to pronounce strategic contestation and which could be a place where quiet defence diplomacy can build the necessary shared understanding about ends and means that can ensure competition operates within managed bounds and that the long-term goal of strategic balance is achieved.

Strategic understanding

A necessary feature in securing Asia's future is a much greater capacity of elites in Asia's major powers to understand the worldview, motives and thinking of their peers. To return to the Cold War, both sides were able simultaneously to compete vigorously in a long-term contest while sharing a reasonably clear understanding of how the world looked from the other's perspective. This was not a perfect understanding, but each side went to considerable lengths to get a comprehension of just what the world looked like in the other's shoes. Some have described this as 'strategic empathy', although self-styled realists bristle at the term, leery of its connotations of compassion or fellow feeling. One need not give up one's values or interests when seeking to understand what motivates one's opponents, what experiences shape their worldview and why they act the way they do. But it is vital to understand the other side, to take seriously their perceptions, grievances, hopes and beliefs.

At present, Asia's most significant geopolitical cleavage is between the US and China. Their relations suffer dramatically from mistrust as well as a lack of genuine understanding of each other's outlooks and worldview. Both sides assume the worst of the other. Beijing's elites believe that Washington is intent on preventing the PRC from achieving its potential. The only question in their minds is just how far the US will go – will attacks on champion firms, like Huawei, be the start of efforts to overthrow the Party-state? Certainly, there are some in the second Trump administration who have made exactly that case. For its part, the US sees China as a country that challenges American primacy in the Western Pacific and is undercutting its global role and economic interests. Such views are surprisingly anxious and show a remarkable lack of confidence in the ability of US firms to compete in US diplomatic and military power more broadly. Equally, it seems not to take the many limitations of Chinese power and influence sufficiently seriously.

To be clear, this is not an argument for accommodation or acquiescence by major powers to the will and vision of the other. Rather, it is a plea that they must take one another seriously and understand just what it is in the other's history, economy and politics that drives its ambitions so that better choices can be made. China's sense that the international order was built by others and in their mould is historically understandable. Given its size and importance to the global economy it would be strange if it did not want to change elements of the international operating system. That is not to argue that Beijing should get everything that it wants. But to present Beijing or Washington as the intellectual equivalent of the pantomime villain will make the region's future necessarily much worse than it could or should be. It is equally a mistake for each to assume the worst of the other. This means elites on all sides need to spend a good deal more time supporting research, education and understanding about the other's languages, cultures and histories. The knowledge base about China in countries like the US, Australia and even Japan is low and, in most cases, is declining swiftly. The same must also be said for study and knowledge of India and its complex culture and history.

Growth and integration

On the economic front, Asia must strive to achieve high levels of economic growth and as much integration as is politically and economically feasible. There are twin imperatives here. The first and most urgent is that even though the past few decades have seen a remarkable economic transformation, there remain hundreds of millions of people who need the improvements in human welfare that economic development brings. Rural China, much of India, Indonesia, the Philippines, Vietnam and Central Asia have vast swathes of humanity that live at or below the poverty line. To tear up globalization, to retreat to economic blocs and 21st century mercantilism, of the kind that at least some members of the second Trump administration seek, is to slam the door on those populations. It would return them to a world in which economic opportunity is limited and what gains can be achieved are realized far too slowly.

The other reason to do everything that is possible to ensure growth occurs and that regional economic interdependence is widespread is because it will bind the interests of Asia's states. Experience teaches us that there are limits to the ability of trade and investment to curb nationalism and geopolitical rivalry. This book would not have been written had the global handcuffs of market-led globalization worked in the way many assumed they would in the 1990s. Nonetheless, integration provides some guardrails. It forces states to pause and think, it provides domestic interests in other countries to have a stake in geopolitical stability and to act on these to encourage moderation. If Asia's future is one of pure geopolitics it will be much more dangerous.

So what can be done, given the scepticism about globalization that seems here to stay? Trump's election and the Brexit referendum in 2016 put the old economic model on notice (DeLong, 2022). Biden's government continued to explore policies in the Trumpian mould: tariffs, industrial policy, subsidies and the like. The pandemic years ripped up the old balance between states and markets. If there was any doubt, Trump's 2024 triumph makes it clear that there is no political constituency for a return to market-led globalization in the US, nor is there much enthusiasm elsewhere in the advanced economies. Yet Asian states know how important it has been to them and while some might see advantage in Trump's anti-China stance – investment into Vietnam and Thailand has increased because of this – the larger risks to a more politicized economic environment for developing economies are significant.

In the early 2000s, as the global multilateral negotiations for the post-Uruguay Round ground to a halt, liberally inclined, trading economies saw that relying on the system centred around the new WTO would not advance the cause of trade liberalization. They probably did not realize then just how badly the trading system would get stuck, but it was clear that, if market expansion was to be achieved by lowering trade barriers, economies would have to do it themselves and not rely on the global institution. In principle this was not optimal – the idea of the GATT/WTO system was that reductions in barriers would apply to all participants, thus maximizing the economic benefit. States working out deals themselves would not be as good as they could be, but policy makers recognized that, if they were to remain WTO purists, then there would not be any gains at all. Liberal economies began to sign what came to be called 'free trade agreements'. They were not technically free trade as they did not reduce all barriers and only extended the benefits to the select signatories, but these agreements show perhaps one way forward for Asia's economic reconstruction. States recognized that the old way of increasing opportunities for trade and investment was no longer politically viable and took pragmatic steps to advance their interests. Some were small-scale bilateral agreements while others, notably the Comprehensive and Progressive Agreement for Trans-Pacific Partnership (CPTPP), are quite significant in scale and reach.

These trade agreements marked a break with old principles and created a more complex and less efficient system. But it was one in which overall trade increased, mutually beneficial growth occurred and at least some of the broader benefits accrued. Asia's current circumstances demand a similar kind of pragmatism. The old political consensus has broken down and Asia's states need to take some inspiration from the Free Trade Agreement world and find a way to achieve at least some kind of increased economic openness and integration, even if it falls short of the market-led system of the pre-2020 period. The CPTPP's conclusion showed that middle-ranking powers can have leadership and influence. Most assumed that without the US what had been the TPP would effectively die. Instead, the remaining parties finalized an agreement. And in the same way Asia's states need to do a combination of advocacy work for openness and create structures, rules and agreements to undergird that, while also experimenting with ways of supporting internationalized production and investment in a world where politics and security concerns play a much greater role than they have since at least the 1970s. One possibility is using the CPTPP as a springboard to defend a liberal approach to trade in cooperation with the EU. The combined size of the two groupings is large, around one-third of global GDP, and the spillover effects of a liberal model of trade that such a block would create as external parties align themselves with the opportunities of accessing the group, would be significant.

There is also a lesson from the decades of economic growth after World War II that was experienced in the advanced industrial economies. Under the Bretton Woods system, countries began to liberalize trading relations and opened their economies on a reciprocal basis. The belief was that freer trade would generate growth and national wealth. But it was not just that economies would grow; all would in some broad sense benefit. The post-war planning was predicated on economic liberalization serving domestic social goals and especially the construction of a series of redistributive economic policies. In many countries this included the creation of national health insurance schemes, welfare states, the expansion of secondary and tertiary education and the development of national infrastructure. Liberalization served a domestic social purpose. The economic benefits of early economic interdependence were spread around through what were, in effect, mechanisms to provide broader social advancement, whether through improved health, education or infrastructure.

One of the unrecognized steps that was taken while liberalization accelerated during the era of markets from the 1980s through into the 21st century was to cut economies loose from some or all sense of domestic social purpose. The anti-globalization sentiment that has become very widespread is fuelled in part by the social consequences of the severing of the domestic function that growing economic growth drove. Asian states and societies need globalization and interdependence. A critical means to provide the political foundations for that is to rediscover the domestic purpose that the growth it generates serves. Redistributive domestic social policies are needed not just to serve broader societal goals but to anchor economic interdependence politically.

Climate cooperation

Addressing the changing climate must be a priority for the region if it is to have a peaceful and prosperous future. While competition will be with us for decades to come, the very real security differences and concerns states have should not be broadened out and used to check the imperative that we all must deal with the biggest security challenge of them all, the warming planet.

Asia is particularly exposed to the implications of shifts in the weather patterns. Populations are already being severely affected by rising sea levels, increased typhoons and more oscillating monsoonal patterns. In the short term, the focus must be on building the capacity to adapt to changes in climate, strengthening societal resilience and improving disaster responses.

Over the longer term, Asia must be at the forefront of decarbonization. One of the most immediate challenges is that firms see a massive economic advantage to be had from developing technologies that advance that goal and that this has become caught up in geopolitical contestation. Regional powers need to work out how to harness commercial endeavour to advance the urgent agenda of decarbonization and bracket out their security concerns. While it is difficult to see US–China cooperation on this front in the early years of the second Trump administration, there is considerable scope for second-tier powers to work to that end. Equally, universities, research institutions and other NGOs can and should work together to drive forward a decarbonized future.

Resisting nationalism

The most powerful force in modern politics is nationalism. It fuelled the hatreds and ambitions of the fascist powers. It was harnessed by colonized Asian peoples to mobilize their struggle for independence. Seeing off its dangers was at the heart of the post-World War II order. The Bretton Woods system deliberately sought to take economic policy levers out of the hands of politicians precisely because nationalist sentiments could generate catastrophic policy choices. In contemporary Asia, nationalism once again has the wind in its sails. A less well-recognized feature of the long Asian peace was the relative quietude of nationalist sentiment. While it was never fully banished – the nation building in many parts of developing Asia meant that these sentiments were being mobilized and burnished – it lacked the grievance-laden and bellicose tones that are its hallmarks today.

Nationalism is an emotional wild card that will be a part of Asia's future. Those who see its cultural power as subordinate to material forces, such as economic welfare, must learn the lesson of communist and liberal polities alike. Those of a Marxist persuasion believed that nationalism was a product of capitalist modes of production and that it would fade from view once class relations were reconfigured by a shift towards communist models of economic organization. Experience in the USSR and elsewhere showed how mistaken those beliefs were. Equally, liberals who thought that globalization and common prosperity would forge a greater sense of a shared humanity and teach us to leave parochial differences behind learned that they were just as wrong as Marxists. To forge a peaceful and stable Asian future will require us to learn how to live with nationalism, resist the worst instincts that it brings out, beat back the temptation it presents to wallow in a victimized view of the world where foreigners are always making life worse and be ever on guard for its violent encouragements.

An Asia of backward-looking nationalist grievance is one that will be doomed to fight. The long Asian peace showed that the region could match its historical and cultural legacy with commensurate achievements in human development. The challenge is to break out of the current cycle of competition, nationalism and disintegration. We know what can be achieved when that occurs; the imperative is to find the imagination and courage to do so again.

Asia's future

The making of modern Asia is one of the great tales of humanity. For thousands of years the continent had been home to the greatest concentrations of human population and consequently was the location of the most wealth and power in the world. With industrialization, the North Atlantic became the locus of the global economy and its countries the most powerful and prosperous. At the end of World War II, Asia remained desperately poor, and it seemed as if it were doomed to remain stuck in a cycle of poverty and underdevelopment.

Within a human lifetime the continent was transformed utterly. The resilience of its peoples, their entrepreneurship, creativity, hard work and ingenuity were the cornerstones of the greatest story of human development ever told. This book has shown that the way in which Asia was able to grow so fast – through the opportunities created by market-led globalization and supply chain production – integrated the region. But as it did so it fostered ambition and nationalism; geopolitics has reanimated violent disintegrative forces. These were accelerated by the COVID-19 years and now Asia is on the precipice. There are still extraordinary opportunities for this great continent but there are also immense risks. The coming decade will be critical to ensure peace and prosperity prevails. The paths forward beckon either conflict or peace. The choices we face will be difficult and finding the best way forward will require the same kind of creativity, energy and resilience that propelled the region's growth. War is not inevitable. It is imperative that it is avoided. This book is an effort to better understand where we have come from so that smart choices can be made to drive a better future for us all.

Sources and Further Reading

This book has been written with a general audience in mind. As such, I opted to provide a light touch to references placed in the main body of the text. Those references direct readers to the sources of data or specific facts as well as arguments of scholars, analysts or political leaders. Readers can find below further information about sources consulted in preparing this book and, while they may not be cited directly, each has had a bearing on the thinking and ideas explored here. Almost all of them have further references and bibliographies for those who wish to pursue topics in more detail.

Chapter 1: Introduction

For a good overview of the East China Sea disputes, see the detailed report from the International Crisis Group (ICG, 2014). There are lots of contemporaneous media reports of the September 10 event available online; some interesting coverage includes reports from *The Guardian* (UK; McCurry, 2010), *The Japan Times* (Ito and Aoki, 2010), the *Asia Times* (Takahashi, 2010) and the *Australian Broadcasting Corporation* (ABC, 2010).

There is an extensive literature on the economic dynamism of Asian economies that began to emerge widely in the first decade of the 21st century. Some of the more interesting books of the first iteration of this literature include Kishore Mahbubani's *The New Asian Hemisphere* (2008) and Bill Emmott's *Rivals* (2008), written by a pugnacious former Singaporean diplomat and a former editor of *The Economist* respectively. More recent additions include Parag Khanna's *The Future Is Asian* (2019) and Bruno Macaes' *Dawn of Eurasia* (2018).

On state efforts to drive regional cooperation and integration in Asia, see an interesting set of essays from a one-time director of Australia's Lowy Institute for International Policy, Michael Wesley's *Regional Organizations of the Asia Pacific* (2003). Mark Beeson's *Institutions of the Asia-Pacific* (2009) provides a broader set of reflections on regionalism in Asia. On the Sino-centric order of the pre-modern period, see Ji-Young Lee's *China's Hegemony* (2016).

There is a vast literature on globalization. For some illustrative examples of the positive assessment of its virtues and the broader intellectual consensus at the turn of the 21st century, see Martin Wolf's *Why Globalization Works* (2004) and Held et al's *Global Transformations* (1999). Wolf is a very influential columnist from the *Financial Times*, while *Global Transformations,* written by four leading British political scientists, was by some margin the most influential early scholarly work on globalization from this period.

Chapter 2: Imperialism and Its Aftermath

University of Cambridge International Relations Professor Ayse Zarakol's *Before the West* (2022) is a particularly original assessment of Asia before the arrival of European powers. Other interesting works include David Kang's *East Asia Before the West* (2012) and Pardesi's excellent, broad-sweeping essay 'Regards geopolitiques sur l'Indo-Pacifique' (2023), while Kenneth Swope and Tonio Andrade's *Early Modern Asia* (2018) provides a thorough academic analysis of the period.

There have been several excellent studies of the EIC. Ian Barrow's *The East India Company* (2017) provides a short but inclusive history supported with primary documents. The renowned British writer William Dalrymple's *The Anarchy* (2020) is an expansive and engagingly written history of the EIC, while Nick Robbins' *The Corporation That Changed the World* (2012) provides an account that puts the company in the longer run history of multinational corporations and draws some important lessons for contemporary circumstances.

For broader works on British rule in India, including the period of direct rule known as 'the Raj', David Gilmour's *The British in India* (2019) provides an approachable broad ranging history. Jon Wilson's *The Chaos of Empire* (2016) gives a comprehensive history of British rule from the EIC through until independence in 1947, while Denis Judd's *The Lion and the Tiger* (2005) provides a scholarly account of the period.

For an accessible history of China's last imperial dynasty, the Qing, William Rowe's *China's Last Empire* (2009) provides a comprehensive and briskly written account that counters some of the conventional histories of the Qing. For works that look at the Opium Wars and foreign entanglements, see the English translation of Hajian Mao's *The Qing Empire and the Opium War* (2018) and Julia Lovell's *The Opium War* (2012), which provides an excellent balance of scholarship and detail with a fine sense of narrative.

The classical account of the Meiji restoration in English is W.G. Beasley's *The Meiji Restoration* (2018). Originally published in 1972, this new edition retains its relevance. See also Ellen Trimberger's *Revolution From Above* (1978) for an influential interpretation of the transformation of Japan's society as a 'revolution' imposed by state elites.

America's approach to Asia in the 19th and early 20th century is well examined in chapters two and three of Michael Green's *By More Than Providence* (2017), a magisterial history of the US in Asia since the 18th century. Green served in the George W. Bush administration as a senior national security staff member. The classic *America's Road to Empire* (Morgan, 1965) puts the early period of the US presence in Asia in the context of the Spanish–American war, while the account of America being dragged into a global role in Ernest May's *Imperial Democracy* (1961) places the early Asia policy as part of the larger story of Washington's emerging global power strategy.

While there is an immense literature on World War II in the Pacific, as it is usually described in the anglophone literature, the works that are of particular salience to this book are as follows. For a broader assessment of World War II in Asia, see Jonathan Clements' *Japan at War in the Pacific* (2022), which provides a detailed examination of Japan's approach to the war, linking it directly to the Meiji Restoration. A more scholarly account of this period can be found in S.C.M. Paine's *The Japanese Empire* (2017). The exhaustive three-volume study of the war from Ian Toll – *Pacific Crucible* (2012), *The Conquering Tide* (2016) and *Twilight of the Gods* (2021) – presents a distinctly American perspective. Paine's *The Wars for Asia* (2014) draws interesting threads between the Chinese Civil War, Japan's war with China and the global conflict of World War II. Paine is a historian based at the US Naval War College.

On decolonization in Asia, Thomas and Thompson's *The Oxford Handbook of the Ends of Empire* (2018) has extensive essays on the global context and the chapters by Chatterji, Goscha and Thomas are particularly relevant to Asia. The division of Korea is examined in some detail in the central chapters of Donald Clark's *Korea in World History* (2012). The book is a broad-ranging and influential history of Korea from a US historian. The creation of Taiwan as the nationalist Republic of China is examined in chapters by Philips and Wang in the edited volume *Taiwan: A New History* (Rubinstein, 2007), a collection that provides a detailed and long-term historical assessment of the island. For more on American rule of the Philippines, see Go and Foster's *The American Colonial State in the Philippines* (2003) and for the period of independence, see chapter four of the approachable history of the country by Luis Francia *A History of the Philippines* (2014). France's ill-fated efforts to retain its colony and the subsequent conflict are the subject of Shawn McHale's *The First Vietnam War* (2021), a detailed historical work. Indonesia's independence and the conflicts that accompanied its struggle is well covered in the first few chapters of Vickers' *A History of Modern Indonesia* (2005), a highly regarded history of Indonesia that tells the story from Dutch imperialism to the turn of the 21st century. David Van Reybrouck's *Revolusi* (2024) focuses primarily on the period from 1930 to 1950, telling the story of the fight for independence in a vivid piece of historical narrative.

The end of Britain's empire in India and the creation of the successor states has created a vast literature. *The Great Partition* (2017) is Oxford historian Yasmin Khan's telling of the story with a focus on the everyday people affected, while Chandra et al's *India's Struggle for Independence, 1857–1947* (2016) is a bestselling account of Indian independence written by influential historians all based at Delhi's Jawaharlal Nehru University.

Chapter 3: Cold War to Long Peace

There are many good overall surveys of the Cold War. Among the more notable is Odd Ane Westad's *The Cold War: A World History* (2017), a global history of the conflict from one of the world's leading international historians. John Lewis Gaddis is regarded as the dean of Cold War history in the US and his *The Cold War: A New History* (2005) is a relatively short work that provides his final assessment of the contest. Carole Fink's *Cold War: An International History* (2018) is a comprehensive study that sees the Cold War as a product of the Russian Revolution, covering the period from 1917 to 1991.

Fischer-Tiné, Boskovska and Miskovic's *The Non-Aligned Movement and the Cold War* (2014) is an edited volume that puts the movement in its broader historical context and draws links across diverse national experiences in Asia, Africa and Europe. Tan and Acharya's *Bandung Revisited* (2008) is an edited volume brought together by two leading Singaporean scholars that discusses Bandung in historical perspective and argues that it laid the foundations for many aspects of modern Asia's international relations.

There is a voluminous literature on the Second Indochina War or Vietnam War. David Anderson's *The Columbia Guide to the Vietnam War* (2002) provides a thorough narrative history largely from an American perspective. Mark Atwood Lawrence's *Vietnam War* (2010) is an excellent short and sharp account of the conflict that has a distinctly international perspective. Daum, Gardner and Mausbach's *America, the Vietnam War and the World* (2003) is an edited collection from the German Historical Institute that provides a historiographical reflection on the war and takes a comparative perspective on the conflict itself and the way it reverberated around the world. Ang Cheng Guan's *The Vietnam War from the Other Side* (2002) tells the story from the perspective of Vietnam's communists.

The best discussions of US strategy in the first phase of the Cold War locate US policy in the context of its larger approach to the region. For a good overview, see Roger Buckley's *The United States in the Asia-Pacific since 1945* (2002), particularly the book's first half. This period is covered in depth in chapters seven and eight of Michael Green's *By More Than Providence* (2017). On the shifting role of China in US thinking at the time, see Tom Christensen's *Useful Adversaries* (1996).

There is an extensive literature that examines the Asian economic 'miracle'. For a journalist's account, see Michael Schuman's *The Miracle* (2009). Berger and Borer's *The Rise of East Asia* (1997) is a broad-ranging set of essays from a political economy perspective, while Birdsall et al's *The East Asian Miracle* (1993) remains the seminal account from a neoclassical economic point of view.

For an excellent assessment of the early Cold War period in South Asia, see the University of Nottingham historian Paul McGarr's *The Cold War in South Asia* (2013), which focuses on the interaction between the dominant Western powers with local dynamics. For a first-rate account of Nixon's groundbreaking visit to China in 1972, see Margaret MacMillan's *Nixon in China* (2006). Evelyn Goh's *Constructing the US Rapprochement with China* (2005) provides an impressive academic framework for understanding this period. Anne Thurston's *Engaging China* (2021) provides a comprehensive overview of five decades of US–China relations that puts the normalization of relations in a longer historical context.

It took some time for scholars to focus on the remarkable duration of Asia's long peace, but there is a growing literature on this phenomenon. Thompson and Volgy's *Reconsidering the East Asian Peace* (2025) is a recent edited volume that presents a series of excellent chapters looking at the various explanations of the peace and the challenge that the US–China rivalry presents. Mikkel Weissmann's *The East Asian Peace* (2012) explains the peace rooted in terms of the broad ranging practices of Asian states, not just American military primacy.

ASEAN's longevity and its importance in Southeast Asia and across the region has launched an extensive body of work. The following provide good introductions to the history and development of the Southeast Asian grouping. Don Weatherbee's *ASEAN's Half Century* (2019) is an authoritative history of the body by a veteran scholar of Southeast Asia, published to coincide with the association's 50th anniversary, while Shaun Narine's *Explaining ASEAN: Regionalism in Southeast Asia* (2002) remains the standard work on the topic. Amitav Acharya's *ASEAN and Regional Order* (2021) is an excellent overview of ASEAN, examining its origins, the role it plays in the regional order and its offshoot organizations; it is from one of the world's most influential scholars of Southeast Asia. For details on ASEAN's expansion in the 1990s, see Gates and Than's *ASEAN Enlargement* (2001), published by one of Southeast Asia's leading think tanks. The collection of influential essays, edited by one of the leading proponents for Asia-Pacific integration, Yamazawa Ippei's *Asia Pacific Economic Cooperation (APEC),* published in 2001, provides an authoritative depiction of the grouping from the perspective of the early 21st century.

The US–Pakistan relationship is examined in comprehensive detail in Dennis Kux's *The United States and Pakistan, 1947–2000* (2001). The excellent Sergey Radchenko's *Unwanted Visionaries* (2014) explores Asia's part in the end of the Cold War as well as Gorbachev's failure to advance his ambitions in the region. Stuart Harris and James Cotton's *The End of the Cold War in Northeast Asia* (1991) is an edited volume that provides a near contemporaneous account of developments and consequences in Northeast Asia.

Chapter 4: Asia Integrated

Liberal triumphalism was widespread in the 1990s. Illustrative examples of this work include the Francis Fukuyama's 'end of history' argument that appeared first as an article in the journal *National Interest* and was then elaborated in book form (Fukuyama, 1992). Other examples include Thomas Friedman's *The Lexus and the Olive Tree* (1999), a bestseller book from the *New York Times* columnist, which sets out to explain globalization but is more usefully understood as a reflection of the complacency of the age.

On the trans-Pacific regionalism that was the dominant mode in the 1990s, see John Ravenhill's *APEC and the Construction of Pacific Rim Regionalism* (2002). Deng's *Promoting Asia-Pacific Economic Cooperation* (1997) is an edited volume that takes APEC as its starting point and provides a good introduction to the broader trends relating to regionalism during this period.

The Indo-Pacific has become a widely used term but one that is primarily focused on military and strategic affairs. Head of the ANU's National Security College Rory Medcalf was a tireless advocate of the term and his *Contest for the Indo-Pacific* (2020) is the clearest and most detailed piece of advocacy, while

Timothy Doyle and Dennis Rumley's *The Rise and Return of the Indo-Pacific* (2019) presents a critical account of the emergence of the idea and its competing conceptualizations.

For a good series of detailed but approachable essays about the more 'traditional' modes of international production, see Kozul-Wright and Rowthorn's *Transnational Corporations and the Global Economy* (1998). Much of the literature on the changes in international production from the traditional model to the 'value chain' model is quite technical. Neilson et al's *Global Value Chains and Global Production Networks* (2017) is an edited volume that presents a range of perspectives, both explanatory and interpretive, of the value-chain model, while Gereffi's *Global Value Chains and Development* (2019) examines the process with a particular focus on developing economies, especially China and Mexico, countries that are at the heart of global production chains. For more on global value chains see the many essays in *The Routledge Companion to Global Value Chains* (Bajada, Skellern, Agarwal and Green, 2021). Kawai and Wignaraja's *Asia's Free Trade Agreements* (2011) provides a set of critical evaluations of free trade agreements in the region and recommendations to make them more effective, see particularly Part III on the ASEAN economies.

The return of geopolitics as a key part of the region's larger strategic environment has led to a wide range of work. Ball et al's *Asia's New Geopolitics* (2021) provides a good survey of the key issues and dynamics with a military focus from the International Institute of Strategic Studies, an authoritative London-based think tank. Felix Heiduk's *Asian Geopolitics and the US-China Rivalry* (2022) provides a wide range of perspectives with a particular focus on US–China rivalry, from leading scholars in the region. Robyn Lim's *The Geopolitics of East Asia* (2003) presents a longer historical perspective and is notable both for its gloomy outlook and its prescience.

For an excellent reflection on US policy during the period from 1991 to 2020, see Bob Davis' *Broken Engagement* (2025), a series of interviews between key policy makers overseeing US–China policy and the veteran *Wall Street Journal* correspondent. Kurt Campbell's *The Pivot* (2016) provides an insider's perspective on the Obama era pivot. Campbell was an influential figure in Asia policy in the Biden administration. Feigenbaum and Manning's *The United States in the New Asia* (2009), from senior American scholars with Republican credentials, illustrates the outlook from mainstream conservative policy makers. For more on the first Trump administration's approach to Asia, see Richard Javad Heydarian's *The Indo-Pacific: Trump, China, and the New Struggle for Global Mastery* (2019), which puts Washington's hardening attitudes to China in its historical context. Akaha et al's *Trump's America and International Relations in the Indo-Pacific* (2021) is an edited volume written at the end of Trump's first term that includes chapters that examine key bilateral relations with allies and competitors as well as thematic issues related to strategic dynamics.

The ambitious and assertive turn in Chinese foreign and strategic policy is the subject of extensive commentary and scholarly debate. Dan Blumenthal's *The China Nightmare* (2020) is a good example of the hawkish assessment of China's foreign policy from a think tank scholar based at the conservative American Enterprise Institute. Hoo Tiang Boon's *Chinese Foreign Policy Under Xi* (2017) presents a more moderate assessment of Xi's approach that was published after his first five years in office. Bates Gill's *Daring to Struggle* (2022) is an excellent work by a veteran China watcher that provides an insightful account of China's foreign policy under Xi and its global ambitions.

Indian ambitions on the global stage are the subject of extensive writing. Khilnani et al's *Non-Alignment 2.0* (2012) sets out a vision for the future as it was styled by the ambitious but middle-of-the-road establishment linked to the Congress

Party. Bharat Karnad's *Staggering Forward* (2018) provides an analysis by a hawkish think tank scholar of India's ambitions and the policy of Prime Minister Modi, published toward the end of his first term. In Shivshankar Menon's *India in a World Adrift* (2025) a former Indian national security advisor assesses India's likely future trajectory and its alignment with Western interests. Bekkevold and Kalyanaraman's *India's Great Power Politics* (2021) is a set of scholarly essays that examines different aspects of India's foreign policy evolution, with China's rise as the key organizational focus.

The expansion of Asia's multilateral institutions is thoroughly examined in Ellen Frost's *Asia's New Regionalism* (2008). Brookings Institution's Andrew Yeo's *Asia's Regional Architecture* (2019) examines these institutions in the context of the alliance structures and regional order. For more on the topic of Asian multilateralism, see Bates Gill and Mike Green's *Asia's New Multilateralism* (2009), a seminal book from two leading Asia scholars.

Chapter 5: The Pandemic Years and the End of Globalization

Micklethwait and Wooldridge's *A Future Perfect* (2000) is a good example of the optimistic assessment of globalization's promise by two journalists, then based at the *Economist,* a publication founded in the mid-19th century to support free trade. Manfred Steger's *Globalization* (2023) provides a more contemporary view by a US social theorist, discussing both the sense of opportunity in the post-Cold War period and more recent headwinds facing globalization.

Stephen Haggard's *The Political Economy of the Asian Financial Crisis* (2010) by a leading scholar of Asia's political economy is among the most comprehensive analyses of the Asian Financial Crisis. Sheng's *From Asian to Global Financial Crisis* (2009) provides an insider's account by a former regulator of the crisis and its links to the 2007–08 GFC. To get more detail about specific countries' experiences in the crisis, see Noble and Ravenhill's *The Asian Financial Crisis and the Architecture of Global Finance* (2000). The crisis led directly to the end of dictatorship in Indonesia. Purdey et al's *Indonesia* (2020) explores this process and the subsequent transition of its state and society through to the 2010s.

For more on Brexit, see the comprehensive set of essays in Sophie Loussouarn's *Brexit and Its Aftermath* (2022). Kevin O'Rourke's *A Short History of Brexit* (2019) is a concise but engaging book that provides a good overview of the key issues leading up to Brexit.

To read more on Trump's 2016 election Sabato et al's *Trumped* (2017) is an excellent edited book that provides detailed analysis from leading political scientists and journalists on how exactly it happened. Sides et al's *Identity Crisis* (2018) examines the shifting electoral coalitions in the US and how they drove the 2016 election outcome.

To get a sense of the logic behind the first Trump administration's trade policy and approach to China, see Moore and Laffer's *Trumponomics* (2018), written by two conservative American economists, while Liang and Ding's *The China–US Trade War* (2020) provides a thorough analysis of the causes and consequences of the first Trump administration's US–China trade war.

It is surprising how few general overviews of the COVID-19 pandemic have been written. Scott Gottlieb's *Uncontrolled Spread* (2022), by a former US Food and Drug Administration Commissioner, provides a fine macro-level assessment, focusing in particular on the US. Zhao et al's *COVID-19 Pandemic, Crisis Responses and the Changing World Perspectives in Humanities and Social Sciences* (2021) is an edited volume that provides a comprehensive set of scholarly analyses of the causes and consequences of COVID-19, looking at issues such as disaster management as well as country studies, examining the US,

India, Singapore, Ghana, Brazil and Japan. Cafruny and Talani's *The Political Economy of Global Responses to COVID-19* (2024) provides a comparative political economy assessment of the pandemic with a particular focus on why some countries coped better than others.

The economic response to the pandemic was as remarkable as the pandemic itself. Columbia University economic historian Adam Tooze's *Shutdown* (2021) remains the best single account of the economic responses to and implications of COVID-19. University of Toronto economist Joshua Gans' *Economics in the Age of COVID-19* (2020) provides a short and very approachable assessment of the economic responses to COVID-19 as a 'first take' of the policy written in the early months of the pandemic in 2020. Former chair of the US Federal Reserve Ben Bernanke's *21st Century Monetary Policy* (2022) presents a fascinating analysis of the Fed's response to the COVID-19 crisis and its longer-term impacts. Strauss and Jones' *Europe's Economic Response to the Covid-19 Pandemic* (2020) is an edited collection that provides an initial assessment of European economic responses to COVID-19, published in late 2020. For a detailed assessment of fiscal and monetary policy responses to COVID-19, see Andreosso-O'Callaghan et al's *Economic Policy and the Covid-19 Crisis* (2021), a scholarly edited volume that examines countries from Asia, Europe and North America.

On the complexity of global supply chains and the chaos that COVID-19 created, see Peter Goodman's *How The World Ran Out of Everything* (2024), an excellent book by a *New York Times* global economics correspondent. While China ultimately suffered significantly from COVID-19, in the first phase of the pandemic it seemed to be faring well. Almighini's *China After COVID 19* (2021) is a set of essays that provides a good contemporaneous assessment of its success as well as imminent challenges.

For a relatively concise analysis of China's economic reform and 'dual circulation', see Andrew Cainey and Christiane Prange's *Xiconomics* (2023), which is pitched at a business audience but provides a good assessment of the combined economic and ideological aspects of what the authors call 'Xiconomics'.

The best account of Trump's first term approach to China, culminating in the COVID-19-prompted unleashing of the China hawks, is Josh Rogin's *Chaos under Heaven* (2021) from a veteran foreign policy journalist. It is based on excellent sourcing within Trump's administration. On the Biden administration's use of industrial and tariff policy to respond to China, see Schild and Schmidt's *EU and US Foreign Economic Policy Responses to China* (2024), particularly chapter five. On US economic coercion towards China put in the context of the larger turn to politicization of economic relations, see Edward Fishman's *Chokepoints* (2025), a best-selling book by a former US State Department official. On Western responses to the challenge of China's infrastructure funding, see the chapter by the Lowy Institute's Roland Rajah 'Mobilizing the Indo-Pacific Infrastructure Response to China's Belt and Road Initiative in Southeast Asia' (2021).

Chapter 6: Geopolitics and the Great Powers

Several recent books provide good examples of the ways the return of geopolitics has been interpreted. The most interesting ones related to the subject of this book are Robert Kaplan's *Waste Land* (2025) from the veteran Brookings Institution commentator and Hal Brands' *The Eurasian Century* (2025) from the prolific scholar based at the Johns Hopkins University.

For introductory work on geopolitics, definitions of the concept and a broader discussion, see Jeremy Black's *Rethinking Geopolitics* (2024), an erudite book from an eminent British historian. John Short's *Geopolitics* (2021) is a useful and concise book that provides further introduction with a sharper focus on the scholarly concept.

For a survey of what great powers are and the roles they are thought to play in international politics, see the opening chapters of Bisley's *Great Powers in the Changing International Order* (2012).

Bear Braumoeller's *The Great Powers and the International System* (2013) examines the role of great powers in the international system, with a focus on the competing role of individuals and international pressures. Jeremy Black's *Great Powers and the Quest for Hegemony* (2007) provides a good historical overview of great powers from the 1500s onwards.

One of the most authoritative scholarly studies of alliances is Stephen Walt's *The Origins of Alliances* (1990). Glen Snyder's *Alliance Politics* (1997) is the other seminal academic work on alliances, while O'Neil and Fruhling's *Alliances, Nuclear Weapons and Escalation* (2021) looks at the contemporary nature of alliances and the particular challenge of nuclear weapons.

For more on China's rise to power and its ambitions, see Oriana Skylar Mastro's *Upstart* (2024). For an analysis of how Chinese elites perceive the country's standing and its ambitions, see the collection of essays edited by US-based scholar Suisheng Zhao titled *China's Big Power Ambition under Xi Jinping* (2022). This is complemented by the excellent edited collection *Chinese Scholars and Foreign Policy: Debating International Relations* (2020) by Feng, He and Xuetong. Geoff Raby's *China's Grand Strategy and Australia's Future in the New Global Order* (2020), by a former Australian ambassador to China, examines China's ambitions from a distinctly Australian perspective, while Rush Doshi's *The Long Game* (2023), by a former Biden administration senior National Security advisor, argues that the PRC has had a multi-decade ambition to displace US global power.

America's ambitions for Asia, which has increasingly been described as the 'Indo-Pacific' since 2017, is the subject of a lively literature. David Kang's *American Grand Strategy and East Asian Security in the Twenty-First Century* (2017) argues for an economy-first grand strategy for East Asia, but it is an approach that feels somewhat out of touch from the geopolitical risks of the post-COVID-19 world. Each year the Washington-based National Bureau of Asian Research publishes its *Strategic Asia* volume that canvasses key issues in the region as they pertain to US strategy. Abe Denmark's *US Strategy in the Asian Century* (2020), by the lead AUKUS official in the US Department of Defence under the Biden administration, presents a Democratic assessment of how the US should approach Asia. Elbridge Colby's *The Strategy of Denial* (2021) argues for a fundamental reorientation of US defence policy focused on seeing off the China challenge through what the author describes as a 'strategy of denial'. Colby served in the first Trump administration and, at the time of writing, is the Undersecretary for Defence for Policy in the second Trump administration. As well as these books, readers should consult the pages of the following journals where Asia policy is regularly discussed and advocated for: *Foreign Affairs*, *Foreign Policy*, *Asia Policy* and *The Washington Quarterly*.

For more on Indian foreign policy and its longer-term ambitions it is good to start with Harsh Pant's *New Directions in India's Foreign Policy* (2019), a comprehensive scholarly account of Indian foreign policy since the end of the Cold War. For more on the challenges and complex environment India faces, see Singh et al's *The New Great Game in the Indo-Pacific* (2023). On the domestic determinants of India's ambitions and its many challenges, see Aparna Pande's *Making India Great* (2020). For an early account of Prime Minister Modi's ambitions for India's global role that retains its relevance a decade on from publication, see Raja Mohan's *Modi's World* (2015). To keep up with the vibrant contemporary debates, consult the websites of the many foreign policy think tanks in Delhi that produce interesting and provocative works. Among the more notable are the Observer Research Foundation, the Delhi Policy Group, the Foreign Policy Research Centre and the Indian Council of World Affairs.

Chapter 7: Flashpoints and Zones of Contestation

Taylor's *The Four Flash Points* (2018), by the head of the Australian National University's Strategic and Defence Studies

Centre, provides an excellent overview and analysis of Asia's main flashpoints. On the longer-run challenges of the Taiwan crisis, see Elleman's *Taiwan Straits* (2015). For an interesting account of the risks of war and the need for the US to shift its posture on Taiwan from two influential former US senior officials, see Blackwill and Zelikow's *The United States, China and Taiwan* (2021). Bill Emmott's *Deterrence, Diplomacy and the Risk of Conflict Over Taiwan* (2024) is an excellent short book from the former editor of *The Economist*, which provides an incisive analysis of the risks of a Taiwan conflict and the need to focus on deterrence to manage the immense dangers it presents. For a contrary view that Taiwan's strategic importance is overstated, see an interesting report from two leading realist scholars Pat Porter and Michael Mazarr titled *Countering China's Adventurism over Taiwan* (2021).

For a thorough analysis of North Korea's nuclear ambitions and how to respond to the challenges it presents by two of America's leading Korea scholars, see Victor Cha and David Kang's *Nuclear North Korea* (2018). Cohen and Kim's *North Korea and Nuclear Weapons* (2017) is an edited volume that includes essays from both American and Korean scholars and analyses how to maintain strategic stability on the Korean Peninsula. On the risks of the collapse of the US–ROK alliance and its regional implications, see Scott Snyder's *The United States–South Korea Alliance* (2023).

For an excellent historical overview of the South China Sea disputes, see Bill Hayton's *The South China Sea* (2014), a comprehensive work from a BBC journalist and long-time Asia analyst. Zou's *Routledge Handbook of the South China Sea* (2021) is a source with extensive essays on the South China Sea. Nehginpao Kipgen's *The Politics of South China Sea Disputes* (2020) provides a thorough survey of the issues, including the Permanent Court of Arbitration ruling. On the Code of Conduct process, see chapter three in Buszynski and Hai's *The South China Sea* (2020).

SOURCES AND FURTHER READING

On great power rivalry in the Indian Ocean, see the excellent work from one of India's most astute scholars of maritime security Darshana Baruah, *The Contest for the Indian Ocean and the Making of a New World Order* (2024). On the India–China maritime competition, see Basrur, Mukerjee and Paul's *India–China Maritime Competition* (2019), a collection of essays from leading Indian scholars.

Central Asia has taken on a new but underappreciated role in geopolitical competition. Geoff Raby's *Great Game On* (2024) is a detailed work by a former Australian diplomat that looks at the zone from the perspective of Sino–Russian rivalry, while Patnaik's *Central Asia* (2016) is a work from a prominent Indian scholar of the region that examines Central Asia's engagement with the major powers and its efforts to maintain autonomy and stability.

On India–China rivalry, see TV Paul's *The China–India Rivalry in the Globalization Era* (2019), an excellent collection of essays edited by one of India's most influential scholars based at McGill University in Canada. For more on the contest in the high Himalayas, see Thapliyal's *India, China and the Strategic Himalayas* (2024) and on the 2020 dispute in particular, see Verma's *Why Did China Intrude Along the Disputed Border with India in May 2020* (2025). Since India and Pakistan acquired nuclear weapons in the late 1990s scholars have debated the impact of this on South Asia's strategic stability. For a good discussion of this issue from two US-based scholars, see Ganguly and Kapur's *India, Pakistan and the Bomb* (2010). Devin Hagerty's *Nuclear Weapons and Deterrence Stability in South Asia* (2019) provides a thorough analysis of and recommendations to enhance nuclear deterrence in South Asia.

For more on warming US–India ties, the edited volume by Ian Hall *The Engagement of India* (2014) provides a historical overview of India's growing appeal to many powers, most especially the US. On Washington–New Delhi ties, see Jaffrey's *US–India Partnership in the Indo-Pacific* (2025), which puts the warming bilateral relationship in the context of the competitive strategic setting in Asia. Ahamed's *A Matter of Trust* (2021) provides an engaging historical examination of the relationship since 1945 written by a prominent Indian journalist.

Chapter 8: Sources of Risk and Volatility

There is a large body of scholarship on modern nationalism. The following are among the most influential works: Anderson's *Imagined Communities* (2006), Kedourie's *Nationalism* (1993) and Smith's *Nations and Nationalism in a Global Era* (1995). Breuilly's *The Oxford Handbook of the History of Nationalism* (2013) also has a wide range of illuminating essays on the topic.

For an expansive set of essays on nationalism in Asia, see Zhouxiang's *The Routledge Handbook of Nationalism in East and Southeast Asia* (2023). On Hindu nationalism in Asia, see Sarkar's *Hindu Nationalism in India* (2022). Nationalism in Japan is the subject of Stockwin and Ampiah's *Rethinking Japan* (2017), written by two prominent British scholars. Chinese nationalism and its ties to the Communist Party are thoroughly examined in Suisheng Zhao's *A Nation-State by Construction* (2004), while Zeng Wang's *Never Forget National Humiliation* (2012) looks at the use of the idea of 'national humiliation' by the CPC.

For more on nationalism in Southeast Asia, see Liow's *Religion and Nationalism in Southeast Asia* (2016) that examines the interplay of religion and nationalism and is written by the Dean of Humanities and Social Sciences at Singapore's Nanyang Technological University. Nationalism is often seen as a positive force in Southeast Asia, due to its role in helping to advance decolonization. Christie's *A Modern History of Southeast Asia* (2000) provides a good introduction to this process, covering the period from the turn of the 20th century to 1980.

Mietzner's *Democratic Deconsolidation in Southeast Asia* (2021) is an incisive book from one of the world's leading authorities on Indonesian politics and provides a good analysis of democratic decline in Southeast Asia. Croissant and Haynes' *Democratic Regressions in Asia* (2023) is an edited book by leading scholars of democratic decline, with chapters that look at both conceptual issues as well as country-specific analysis, including states in South, Southeast and Northeast Asia. Edward Luce's *The Retreat of Western Liberalism* (2017) is an accessible analysis of the broader decline of liberalism by a columnist for the *Financial Times*. A good survey of populism across Asia can be found in Wang's *Three Faces of Populism in Asia* (2024), an edited book that provides case studies from across the region. For a number of studies on illiberalism in Asia, see chapters 44 to 47 in Sajo, Uitz and Holmes' *The Routledge Handbook of Illiberalism* (2022).

For more on climate change in Asia, see Pereira, Zain and Shaw's *Climate Change Adaptation in Southeast Asia* (2022). On the intersection of environmental issues and conflict in Northeast Asia, see Park's *Regional Environmental Politics in Northeast Asia* (2019), while Kar et al's *South Asia and Climate Change* (2022) provides a detailed set of chapters looking at the changing climate in South Asia.

Chapter 9: Three Paths to the Future

The Cold War was a period of bipolarity, and the era of markets was largely dominated by the US. But for some time, scholars have argued about an emerging order of multiple great powers, or what scholars call 'multipolarity'. Amitav Acharya's *The End of the American World Order* (2014) is an influential early account of what the author describes as 'the world's emerging multiplex setting'. Blackwill and Wright's *The End of World Order and America Foreign Policy* (2020) is a short work published by two leading American foreign policy commentators that assesses the distribution of power and instability in the world at the start of the pandemic period.

On the post-1945 liberal international order, see G. John Ikenberry's *A World Safe for Democracy* (2020), a book written by one of the most influential scholars of liberalism, particularly chapters five to seven. On the future of the US dollar system and how it might be challenged, see Kenneth Roggoff's *Our Dollar, Your Problem* (2025), an impeccably timed book from one of the world's leading authorities on the topic and former chief economist at the IMF.

The relative decline of the West has become the subject of some introspection. Ikenberry et al's *The End of the West? Crisis and Change in the Atlantic World Order* (2016) is an edited volume that includes leading liberal scholars in International Relations and focuses on fissures emerging within the West. Fabbrini and Marchetti's *Still a Western World?* (2017) brings together scholars from across the world, who reflect on the shifting patterns of global order. Cooley and Nexon's *Exit from Hegemony* (2020) is an excellent book that assesses the long-term decline of the US-led order and puts it in the context of longer-term patterns of hegemony.

On the tension in the UN system between state purpose and rights, see Edward Keene's *Beyond the Anarchical Society* (2002), an outstanding revisionist work on the foundations of the contemporary order. For around a decade or so the G20 appeared to have promise as a major new institution, although the geopolitical divisions between China and the US in particular have stymied this potential. Cooper and Thakur's *The Group of Twenty (G20)* (2012) is an authoritative account of its origins, purpose and possibilities by two of the world's leading scholars of multilateralism.

Chapter 10: Securing Asia's Future

The Concert of Europe is regularly seen as a highly effective mechanism to share power and reduce the risks of international conflict. For more on the Concert system and its operation, see Glenda Sluga's *The Invention of International Order* (2021). On the way concerts manage power relations and improve collaboration, see Jennifer Mitzen's *Power in Concert* (2013). The possibilities of a concert-like grand bargain are explored among the chapters in Dean et al's *After American Primacy* (2019). George Washington University's Charles Glaser caused immense consternation when he published an article advocating a US–China grand bargain in the influential journal *International Security* (2015).

On crisis management and confidence building measures, see Desjardins' *Rethinking Confidence-Building Measures* (2004), a critical account published by the London-based International Institute for Strategic Studies. Alan Chong's *International Security in the Asia-Pacific* (2017) brings together a wide range of perspectives from leading scholars in Asia on ways in which security concerns and conflict risks can be addressed and better managed across the continent. Strategic empathy is not widely studied, however, the essay by Yorke 'Is empathy a strategic imperative' (2023) in the *Journal of Strategic Studies* provides a thorough review of the state of the literature and can point readers in the direction of historical and more contemporary studies.

There is an extensive literature on the balance of power and the importance of strategic equilibrium in international relations. Kaufman et al's *Balance of Power in World History* (2007) examines the idea of the balance of power in the context of a world history with a focus on the non-Western world. The essays in Paul et al's *Balance of Power* (2004) reflect on the prospects and benefits of a return to a balanced world order from the setting of American primacy in the early 21st century.

References

ABC (2010) 'China Demands Compensation over Captured Sailor', *ABC News (Australia)* 26 September, https://web.archive.org/web/20101109122553/http://www.abc.net.au/news/stories/2010/09/26/3022074.htm.

Acharya, A. (2014) *The End of the American World Order*, Cambridge: Polity.

Acharya, A. (2021) *ASEAN and Regional Order: Revisiting Security Community in Southeast Asia*, London: Routledge.

Acheson, D (1950) 'Speech on the Far East' National Press Club, January 12, Washington, DC, https://www.cia.gov/library/readingroom/docs/1950-01-12.pdf.

Agarwal, S., He, Z. and Yeung, B. (eds) (2020) *The Impact of Covid-19 on Asian Economies and Policy Responses,* Singapore: World Scientific Publishing.

Ahamed, M. (2021) *A Matter of Trust: India-US Relations from Truman to Trump*, New Delhi: Harper Collins.

Akaha, T., Yuan, J.D. and Liang, W. (eds) (2021) *Trump's America and International Relations in the Indo-Pacific: Theoretical Analysis of Changes and Continuities*, Berlin: Springer Nature.

Almighini, A. (ed.) (2021) *China after COVID 19: Economic Revival and Challenges of the World*, Milan: Ledizioni with support from Ministry of Foreign Affairs and International Cooperation and ISPI.

Anderson, B.R. (2006) *Imagined Communities: Reflections on the Origins and Spread of Nationalism* (2nd edn), London: Verso.

Anderson, D.L. (2002) *The Columbia Guide to the Vietnam War*, New York: Columbia University Press.

REFERENCES

Andreosso-O'Callaghan, B., Sohn, W. and Moon, W. (eds) (2021) *Economic Policy and the Covid-19 Crisis: The Macroeconomic Response in the US, Europe and East Asia*, London: Routledge.

Aspinall, E. (2005) *Opposing Suharto: Compromise, Resistance, and Regime Change in Indonesia*, Stanford: Stanford University Press.

Auslin, M.R. (2020) *Asia's New Geopolitics: Essays on Reshaping the Indo-Pacific*, Stanford: Hoover Institution Press.

Ayyangar, S. (2024) 'Populisms in India: Conditions and a Concept', in S. Wang (ed.) *Three Faces of Populism in Asia: Populism as a Multifaceted Political Practice,* London: Routledge, pp 27–43.

Ball, D., Beraud-Sudreau, L., Huxley, T., Mohan, C.R. and Taylor, B. (2021) *Asia's New Geopolitics: Military Power and Regional Order*, London: Routledge for IISS, Adelphi, pp 478–80.

Bajada,C., Skellern, K., Agarwa, R. and Green, R. (eds) (2021) *The Routledge Companion to Global Value Chains: Reinterpreting and Reimagining Megatrends in the World Economy*, London: Routledge.

Barr, M.D. (2002) *Cultural Politics and Asian Values: The Tepid War*, London: Routledge.

Barrow, I. (2017) *The East India Company: A Short History with Documents*, Indianapolis: Hackett.

Baruah, D.M. (2024) *The Contest for the Indian Ocean and the Making of a New World Order*, New Haven: Yale University Press.

Basrur, R., Mukherjee, A. and Paul, T.V. (2019) *India-China Maritime Competition: The Security Dilemma at Sea*, London: Routledge.

Beasley, W.G. (1991) *Japanese Imperialism: 1894–1945*, Oxford: Oxford University Press.

Beasley, W.G. (2018) *The Meiji Restoration*, Stanford: Stanford University Press.

Beck, U. (1999) *World Risk Society*, Cambridge: Polity.

Beeson, M. (2009) *Institutions of the Asia-Pacific: ASEAN, APEC and Beyond*, London: Routledge.

Beeson, M. (2014) *Regionalism and Globalization in East Asia*, London: Bloomsbury.

Beetham, D. (2013) *The Legitimation of Power* (2nd edn), London: Bloomsbury.

Bekkevold. J.I. and Kalyanaraman, S. (eds) (2021) *India's Great Power Politics: Managing China's Rise*, London: Routledge.

Bellamy, A.J. (2017) *East Asia's Other Miracle: Explaining the Decline of Mass Atrocities*, Oxford: Oxford University Press.

Benson, J. and Matsumura, T. (2001) *Japan 1848 to 1945: From Isolation to Occupation*, London: Routledge.

Berger, M. and Borer, D. (eds) (1997) *The Rise of East Asia: Critical Visions of the Pacific Century*, London: Routledge.

Berger-Thomson, L. and Doyle, M-A. (2013) 'Shifts in Production in East Asia', *Bulletin of the Reserve Bank of Australia* June Quarter, https://www.rba.gov.au/publications/bulletin/2013/jun/pdf/bu-0613-4.pdf.

Bernanke, B.S. (2022), *21st Century Monetary Policy: The Federal Reserve from the Great Inflation to COVID-19*, New York: W.W. Norton.

Birdsall, N.M., Campos, J.E.L., Corden, W.M., Kim, C-S., MacDonald, L., Pack, H., et al (1993), *The East Asian Miracle: Economic Growth and Public Policy*, Washington, DC: World Bank Group.

Bisley, N. (2009) *Building Asia's Security* Adelphi No. 408, London: Routledge for IISS.

Bisley, N. (2012) *Great Powers in the Changing International Order*, Boulder: Lynne Rienner.

Bisley, N. (2020), 'Security Policy in Asia from Obama to Trump: Autopilot, Neglect or Worse?', in O. Turner and I. Parmar (eds) *The United States in the Indo-Pacific: Obama's Legacy and the Trump Transition*, Manchester: Manchester University Press, pp 161–76.

Bisley, N. (2024) 'The Quad, AUKUS and Australian Security Minilateralism: China's Rise and New Approaches to Security Cooperation', *Journal of Contemporary China*, June, https://www.tandfonline.com/doi/epdf/10.1080/10670564.2024.2365241?needAccess=true.

Black, J. (2007) *Great Powers and the Quest for Hegemony: The World Order since 1500*, London: Routledge.

Black, J. (2024) *Rethinking Geopolitics*, Bloomington: Indiana University Press.

REFERENCES

Blackwill, R.D and Harris, J.M. (eds) (2016) *War by Other Means: Geoeconomics and Statecraft*, Cambridge: Harvard University Press.

Blackwill, R.D. and Wright, T. (2020) *The End of World Order and America Foreign Policy*, New York: Council on Foreign Relations.

Blackwill, R.D. and Zelikow, P. (2021) *The United States, China and Taiwan: A Strategy to Prevent War*, New York: Council on Foreign Relations.

Blumenthal, D. (2020) *The China Nightmare: The Grand Ambitions of a Decaying State*, Washington, DC: AEI Press.

Boillot, J-J. and Labbouz, M. (2006) 'India-China Trade: Lessons Learned and Projections for 2015', *Economic and Political Weekly* 41(26): 2893–901.

Booth, K. and Wheeler, N. (2008) *The Security Dilemma: Fear, Cooperation and Trust in World Politics*, Basingstoke: Macmillan.

Bradley, C., Seong, J., Smith, S. and Woetzel, J. (2022) *On the Cusp of a New Era?* McKinsey Global Institute, Discussion Paper, https://www.mckinsey.com/~/media/mckinsey/business%20functions/risk/our%20insights/on%20the%20cusp%20of%20a%20new%20era/on-the-cusp-of-a-new-era.pdf?shouldIndex=false.

Brands, H. (2025) *The Eurasian Century: Hot Wars, Cold Wars and the Making of the Modern World*, New York: W.W. Norton.

Braumoeller, B.F. (2013) *The Great Powers and the International System: Systemic Theory in Empirical Perspective*, Cambridge: Cambridge University Press

Breuilly, J. (ed.) (2013) *The Oxford Handbook of the History of Nationalism*, Oxford: Oxford University Press.

Brown, C. (2022), 'Four Years into the Trade War, Are the US and China Decoupling?' Peterson Institute for International Economics Washington, DC, 20 October, https://www.piie.com/blogs/realtime-economics/four-years-trade-war-are-us-and-china-decoupling.

Brown, M.E., Cote, O.R., Lynn-Jones, S.M. and Miller, S.E. (eds) (2000) *The Rise of China*, Cambridge: MIT Press.

Brzezinskwi, Z. (1997) *The Grand Chessboard: American Primacy and Its Geostrategic Imperatives*, New York: Basic Books.

Buckley, R. (2002) *The United States in the Asia-Pacific since 1945*, Cambridge: Cambridge University Press.

Burns-Murdoch, J. (2024) 'What the "Year of Democracy" Taught Us, in Six Charts', *Financial Times* 30 December, https://www.ft.com/content/350ba985-bb07-4aa3-aa5e-38eda7c525dd.

Buszynski, L. (1983) *SEATO: The Failure of an Alliance Strategy*, Singapore: Singapore University Press.

Buszynski, L. and Hai, D. T. (eds) (2020) *The South China Sea: From a Regional Maritime Dispute to a Geo-Strategic Competition*, London: Routledge.

Cafruny, A.W. and Talani, L.S. (eds) (2024) *The Political Economy of Global Responses to COVID-19*, London: Palgrave.

Cainey, A. and Prange, C. (2023) *Xiconomics: What China's Dual Circulation Strategy Means for Global Business*, London: Agenda.

Camilleri, J.A. and Falk, R. (1992) *The End of Sovereignty: The Politics of a Shrinking and Fragmenting World*, London: Edward Elgar.

Campbell, K. (2016) *The Pivot: The Future of American Statecraft in Asia*, New York: Twelve.

Cardoso, R. (2009) 'Close Encounters at Sea: The USNS Impeccable Incident', *Naval War College Review* 62(3): 101–12.

Cha, V.D. and Kang, D.C. (2018) *Nuclear North Korea: A Debate on Engagement Strategies*, New York: Columbia University Press.

Chan, S., Feng, H., He, K. and Hu, W. (2021) *Contesting Revisionism: China, the United States and the Transformation of International Order*, Oxford: Oxford University Press.

Chandra, B., Mukerjeee, M., Mukerjee, A., Panikkar, K.N. and Mahajan, S. (2016) *India's Struggle for Independence, 1857–1947*, London and Delhi: Penguin.

Chen, W-C., Ou, C-H., Yang, M-H., Shi, Y-C. (2024) 'China's Grey Zone Actions in the East China Sea, Taiwan Strait, and South China Sea: A Comparative Study and Impact on Fisheries', *Marine Policy* 167, September, https://www.sciencedirect.com/science/article/pii/S0308597X24002446.

Cheng, T-J. and Chu, Y-H. (eds) (2018) *The Routledge Handbook of East Asian Democratization*, London: Routledge.

REFERENCES

Chiang, M-H. (2019) 'China–ASEAN Economic Relations after Establishment of Free Trade Area', *The Pacific Review* 32(3): 267–90.

Chin, J. and Lin, L. (2022) *Surveillance State: Inside China's Quest to Launch a New Era of Social Control*, New York: St Martin's Press.

Chong, A. (ed.) (2017) *International Security in the Asia-Pacific: Transcending ASEAN towards Transitional Polycentrism*, London: Palgrave Macmillan.

Christensen, T.J. (1996) *Useful Adversaries: Grand Strategy, Domestic Mobilization and Sino-American Conflict, 1947–58*, Princeton: Princeton University Press.

Christie, C.J. (2000) *A Modern History of Southeast Asia: Decolonization, Nationalism*, Singapore: ISEAS Press.

Clark, C. (2012) *The Sleepwalkers: How Europe Went to War in 1914*, London: Penguin.

Clark, D. (2012) *Korea in World History*, New York: Columbia University Press.

Clarke, H.D., Goodwin, M. and Whiteley, P. (2017) *Brexit: Why Britain Voted to Leave the European Union*, Cambridge: Cambridge University Press.

Clarke, M., Sussex, M. and Bisley, N. (eds) (2020) *The Belt and Road Initiative and the Future of Regional Order in the Indo-Pacific*, Lanham: Lexington Books.

Clements, J. (2022) *Japan at War in the Pacific: The Rise and Fall of an Empire, 1869–1945*, Tokyo: Tuttle.

Clinton, W.J. (2000), 'Remarks to the World Economic Forum and a Question-and-Answer Session in Davos, Switzerland', Davos, Switzerland, 29 January, https://www.presidency.ucsb.edu/documents/remarks-the-world-economic-forum-and-question-and-answer-session-davos-switzerland.

Coe, N.M. and Yeung, H.W-C. (2015) *Global Production Networks: Theorising Economic Development in an Interconnected World*, Oxford: Oxford University Press.

Cohen, M.D. and Kim, S.C. (2017) *North Korea and Nuclear Weapons: Entering the New Era of Deterrence*, Washington, DC: Georgetown University Press.

Colby, E.A. (2021) *The Strategy of Denial: American Defense in the Age of Great Power Conflict*, New Haven: Yale University Press.

Cooley, A. and Nexon, D.H. (2020) *Exit from Hegemony: The Unravelling of the American Global Order*, Oxford: Oxford University Press.

Cooper, A.F. and Thakur, R. (2012) *The Group of Twenty (G20)*, London: Routledge.

Copland, I. (1986) *Europe's Great Game: Imperialism in Asia Vol. 1*, Oxford: Oxford University Press.

Coppedge, M., Gerring, J., Glynn, A., Knutsend, C.J., Lindberg, S.I., Pemstein, D., et al (2020) *Varieties of Democracy: Measuring Two Centuries of Political Change*, Cambridge: Cambridge University Press.

Cordesman, A.H, Hess, A. and Yarosh, N.S. (2013) *Chinese Military Modernization and Force Development: A Western Perspective*, Washington, DC: CSIS.

Croissant, A. and Haynes, J. (2021) 'Democratic Regression in Asia: Introduction', *Democratization* 28(2): 1–21.

Croissant, A. and Haynes, J. (eds) (2023) *Democratic Regressions in Asia*, London: Routledge.

CSIS (2018) 'Economic Security as National Security: A Discussion with Dr. Peter Navarro', Washington, DC, 18 November, https://www.csis.org/analysis/economic-security-national-security-discussion-dr-peter-navarro.

Cummings, B. (2011) *The Korean War: A History*, New York: Random House.

Dahm, B. (1969) *Sukarno and the Struggle for Indonesian Independence*, Ithaca: Cornell University Press.

Dalrymple, W.D. (2020) *The Anarchy: The Relentless Rise of the East India Company*, London: Bloomsbury.

Daum, A.W., Gardner, L.C. and Mausbach, W. (eds) (2003) *America, the Vietnam War and the World: International and Comparative Perspectives*, Cambridge: German Historical Institute and Cambridge University Press.

Davis, B. (2025) *Broken Engagement: Interviews with Those Who Have Made — and Remade — the U.S.'s Policy Towards China*, Boston: The Wire China.

REFERENCES

Day, I. and Simon, J. (eds) (2016) *Structural Change in China: Implications for Australia and the World*, Canberra: Reserve Bank of Australia.

Dean, P.J., Taylor, B. and Fruhling, S. (eds) (2019) *After American Primacy: Imagining the Future of Australia's Defence*, Melbourne: Melbourne University Press.

Defence, Department of (Australia) (2016) *2016 Defence White Paper*, Canberra: Commonwealth of Australia.

Defense, Department of (US) (1995), *The United States Security Strategy for the East Asia-Pacific Region, 1995*, Washington, DC: USGPO, https://apps.dtic.mil/sti/citations/ADA298441.

DeLong, J.B. (2022) *Slouching towards Utopia: An Economic History of the Twentieth Century*, London: Basic Books.

Deng, Y. (ed.) (1997) *Promoting Asia-Pacific Economic Cooperation: Perspectives from East Asia*, Basingstoke: Macmillan.

Denmark, A.M. (2020) *US Strategy in the Asian Century: Empowering Allies and Partner*, New York: Columbia University Press.

Dennis, P. (1987) *Troubled Days of Peace: Mountbatten and South East Asia Command, 1945–46*, New York: St. Martin's.

Desjardins, M-F. (2004) *Rethinking Confidence-Building Measures*, Oxford: Oxford University Press for IISS, Adelphi No. 307.

Diamond, L. (2015) 'Facing up to the Democratic Recession', *Journal of Democracy* 26(1): 141–55.

Dicken, P. (2015) *Global Shift: Mapping the Changing Contours of the Global Economy* (7th edn), New York: Guilfoyle.

Doshi, R. (2023) *The Long Game: China's Grand Strategy to Displace American Order*, Oxford: Oxford University Press.

Dower, J.W. (1999) *Embracing Defeat: Japan in the Wake of World War II*, New York: W.W. Norton.

Doyle, T. and Rumley, D. (2019) *The Rise and Return of the Indo-Pacific*, Oxford: Oxford University Press.

Dreher, A., Gastons, N. and Martens, P. (2008) *Measuring Globalization: Gauging Its Consequences*, London: Springer.

Duiker, W.J. (2012) *Ho Chi Minh: A Life*, New York: Hachette.

Eatwell, R. and Goodwin, M. (2018) *National Populism: The Revolt Against Liberal Democracy*, London: Penguin.

Economist (2023) 'How Asia Is Reinventing Its Economic Model', *The Economist* 19 September, https://www.economist.com/finance-and-economics/2023/09/19/how-asia-is-reinventing-its-economic-model.

Elleman, B.A. (2015) *Taiwan Straits: Crisis in Asia and the Role of the US Navy*, Lanham: Rowman and Littlefield.

Emmott, B. (2008) *Rivals: How the Power Struggle between China, India and Japan Will Shape Our Next Decade*, London: Allen Lane.

Emmott, B. (2024) *Deterrence, Diplomacy and the Risk of Conflict Over Taiwan*, London: Routledge for IISS, Adelphi No. 508–10.

Fabbrini, S. and Marchetti, R. (eds) (2017) *Still a Western World? Continuity and Change in Global Order*, London: Routledge.

Feigenbaum, E.A. and Manning, R.A. (2009) *The United States in the New Asia*, New York: Council on Foreign Relations.

Feng, H., He, K. and Xuetong, Y. (eds) (2020) *Chinese Scholars and Foreign Policy: Debating International Relations*, London: Routledge.

Feng, Z. (2021) 'The Trump Administration's Policy Changes on China and Their Destructive Ramifications for US–China Relations', *Asian Perspective* 45(1): 123–45.

Fink, C.K. (2018) *Cold War: An International History*, London: Routledge.

Fischer-Tiné, H., Boskovska, N. and Miskovic, N. (eds) (2014) *The Non-Aligned Movement and the Cold War: Delhi – Bandung – Belgrade*, London: Routledge.

Fishman, E. (2025) *Chokepoints: American Power in the Age of Economic Warfare*, New York: Portfolio.

Forsberg, A. (2000) *America and the Japanese Miracle: The Cold War Context of Japan's Economic Revival, 1950–1960*, Chapel Hill: University of North Carolina Press.

Francia, L. (2013) *A History of the Philippines: From Indios Bravos to Filipinos*, New York: Abrams Press.

Frank, R.B. (2021) *The Tower of Bones: From the Marco Polo Bridge Incident to the Fall of Corregidor*, New York: W.W. Norton.

REFERENCES

Fravel, M.T. (2009) *Strong Borders, Secure Nation: Cooperation and Conflict in China's Territorial Disputes*, Princeton: Princeton University Press.

Fravel, M.T. (2019) *Active Defense: China's Military Strategy since 1949*, Princeton: Princeton University Press.

Friedberg, A.L. (2011) *A Contest for Supremacy: China, America and the Struggle for Mastery in Asia*, New York: W.W. Norton.

Friedman, E. (ed.) (2019) *The Politics of Democratization: Generalizing East Asian Experience*, London: Routledge.

Friedman, T.L. (1999) *The Lexus and the Olive Tree*, New York: Harper Collins.

Frost, E. (2008) *Asia's New Regionalism*, Boulder: Lynne Rienner.

Fukuyama, F. (1992) *The End of History and the Last Man*, New York: The Free Press.

Gaddis, J.L. (2005) *The Cold War: A New History*, New York: Penguin.

Ganguly, S. and Kapur, S.P. (2010), *India, Pakistan and the Bomb: Debating Nuclear Stability in South Asia*, New York: Columbia University Press.

Ganguly, S. and Pardesi, M.S. (2009) 'Explaining Sixty Years of India's Foreign Policy', *India Review* 8(1): 4–19.

Gans, J. (2020) *Economics in the Age of COVID-19*, Cambridge: Cambridge University Press.

Garcia-Herrero, A. (2021), 'What Is Behind China's Dual Circulation Strategy', *China Leadership Monitor* 69, Fall.

Garnaut, R., Song, L. and Fang, C. (eds) (2018) *China's Forty Years of Reform and Development: 1978–2018*, Canberra: ANU Press.

Gates, C. and Than, M. (2001) *ASEAN Enlargement: Impacts and Implications*, Singapore: ISEAS Press.

Gereffi, G. (2019) *Global Value Chains and Development: Redefining the Contours of 21st Century Capitalism*, Cambridge: Cambridge University Press.

Gerschewski, J. (2021) 'Erosion or Decay? Coneptualizing Causes and Mechanisms of Democratic Regression', *Democratization* 28(1): 43–62.

Gerstle, G. (2022) *The Rise and Fall of the Neoliberal Order: America and the World in the Free Market Era*, Oxford: Oxford University Press.

Gill, B. (2022) *Daring to Struggle: China's Global Ambitions under Xi Jinping*, Oxford: Oxford University Press.

Gill, B. and Green, M.J. (eds) (2009) *Asia's New Multilateralism: Cooperation, Competition, and the Search for Community*, New York: Columbia University Press.

Gilmour, D. (2019) *The British in India: Three Centuries of Ambition and Experience*, London: Penguin.

Glaser, C.L. (2015) 'A US-China Grand Bargain? The Hard Choice between Military Competition and Accommodation', *International Security* 39(4): 49–90.

Glasser, R., Kapetas, A., Leben, W. and Johnstone, C. (2022) 'The Geopolitics of Climate and Security in the Indo-Pacific', Canberra: Australian Strategic Policy Institute, https://www.aspi.org.au/report/geopolitics-climate-and-security-indo-pacific.

Go, J. and Foster, A.L. (eds) (2003) *The American Colonial State in the Philippines: Global Perspectives*, Durham: Duke University Press.

Godehart, N. (2024) 'China's Geopolitical Code: Shaping the Next World Order' *Mapping China's Strategic Space Project*, National Bureau of Asian Research 24 January, https://strategicspace.nbr.org/chinas-geopolitical-code-shaping-the-next-world-order/.

Goh, E. (2005) *Constructing the US Rapprochement with China: 1961–1974: From Red Menace to 'Tacit Ally'*, Cambridge: Cambridge University Press.

Goldberg, P. and Reed, T. (2023) 'Is the Global Economy Deglobalizing? And If So, Why? And What Is Next?' *Brookings Papers of Economic Activity* 31 March, https://www.brookings.edu/wp-content/uploads/2023/03/BPEA_Spring2023_Goldberg-Reed_unembargoed.pdf.

Goodman, P.S. (2024) *How the World Ran Out of Everything: Inside the Global Supply Chain*, New York: Harper Collins.

REFERENCES

Goscha, C.E. (1995) *Vietnam or Indochina? Contesting Concepts of Space in Vietnamese Nationalism, 1887–1954*, Copenhagen: Nordic Institute of Asian Studies.

Gottlieb, S. (2021) *Uncontrolled Spread: Why Covid-19 Crushed Us and How We Can Defeat the Next Pandemic*, New York: Harper.

Gray, C.S. and Sloan, G. (2014) *Geopolitics, Geography and Strategy*, London: Routledge.

Green, M.J. (2017) *By More Than Providence: Grand Strategy and American Power in the Asia Pacific since 1783*, New York: Columbia University Press.

Guan, A.C. (2002) *The Vietnam War from the Other Side: Vietnamese Communists' Perspectives*, London: Routledge Curzon.

Gudavarthy, A. (2019) *India after Modi: Populism and the Right*, London: Bloomsbury.

Hagerty, D.T. (2019) *Nuclear Weapons and Deterrence Stability in South Asia*, London: Palgrave Macmillan.

Haggard, S. (2010) *The Political Economy of the Asian Financial Crisis*, Washington, DC: International Institute for Economics Press.

Haggard, S. and Noland, M. (2005) *Hunger and Human Rights: The Politics of Famine in North Korea*, Washington, DC: Committee for Human Rights in North Korea. https://www.hrnk.org/uploads/pdfs/Hunger_and_Human_Rights.pdf.

Hall, I. (2014) *The Engagement of India: Strategies and Responses*, Washington, DC: Georgetown University Press.

Hall, I. (2019) *Modi and the Reinvention of Indian Foreign Policy*, Bristol: Bristol University Press.

Hall, P.A. and Soskice, D. (eds) (2001) *Varieties of Capitalism: The Institutional Foundations of Comparative Advantage*, Oxford: Oxford University Press.

Hara, K. (ed.) (2015) *The San Francisco System and Its Legacies: Continuation, Transformation and Historical Reconciliation in the Asia-Pacific*, London: Routledge.

Harris, S. (2014) *Chinese Foreign Policy*, Cambridge: Polity.

Harris, S. and Cotton, J. (eds) (1991) *The End of the Cold War in Northeast Asia*, London: Longman.

Haruki, W. (2014) *The Korean War: An International History* translated by F. Baldwin, Lanham: Rowman and Littlefield.

Hastings, M. (2008) *Nemesis: The Battle for Japan, 1944–45*, London: Harper Collins.

Hattori, R. (2023) *Fighting Japan's Cold War: Prime Minister Yasuhiro Nakasone and His Times*, London: Routledge.

Hayton, B. (2014) *The South China Sea: The Struggle for Power in Asia*, New Haven: Yale University Press.

Heiduk, F. (ed.) (2022) *Asian Geopolitics and the US–China Rivalry*, London: Routledge.

Held, D., McGrew, A., Goldblatt, D. and Perraton, J. (1999) *Global Transformations: Politics, Economics and Culture*, Cambridge: Polity.

Hellyer, R. and Fuess, H. (2020) *The Meiji Restoration: Japan as a Global Nation*, Cambridge: Cambridge University Press.

Heydarian, R.J. (2019) *The Indo-Pacific: Trump, China, and the New Struggle for Global Mastery*, London: Palgrave Macmillan.

Hille, K. (2024) 'China's Show of Force in Massive Military Exercises Alarms Taiwan', *Financial Times* 17 October, https://www.ft.com/content/b1935d18-7059-4229-9137-2f3d6042a97e.

Hiro, D. (2015) *The Longest August*, New York: Nation Books.

Hobsbawm, E.J. (1992) *Nations and Nationalism since 1780*, Cambridge: Cambridge University Press.

Holbraad, C. (1971) *The Concert of Europe: A Study in German and British International Theory, 1815–1914*, New York: Barnes and Noble.

Hoo, T.B. (ed.) (2017) *Chinese Foreign Policy under Xi*, London: Routledge.

Hur, M-Y. (2018) *The Six-Party Talks on North Korea: Dynamic Interactions among Principal States*, London: Palgrave Macmillan.

Hutchison, J. (2017) *Nationalism and War*, Oxford: Oxford University Press.

ICG (2014) 'Old Scores, New Grudges: Evolving Sino-Japanese Tensions', *Asia Report* 258, 24 July: 3–14.

IISS (2022) *China's Belt and Road Initiative: A Geopolitical and Geo-economic Assessment*, London: Routledge for IISS.

IISS (2024) *The Military Balance 2024*, London: Routledge for IISS.

REFERENCES

Ikenberry, G.J. (2020) *A World Safe for Democracy: Liberal Internationalism and the Crises of Global Order*, New Haven: Yale University Press.

Ikenberry, G.J., Anderson, J.J. and Risse, T. (eds) (2016) *The End of the West? Crisis and Change in the Atlantic World Order*, Ithaca: Cornell University Press.

Ishikawa, K. (2021) 'The ASEAN Economic Community and ASEAN Economic Integration', *Journal of Contemporary East Asian Studies* 10(1): 24–41.

Ito, M. and Aoki, M. (2010) 'Senkaku Collisions Video Leak Riles China', *Japan Times* 6 November, https://web.archive.org/web/20101109002022/http://search.japantimes.co.jp/cgi-bin/nn20101106a1.html.

Jaffrelot, C. (2023) *Modi's India*, Princeton: Princeton University Press.

Jaffrey, T. (2025) *US-India Partnership in the Indo-Pacific: Implications for China*, London: Routledge.

James, L. (2010) *Raj: The Making and Unmaking of British India*, New Edition, London: Abacus.

Javits, J.K. (1981) 'Congress and Foreign Relations: The Taiwan Relations Act', *Foreign Affairs* 60(1): 54–62.

Ju, H. (2015) *China's Maritime Power and Strategy: History, National Security and Geopolitics*, Singapore: World Scientific Press.

Judd, D. (2005) *The Lion and the Tiger: The Rise and Fall of the British Raj, 1600–1947*, Oxford: Oxford University Press.

Kang, D.C. (2012) *East Asia before the West: Five Centuries of Trade and Tribute*, New York: Columbia University Press.

Kang, D.C. (2017) *American Grand Strategy and East Asian Security in the Twenty-First Century*, Cambridge: Cambridge University Press.

Kaplan, R.D. (2025) *Waste Land: A World in Permanent Crisis*, London: Hurst.

Kar, M., Mukhopadhyay, J. and Sarkar, M.D. (eds) (2022) *South Asia and Climate Change: Unravelling the Conundrum*, London: Routledge.

Karnad, B. (2015) *Why India Is Not a Great Power (Yet)*, Delhi: Oxford University Press.

Karnad, B. (2018), *Staggering Forward: Narendra Modi and India's Global Ambition*, Delhi: Penguin India.

Kassim, Y.R. (2012) 'East Asia Summit 2012: Asia's Power Game Unfolds', *East Asia Forum* 12 December, https://eastasiaforum.org/2012/12/12/east-asia-summit-2012-asias-power-game-unfolds/.

Kaufman, S.J., Little, R. and Wohlforth, W.W. (eds) (2007) *Balance of Power in World History*, London: Palgrave Macmillan.

Kawai, M. and Wignaraja, G. (eds) (2011) *Asia's Free Trade Agreements: How Is Business Responding*, Cheltenham: Edward Elgar.

Kedourie, E. (1993) *Nationalism* (4th edn), London: Wiley-Blackwell.

Keene, E. (2002) *Beyond the Anarchical Society: Grotius, Colonialism and Order in World Politics*, Cambridge: Cambridge University Press.

Keohane, R.O. and Nye, J.S. (2011) *Power and Interdependence: World Politics in Transition* (4th edn), London: Pearson.

Khalilzad, Z. (1999) 'Congage China', *RAND Issue Paper* https://www.rand.org/content/dam/rand/pubs/issue_papers/2006/IP187.pdf.

Khan, A. and Patrick, W. (2016) *The Next Pandemic: On the Front Lines Against Humankind's Gravest Dangers*, New York: Public Affairs.

Khan, Y. (2017) *The Great Partition: The Making of India and Pakistan* (2nd edn), New Haven: Yale University Press.

Khanna, P. (2019) *The Future Is Asian*, New York: Simon and Schuster.

Khilnani, S., Kumar, R., Mehta, P.B., Menon, R., Nilekani, N., Srinath, R. et al (2012) *Non-Alignment 2.0: A Foreign and Strategic Policy for India in the Twenty First Century*, Delhi: Centre for Policy Research, https://cprindia.org/wp-content/uploads/2021/12/NonAlignment-2.pdf.

Kim, S.Y. (2016) 'Do Asian Values Exist? Empirical Tests of the Four Dimensions of Asian Values', *Journal of East Asian Studies* 10(2): 315–44.

Kim, Y.C. (1995) *The Southeast Asian Economic Miracle*, London: Routledge.

Kipgen, N. (2020) *The Politics of South China Sea Disputes*, London: Routledge.

Kirby, W.C., Ross, R.S. and Li, G. (eds) (2006) *The Normalization of US–China Relations: An International History*, Cambridge: Harvard University Asia Center.

REFERENCES

Kivimaki, T. (2014) *The Long East Asian Peace*, London: Ashgate.

Kohno, M. (1997) *Japan's Postwar Party Politics*, Princeton: Princeton University Press.

Kozul-Wright, R. and Rowthorn, R. (eds) (1998) *Transnational Corporations and the Global Economy*, Basingstoke: Macmillan for UN University.

Kremlin (2022) *Joint Statement of the Russian Federation and the People's Republic of China on the International Relations Entering a New Era and the Global Sustainable Development*, Beijing, 4 February.

Kux, D. (2001) *The United States and Pakistan, 1947–2000: Disenchanted Allies*, Baltimore: Johns Hopkins University Press.

Lai, C. (2024), 'President Lai Delivers 2024 National Day Address', *Office of the President of the Republic of China* 10 October, https://english.president.gov.tw/News/6816.

Lavelle, K.C. (2020) *The Challenges of Multilateralism*, New Haven: Yale University Press.

Lawrence, M.A. (2010) *Vietnam War: A Concise International History*, New York: Oxford University Press.

Lawrence, R. (2024) *Behind the Curve – Can Manufacturing Still Provide Inclusive Growth?* Washington, DC: Peterson Institute for International Economics.

Leifer, M. (2000) *Asian Nationalism*, London: Routledge.

Lee, J.J. (2006) *The Partition of Korea after World War II*, Basingstoke: Palgrave.

Lee, J-Y. (2016), *China's Hegemony: Four Hundred Years of East Asian Domination*, New York: Columbia University Press.

Lee, S. (2021) 'Monetary and Fiscal Policies in the United States' in B. Andreosso-O'Callaghan, W. Sohn and W. Moon (eds) *Economic Policy and the Covid-19 Crisis: The Macroeconomic Response in the US, Europe and East Asia*, London: Routledge, pp 15–38.

Li, S. (2018) *The Constitution of Ancient China*, edited by Z. Yongle and D.A. Bell, Princeton: Princeton University Press.

Liang, G. and Ding, H. (2020) *The China–US Trade War*, London: Routledge.

Lim, R. (2003) *The Geopolitics of East Asia: The Search for Equilibrium*, London: Routledge.

Lin, J.Y. and Wang, X. (2022) 'Dual Circulation: A New Structural Economics View of Development', *Journal of Chinese Economic and Business Studies* 20(4): 303–22.

Lind, J. and Ueki, C. K. (2021) 'Is Japan Back? Measuring Nationalism and Military Assertiveness in Asia's Other Great Power', *Journal of East Asian Studies* 21: 367–401.

Liow, J.C. (2016) *Religion and Nationalism in Southeast Asia*, Cambridge: Cambridge University Press.

Liu, X. and Zhang, W. (eds) (2010) *China's Three Decades of Economic Reforms*, London: Routledge.

Loussouarn, S. (ed.) (2022) *Brexit and Its Aftermath*, London: Bloomsbury.

Lovell, J. (2012) *The Opium War: Drugs, Dreams and the Making of China*, London: Picador

Luce, E. (2017) *The Retreat of Western Liberalism*, New Haven: Yale University Press.

Macaes, B. (2018) *Dawn of Eurasia: On the Trail of the New World Order*, New Haven: Yale University Press.

MacKenzie, D. (2020), *COVID-19: The Pandemic That Never Should Have Happened, and How to Stop the Next One*, New York: Bridge Street Press.

MacMillan, M. (2006) *Nixon in China: The Week That Changed the World*, London: Penguin.

Mahan, A.T. (1987 [1890]) *Influence of Sea Power on History*, Dover Publications.

Mahbubani, K. (2008) *The New Asian Hemisphere: The Irresistible Shift of Global Power to the East*, New York: Public Affairs.

Makinder, H. (2022) *Heartland: Three Essays on Geopolitics*, London: Spinebill.

Mao, H. (2018) *The Qing Empire and the Opium War: The Collapse of the Heavenly Dynasty*, Cambridge: Cambridge University Press.

Markoff, J. (2016) *Waves of Democracy: Social Movements and Political Change* (2nd edn), London: Routledge.

REFERENCES

Martin, L.L. (2021) *Coercive Cooperation: Explaining Multilateral Economic Sanctions*, Princeton: Princeton University Press.

Mason, P. (2012) *Why It's Kicking Off Everywhere: The New Global Revolutions*, London: Verso.

Mastro, O.S. (2024) *Upstart: How China Became a Great Power*, New York: Oxford University Press.

May, E. (1961) *Imperial Democracy: The Emergence of America as a Great Power*, New York: Harcourt, Brace and World.

Mazarr, M.J. (2015) *Mastering the Gray Zone: Understanding a Changing Era of Conflict*, Washington, DC: US Army War College Press.

McCoy, A. (1981) 'The Philippines' in R. Jeffrey (ed.) *Asia—Winning Independence*, London: Macmillan, pp 19–65.

McCurry, J. (2010) 'Japan-China Row Escalates over Fishing Boat Collision', *The Guardian* 9 September.

McDevitt, M.A. (2013) *The Long Littoral Project: A Summary Report*, Washington, DC: Centre for Naval Analysis, https://www.cna.org/archive/CNA_Files/pdf/irp-2013-u-004654-final.pdf.

McGarr, P.M. (2013) *The Cold War in South Asia: Britain, the United States and the Indian Subcontinent, 1945–1960*, Cambridge: Cambridge University Press.

McGee, P. (2025) *Apple in China: The Capture of the World's Greatest Company*, London: Simon and Schuster.

McHale, S.F. (2021) *The First Vietnam War*, Cambridge: Cambridge University Press.

McVeigh, B.J. (2004) *Nationalisms of Japan: Managing and Mystifying Identity*, Lanham: Rowman and Littlefield.

Medcalf, R. (2020) *Contest for the Indo-Pacific: Why China Won't Map the Future*, Melbourne: La Trobe University Press.

Menon, S. (2025) *India in a World Adrift: A Rising Power Takes Its Place among Rivals*, Sydney: Penguin and Lowy Institute for International Policy.

Micklethwait, J. and Wooldridge, A. (2000) *A Future Perfect: The Challenge and Hidden Promise of Globalization*, London: William Heinemann.

Mietzner, M. (2021) *Democratic Deconsolidation in Southeast Asia*, Cambridge: Cambridge University Press.

Miller, C. (2022) *Chip War: The Fight for the World's Most Critical Technology*, New York: Scribner.

Mishra, A.K. (2015) 'Globalization and South Asian Trade Performance', *The Indian Journal of Political Science* LXXVI(3): 334–40.

Mitzen, J. (2013) *Power in Concert: The Nineteenth-Century Origins of Global Governance*, Chicago: University of Chicago Press.

Mohan, C.R. (2015) *Modi's World: Expanding India's Sphere of Influence*, Delhi: Harper Collins.

Moore, S. and Laffer, A.B. (2018) *Trumponomics: Inside the America First Plan to Revive Our Economy*, New York: St Martin's Press.

Morgan, W.H. (1965) *America's Road to Empire: The War with Spain and Overseas Expansion*, New York: Wiley.

Morris, L.J. and Marcrum, K. (2022), 'Another "Hotline" with China Isn't the Answer', *Pacific Forum* 27 July, https://www.rand.org/pubs/commentary/2022/07/another-hotline-with-china-isnt-the-answer.html.

Mudde, C. (ed.) (2016) *The Populist Radical Right: A Reader*, London: Routledge.

Mudde, C. and Rovira Kaltwasser, C.R (2017) *Populism: A Very Short Introduction*, Cambridge: Cambridge University Press.

Mudde, C. and Rovira Kaltwasser, C. (2018) 'Studying Populism in Comparative Perspective: Reflections on the Contemporary and Future Research Agenda', *Comparative Political Studies* 51(13): 1667–93.

Munro-Leighton, J. (1992), 'A Post-revisionist Scrutiny of America's Role in the Cold War in Asia, 1945—1950', *Journal of American-East Asian Relations* 1(1): 73–98.

Narine, S. (2002) *Explaining ASEAN: Regionalism in Southeast Asia*, Boulder: Lynne Rienner.

Neilson, J., Pritchard, B., Wai-Chung, H.Y. (eds) (2017) *Global Value Chains and Global Production Networks: Changes in the International Political Economy*, London: Routledge.

Ng, K. (2024) 'N Korean Constitution Now Calls South "Hostile State"', *BBC News* 17 November, https://www.bbc.com/news/articles/c1wnxlxxwq2o.

REFERENCES

Noble, G.W. and Ravenhill, J. (eds) (2000), *The Asian Financial Crisis and the Architecture of Global Finance*, Cambridge: Cambridge University Press.

Norris, P. and Inglehart, R. (2019) *Cultural Backlash: Trump, Brexit and Authoritarian Populism*, Cambridge: Cambridge University Press.

O'Brien, K. and Zhao, S. (eds) (2011) *Grassroots Elections in China*, London: Routledge.

O'Neil, A. and Fruhling, S. (eds) (2021) *Alliances, Nuclear Weapons and Escalation: Managing Deterrence in the 21st Century*, Canberra: ANU Press.

O'Rourke, K. (2019) *A Short History of Brexit: From Brentry to Backstop*, London: Penguin.

Ohmae, K. (1995) *The End of the Nation-State: How Regional Economics Will Soon Reshape the World*, New York: Simon and Schuster.

Overholt, W.H. (2018) *China's Crisis of Success*, Cambridge: Cambridge University Press.

Pant, H.V. (2019) *New Directions in India's Foreign Policy: Theory and Praxis*, Cambridge: Cambridge University Press.

Paine, S.C.M. (2014) *The Wars for Asia, 1911–1949*, Cambridge: Cambridge University Press.

Paine, S.C.M. (2017) *The Japanese Empire: Grand Strategy from the Meiji Restoration to the Pacific War*, Cambridge: Cambridge University Press.

Pande, A. (2020) *Making India Great: The Promise of a Reluctant Global Power*, New York: Harper Collins.

Pardesi, M. (2023) 'Regards geopolitiques sur l'Indo-Pacifique', *Herodote: Revue de Geographie et de Geopolitique* 189, www.herodote.org/spip.php?article1087.

Park, J.W.B. (2019) *Regional Environmental Politics in Northeast Asia*, London: Routledge.

Parks, T. (2023) *Southeast Asia's Multipolar Future: Averting a New Cold War*, London: Bloomsbury.

Parthesius, R. (2010) *Dutch Ships in Tropical Waters: The Development of the Dutch East India Company (VOC) Shipping Network in Asia 1595–1660*, Amsterdam: University of Amsterdam Press.

Patnaik, A. (2016) *Central Asia: Geopolitics, Security and Stability*, London: Routledge.

Paul, T.V. (ed.) (2019) *The China-India Rivalry in the Globalization Era*, Washington, DC: Georgetown University Press.

Paul, T.V., Wirtz, J.J. and Fortmann, M. (eds) (2004) *Balance of Power: Theory and Practice in the 21st Century*, Stanford: Stanford University Press.

Peers, D.M. and Gooptu, N. (eds) (2012) *India and the British Empire*, Oxford: Oxford University Press.

Pence, M. (2018) 'Remarks by Vice President Pence on the Administration's Policy Toward China', Hudson Institute, Washington, DC, 4 October, https://trumpwhitehouse.archives.gov/briefings-statements/remarks-vice-president-pence-administrations-policy-toward-china/.

Pereira, J.J., Zain, M.K. and Shaw, R. (eds) (2022) *Climate Change Adaptation in Southeast Asia*, Singapore: Springer Nature.

Phillips, A. (2021) *How the East Was Won: Barbarian Conquerors, Universal Conquest and the Making of Modern Asia*, Cambridge: Cambridge University Press.

Pillsbury, M. (2015) *The Hundred Year Marathon: China's Secret Strategy to Replace America as the Global Superpower*, New York: Henry Holt.

Platt, S.R. (2018) *Imperial Twilight: The Opium War and the End of China's Last Golden Age*, New York: Knopf.

Porter, P. and Mazarr, M. (2021) *Countering China's Adventurism over Taiwan: A Third Way*, Lowy Institute for International Policy, 14 May, https://www.lowyinstitute.org/publications/countering-chinas-adventurism-over-taiwan-third-way-0.

Pottinger, M. and Gallagher, M. (2024), 'No Substitute for Victory: America's Competition with China Must Be Won, Not Managed', *Foreign Affairs* May/June.

Power, T. and Warburton, E. (2020) *Democracy in Indonesia: From Stagnation to Regression?*, Singapore: ISEAS Publishing.

Purdey, J., Missbach, A.J. and McRae, D. (2020) *Indonesia: State and Society in Transition*, Boulder: Lynne Rienner.

REFERENCES

Puri, S. (2024) *Westlessness: The Great Global Rebalancing*, London: Hodder and Stoughton.

Raby, G. (2020) *China's Grand Strategy and Australia's Future in the New Global Order*, Melbourne: Melbourne University Press.

Raby, G. (2024) *Great Game On: The Contest for Central Asia and Global Supremacy*, Melbourne: Melbourne University Press.

Radchenko, S. (2014) *Unwanted Visionaries: The Soviet Failure in Asia at the End of the Cold War*, Oxford: Oxford University Press.

Rajah, R. (2021) 'Mobilizing the Indo-Pacific Infrastructure Response to China's Belt and Road Initiative in Southeast Asia' in J.R. Stromseth (ed.) *Rivalry and Response: Assessing Great Power Dynamics in Southeast Asia*, Washington, DC: Brookings Institution Press.

Ramirez, R. and Wilkinson, A. (2016) *Strategic Reframing: The Oxford Scenario Planning Approach,* Oxford: Oxford University Press.

Ravenhill, J. (2002) *APEC and the Construction of Pacific Rim Regionalism*, Cambridge: Cambridge University Press.

Renzi, W.A. and Roehrs, M.D. (1991) *Never Look Back: History of World War II in the Pacific*, London: Routledge.

Riad, N., Errico, L., Henn, C., Saborowski, C., Saito, M. and Turunen, J. (2012) *Changing Patterns of Global Trade*, Departmental Paper No. 12/1, Washington, DC: International Monetary Fund, https://www.imf.org/external/pubs/ft/dp/2012/dp1201.pdf.

Robbins, N. (2012) *The Corporation That Changed the World*, London: Pluto Press.

Rock, M.T. (2017) *Dictators, Democrats, and Development in Southeast Asia: Implications for the Rest*, Oxford: Oxford University Press.

Rogin, J. (2021) *Chaos under Heaven: Trump, Xi and the Battle for the Twenty-first Century*, New York: Mariner Books.

Rogoff, K. (2025) *Our Dollar, Your Problem: An Insider's View of Seven Decades of Global Finance and the World Ahead*, New Haven: Yale University Press.

Rolland, N. (2020) *China's Vision for a New World Order*, Washington, DC: National Bureau of Asian Research.

Rowe, W.T. (2009) *China's Last Empire: The Great Qing*, Cambridge, MA: Harvard University Press.

Rubinstein, M.A. (ed.) (2007) *Taiwan: A New History*, Abingdon: M.E. Sharpe.

Rudd, K. (2024) *On Xi Jinping: How Xi's Marxist Nationalism Is Shaping China and the World*, Oxford: Oxford University Press.

Sabato, L.J, Kondik, K. and Skelley, G. (2017) *Trumped: The 2016 Election That Broke All the Rules*, Lanham: Rowman and Littlefield.

Sajo, A., Uitz, R. and Holmes, S. (eds) (2022) *The Routledge Handbook of Illiberalism*, London: Routledge.

Salmon, F. (2023) *The Phoenix Economy: Work, Life and Money in the New Not Normal*, New York: Harper Collins.

Sarkar, T. (2022) *Hindu Nationalism in India*, Oxford: Oxford University Press.

Sassen, S. (1998), *Globalization and Its Discontents*, New York: New Books.

Schild, J. and Schmidt, D.H. (2024) *EU and US Foreign Economic Policy Responses to China: The End of Naivety*, London: Routledge and UACES.

Schuman, M. (2009) *The Miracle: The Epic Story of Asia's Quest for Wealth*, New York: Harper Collins.

Seong, J., Bradley, C., Leung, N., Woetzel, J., Ellingrud, K., Kumra, G. et al (2023) *Asia on the Cusp of a New Era*, McKinsey Global Institute, September, https://www.mckinsey.com/mgi/our-research/asia-on-the-cusp-of-a-new-era.

Shellbourne, M. (2021) 'Davidson: China Could Try to Take Control of Taiwan in "Next Six Years"', *USNI News* 9 March, https://news.usni.org/2021/03/09/davidson-china-could-try-to-take-control-of-taiwan-in-next-six-years.

Sheng, A. (2009) *From Asian to Global Financial Crisis: An Asian Regulator's View of Unfettered Finance in the 1990s and 2000s*, Cambridge: Cambridge University Press.

Shepardson, D. (2024), 'US House Passes Bill to Force ByteDance to Divest TikTok or Face Ban', *Reuters* 14 March.

Short, J.R. (2021) *Geopolitics: Making Sense of a Changing World*, Lanham: Rowman and Littlefield.

REFERENCES

Sidel, J.T. (2012), 'The Fate of Nationalism in the New States: Southeast Asia in Comparative Historical Perspective', *Comparative Studies in Society and History* 54(1): 114–44.

Sides, J., Tesler, M. and Vavreck, L. (2018) *Identity Crisis: The 2016 Presidential Campaign and the Battle for the Meaning of America*, Princeton: Princeton University Press.

Singh, B., Khan, A., Thoker, P.A. and Lone, M.A. (2023) *The New Great Game in the Indo-Pacific: Rediscovering India's Pragmatism and Paradoxes*, London: Routledge.

Sluga, G. (2021) *The Invention of International Order: Remaking Europe after Napoleon*, Princeton: Princeton University Press.

Smith, A.D. (1995) *Nations and Nationalism in a Global Era*, Cambridge: Cambridge University Press.

Smith, A.D. (1998) *Nationalism and Modernism*, London: Routledge.

Snyder, G.H. (1997) *Alliance Politics*, Ithaca: Cornell University Press.

Snyder, S.A. (2023) *The United States-South Korea Alliance: Why It May Fail and Why It Must Not*, New York: Columbia University Press.

Song, E. and Sung, Y.W. (1995) *The Fifth Dragon: The Emergence of the Pearl River Delta*, New York: Addison Wesley Publishing Company.

Steger, M. (2023) *Globalization: Past, Present, Future*, Oakland: University of California Press.

Stiglitz, J.E. and Yusuf, S. (eds) (2001) *Rethinking the East Asian Miracle*, Oxford: Oxford University Press and the World Bank.

Stockwin, A. and Ampiah, K. (2017) *Rethinking Japan: The Politics of Contested Nationalism*, Lanham: Lexington Books.

Storey, I. (2017) *The South China Sea Dispute*, Singapore: ISEAS-Yusuf Ishak Institute.

Strauss, Z.K. and Jones, E. (eds) (2020) *Europe's Economic Response to the Covid-19 Pandemic*, South Portland: Perch Press.

Stubbs, R. (2018) *Rethinking the Asian Economic Miracle* (2nd edn), London: Palgrave.

Stuenkel, O. (2016) *Post-Western World: How Emerging Powers Are Remaking Global Order*, Cambridge: Polity.

Sutter, R.G. (2002) *The United States and East Asia: Dynamics and Implications*, Boulder: Lynne Rienner.

Swope, K.M. and Andrade, T. (2018) *Early Modern East Asia: War, Commerce, and Cultural Exchange*, London: Routledge.

Takahashi, K. (2010) 'China Signals V for Victory' *Asian Times* 5 October, https://archive.md/20101031211613/http://atimes.com/atimes/Japan/LJ05Dh01.html.

Tan, S.S. and Acharya, A. (eds) (2008) *Bandung Revisited: The Legacy of the 1955 Asian-African Conference for International Order*, Singapore: NUS Press.

Tarling, N. (1992) 'The Establishment of the Colonial Regimes' in N. Tarling (ed.) *The Cambridge History of Southeast Asia: Volume Two. The Nineteenth and Twentieth Centuries*, Cambridge: Cambridge University Press, pp 5–78.

Tarling, N. and Chen, X. (eds) (2017) *Maritime Security in East and Southeast Asia Political Challenges in Asian Waters*, Basingstoke: Palgrave.

Taylor, B. (2018) *The Four Flash Points: How Asia Goes to War*, Melbourne: La Trobe University Press.

Taylor, J.B. and Baily, M.N. (eds) (2014) *Across the Great Divide: New Perspectives on the Financial Crisis*, Stanford: Hoover Institution Press.

Thapliyal, S. (ed.) (2024) *India, China and the Strategic Himalayas*, London: Routledge.

Thomas, M. and Thompson, T. (eds) (2018) *The Oxford Handbook of the Ends of Empire*, Oxford: Oxford University Press.

Thompson, L. (2021) 'U.S. Shipbuilding Is at Its Lowest Ebb Ever. How Did America Fall So Far?', *Forbes* 23 July, https://www.forbes.com/sites/lorenthompson/2021/07/23/us-shipbuilding-is-at-its-lowest-ebb-ever-how-did-america-fall-so-far/.

Thompson, M. (2023) *The Philippines: From 'People Power' to Democratic Backsliding*, Cambridge: Cambridge University Press.

Thompson, W.R. and Volgy, T.J. (eds) (2025) *Reconsidering the East Asian Peace: Confluences, Regional Characteristics and Societal Transformations*, London: Routledge.

Thurston, A.F. (2021) *Engaging China: Fifty Years of Sino-American Relations*, New York: Columbia University Press.

Tillman, R.O. (1963) 'Malaysia: The Problems of Federation' *The Western Political Quarterly*, 16(4): 897–911.

REFERENCES

Toll, I.W. (2012) *Pacific Crucible: War at Sea in the Pacific, 1941–1942*, New York: W.W. Norton.

Toll, I.W. (2016) *The Conquering Tide: War in the Pacific Islands, 1942–1944*, New York: W.W. Norton.

Toll, I.W. (2021) *Twilight of the Gods: War in the Western Pacific, 1944–1945*, New York: W.W. Norton.

Tooze, A. (2018) *Crashed: How a Decade of Financial Crises Changed the World*, London: Penguin.

Tooze, A. (2021) *Shutdown: How COVID Shook the World Economy*, London: Penguin.

Transco, R., Syktus, J., Allan, R.P., Croke, J., Hoegh-Guldberg, O. and Chadwick, R. (2024) 'Significantly Wetter or Drier Future Conditions for One to Two Thirds of the World's Population', *Nature Communications* 15 (483), https://www.nature.com/articles/s41467-023-44513-3.

Trimberger, E.K. (1978) *Revolution from Above: Military Bureaucrats and Development in Japan, Turkey, Egypt, and Peru*, New York: Transaction.

Tsang, S. and Cheung O. (2024) *The Political Thought of Xi Jinping*, Oxford: Oxford University Press.

Tuan, H.A. (2009) 'Doi Moi and the Remaking of Vietnam', *Global Asia* 4(3): 37–41.

Tudda, C. (2012) *A Cold War Turning Point: Nixon and China, 1969–72*, Baton Rouge: Louisiana State University Press.

Turner, O. and Parmar, I. (eds) (2020) *The United States in the Indo-Pacific: Obama's Legacy and the Trump Transition*, Manchester: Manchester University Press.

Urata, S. (1993) 'Japanese Foreign Direct Investment and Its Effect on Foreign Trade in Asia', in T. Ito and A.O. Krueger (eds) *Trade and Protectionism*, Chicago: University of Chicago Press for NBER, pp 273–304.

Van Reybrouck, D. (2024) *Revolusi: Indonesia and the Birth of the Modern World*, London: Bodley Head.

Verma, R. (ed.) (2025) *Why Did China Intrude Along the Disputed Border with India in May 2020?*, London: Routledge.

Vickers, A. (2005) *A History of Modern Indonesia*, Cambridge: Cambridge University Press.

Vogel, E.G. (2011) *Deng Xiaoping and the Transformation of China*, Cambridge: Harvard University Press.

Waite, J. (2012) *The End of the First Indochina War: A Global History*, London: Routledge.

Walt, S.M. (1990) *The Origins of Alliances*, Ithaca: Cornell University Press.

Walt, S.M. (2005) *Taming American Power: The Global Response to American Primacy*, New York: W.W. Norton.

Wang, S. (ed.) (2024) *Three Faces of Populism in Asia: Populism as a Multifaceted Political Practice*, London: Routledge.

Wang, Z. (2012) *Never Forget National Humiliation: Historical Memory in Chinese Politics and Foreign Relations*, New York: Columbia University Press.

Weatherbee, D.C (2019) *ASEAN's Half Century: A Political History of the Association of Southeast Asian Nations*, Lanham: Rowman and Littlefield.

Weiss, J.C. (2014) *Powerful Patriots: Nationalist Protest in China's Foreign Relations*, Oxford: Oxford University Press.

Weissmann, M. (2012) *The East Asian Peace: Conflict Prevention and Informal Peacebuilding*, London: Palgrave.

Wesley, M. (2003) *Regional Organizations of the Asia-Pacific*, London: Palgrave.

Westad, O.A. (2017) *The Cold War: A World History*, London: Allen Lane.

White, H. (2009) *The China Choice: Why We Should Share Power*, Melbourne: Black Ink.

White House (2017) *The National Security Strategy of the United States*, Washington, DC: USGPO, December, https://trumpwhitehouse.archives.gov/wp-content/uploads/2017/12/NSS-Final-12-18-2017-0905.pdf.

White House (2022) *Indo-Pacific Strategy of the United States*, Washington, DC: White House, https://bidenwhitehouse.archives.gov/wp-content/uploads/2022/02/U.S.-Indo-Pacific-Strategy.pdf.

REFERENCES

White-Spunner, B. (2017) *Partition: The Story of Indian Independence and the Creation of Pakistan in 1947*, London: Simon and Schuster.

Wilkins, T.S. (2020) 'Australia-China Clashes in the COVID-19 Era: Adjusting to a "New Normal" in Bilateral Relations?', *Japan Institute for International Affairs Policy Brief* 19 June, https://www.jiia-jic.jp/en/policybrief/pdf/PolicyBrief_Wilkins_20200619.pdf.

Wilson, J. (2016) *The Chaos of Empire: The British Raj and the Conquest of India*, London: Public Affairs.

Wolf, M. (2004) *Why Globalization Works*, New Haven: Yale University Press.

Xi, J. (2014) *Remarks at the Fourth Summit of the Conference on Interaction and Confidence Building Measures in Asia*, Shanghai Expo Center, Shanghai, 21 May, http://www.china.org.cn/world/2014-05/28/content_32511846.htm.

Xi, J. (2017), 'Jointly Shoulder Responsibility of Our Times, Promote Global Growth', Keynote Speech by H.E. Xi Jinping President of the People's Republic of China at the Opening Session of the World Economic Forum Annual Meeting 17 January, https://america.cgtn.com/2017/01/17/full-text-of-xi-jinping-keynote-at-the-world-economic-forum.

Xiang, L. (2024) 'Biden's Misguided China Policy', *Survival* 66(3): 91–104.

Yahuda, M. (1996) *International Politics of the Asia-Pacific, 1945–1995*, London: Routledge.

Yamazawa, I. (ed.) (2001) *Asia Pacific Economic Cooperation (APEC): Challenges and Tasks for the Twenty First Century*, London: Routledge.

Yeo, A. (2019) *Asia's Regional Architecture: Alliances and Institutions in the Pacific Century*, Stanford: Stanford University Press.

Yorke, C. (2023) 'Is Empathy a Strategic Imperative: A Review Essay', *Journal of Strategic Studies* 46(5): 1082–1102.

Zarakol, A. (2022) *Before the West: The Rise and Fall of Eastern World Orders*, Cambridge: Cambridge University Press.

Zhao, S. (2004) *A Nation-State by Construction: The Dynamics of Modern Chinese Nationalism*, Stanford: Stanford University Press.

Zhao, S. (ed.) (2022) *China's Big Power Ambition under Xi Jinping: Narratives and Driving Forces*, London: Routledge.

Zhao, S.X.B., Wong, J.H.C., Lowe, C., Monaco, E. and Corbett, J. (eds) (2021) *COVID-19 Pandemic, Crisis Responses and the Changing World Perspectives in Humanities and Social Sciences*, Singapore: Springer.

Zhenuan, M. (2023), '2023 Edition of National Map Released', *China Daily* 28 August, https://www.chinadaily.com.cn/a/202308/28/WS64ec91c2a31035260b81ea5b.html.

Zhouxiang, L. (ed.) (2023) *The Routledge Handbook of Nationalism in East and Southeast Asia*, London: Routledge.

Zou, K. (ed.) (2021) *Routledge Handbook of the South China Sea*, London: Routledge.

Zubok, V.M. (2021) *Collapse: The Fall of the Soviet Union*, New Haven: Yale University Press.

Index

References to figures appear in *italic* type; those in **bold** type refer to tables.

9/11 attacks 252
38th parallel 36, 40

A

Abe Shinzo 169
Acheson, Dean 45, 49
ADMM+ 136, 176–7, 270
Afghanistan
 America's 2001 invasion
  of 186
 Soviet invasion of 57
Afro–Asian People's Solidarity
 Organization 46
AFTA (ASEAN Free Trade
 Area) 73–4, 110
AI 119, 141
AIIB (Asian Infrastructure and
 Investment Bank) 90, 147
Aksai Chin 180
allies of the great powers 133–4
American–Philippines War 37
American primacy 256, 259,
 268, 271
Anglo–Dutch treaty 24
Antarctica 222
antisemitism 201
APEC (Asia-Pacific Economic
 Cooperation) 57, 61, 77,
 88, 137
Apple 70, 73, 121
ARF (ASEAN Regional Forum)
 88, 89, 136, 176–7, 266
arms control agreements 266

Arunachal Pradesh 180
ASEAN (Association of Southeast
 Asian Nations) 56, 60, 73–4,
 136, 137
 established in 1967 87, 172
 and China 147
 launched EAS 88–9
 led by anti-communist
  nationalists 52–3
 and the South China Sea
  disputes 175–7
ASEAN+ 3 88, 89
ASEAN Defence Ministers
 Meeting Plus process
 (ADMM+) 89
Asian financial crisis of 1997–98
 96–7, 209, 211, 252
ASML 108
Atlantic Charter 25
AUKUS (Australia, United Kingdom
 and United States pact) 136,
 155, 217, 234
Australia
 in APEC 57
 and China 112
 defined a stable 'rules-based
  order' 217
 and East Asia Summit 89
 and the Quad mechanism 119
 and Southeast Asia 178
 and Southeast Asia Treaty
  Organization 47
 and the US 134

331

Australia, New Zealand and the United States Security Treaty (ANZUS) 133
authoritarianism 211, 214
authoritarian states 216, **216**
autocratization 213
automative sector 69

B

Bandung Conference 46–7
Bangkok Treaty 52
Bangladesh 40, 51, 184, 214
  at risk of inundation as sea levels rise 220
  swing state 135
Beck, Ulrich 109
Belt and Road Initiative (BRI) 84, 85–6, 119, 146–7, 188
Bhutan 180, 184
Biden, Joe 14
  and China 150–1
  hosted US–Central Asia summit 187
bipolarity 46
BJP (Bharatiya Janata Party) 157, 183, 202–3, 205, 208, 213
Boao Forum 91, 147, 148
  and Boao Forum 91
Bretton Woods system 32, 275, 277
Brexit referendum 98, 273
Britain
  and Burma, Malaya and Singapore 24
  and Dutch possessions 24
  and India 39–40
  military force 33
  and Southeast Asia 28
British East India Company (EIC) 19–20, 22
British Empire 19–21, 195
British India 19–21, 28, 39–40, 41
  map of in 1914 *21*
British Malaya 41
British Raj 20
Brunei
  absolutist monarchy 206
  joined ASEAN 60
  part of the British Empire 195
  and the South China Sea 173
  and TPP 80
Burma 24, 32, 40
Bytedance 117

C

Cambodia 47
  and Indochina 195
  and Indochina Wars 172
  swing state 135
Cambodian peace agreements 60
Cameron, David 98
Canada, in APEC 57
car industry 69
Carter, Jimmy 54
Caspian Sea 186
Central Asia 28, 51, 61, 63, 184–90
  political map of *186*
  states declared their independence 59
Central Asia–Gulf Cooperation Council (GCC) Summit 187
Ceylon 40
Chiang-kai Shek 44
Chile, and the TPP 80
China 33–4, 60, 64, 66, 92, **134**, 216–17
  and Australia 112
  and autocratization 213
  and Belt and Road Initiative 119
  border war in 1962 with India 51
  and Central Asia 186, 187–8
  communist victory in 1949 44
  and COVID-19 pandemic 11–12, 100, 101
  Diaoyu 1–2, 163–4
  disputed borders 144
  'dual circulation' economy 205
  and the East China Sea 129
  economic growth 71–3, 76–7, 83, 85, 97, 101, 122
  economic reform programme 6
  foreign policy 83
  global production zone 242

INDEX

as great power 132, 142–51
and green technology 220–1
and grey zone tactics 140
and high technology 242, 248
and India 74, 138–9, 159, 160, 179–82, 205, 221
and Japan 3, 28–9, 35, 205
Leninist regime 206
and liberalism 224
map of in 1927 *23*
and microchips 108
military 239, 240
and nationalism 204, 205
navy 139
and North Korea 167–8
partners and allies **134**, 135–6
political space opened in the late 1990s and early 2000s 211
Qing dynasty 21–3
in Rebalanced Asia 245–6
and the Shanghai Cooperation Organization 89
and the South China Sea 129, 172–3, 175
and Taiwan 37, 78, 83, 163–5, 255
threat of 238–9
and Trump 99
undercuts democracy and liberal rights-based norms in Fractured Asia 243–4
and the US 126–7
and the USSR 52
wants to reduce liberal and Western influence 218–19
in the Western Pacific 138
wishes to controls its maritime approaches 143
see also People's Republic of China (PRC); US–China relationsChina–ASEAN Free Trade Agreement 74
China Association of Military Sciences 90
China–Central Asia summit 187
China Command 32
China Institute of International Strategic Studies 90
Chinese Civil War 29, 37

Chinggis Khan 185
Chipmageddon 108
Clark, Christopher 267
climate adaptive technologies 222
climate change 120, 193–4, 219–23, 246, 251, 253
climate cooperation 276–7
Clinton, Hillary 79, 98, 153
Clinton, President Bill 5
Cold War 35, 43–53, 54, 59, 61, 76, 77–8, 218, 263
and arms control agreements 266
and confidence-building measures 264
and nationalism 196
and Southeast Asia 171
and strategic empathy 271
colonialism 40, 61
communism 44–6, 48
Communist Party of China (CPC) 2, 32, 55, 97, 211
and COVID-19 pandemic 101
and green technology 220–1
and nationalism 196, 197–200
and Taiwan 37, 41, 78, 144
wanted to be able to control the country's supply lines and markets 111
competition 131, 136, 246, 256, 261
and the Cold War 46, 54
and India 206
military 17, 46, 124, 131, 160
protection from foreign 66, 67
in Rebalanced Asia 246
Soviet–American 34–5, 43–4
strategic 16, 75–87, 162, 172, 177–8, 262–4
US with the PRC 14, 15, 111, 169, 223
and zones of contestation 137, 138, 139
see also geopolitical competition; great power competition
Comprehensive and Progressive Agreement for Trans-Pacific Partnership (CPTPP) 274, 275

Concert of Europe 237, 257
Conference on Interaction and Confidence Building Measures in Asia (CICA) 84, 89–90, 147
confidence-building measures (CBMs) 264–6
congagement 79, 80
Congress of Vienna 237, 257
Congress Party 39, 202
contestation zones 137, 138, 139, 190–1
continental zones 139
COVID-19 pandemic 8, 9, 11–12, 13, 92, 94–5, 100–4, 111–12, 252
  economic stimulus and government intervention 104–5
  and globalization 105, 109–10, 260
  and international supply chains 106
  and PPE 107
  and US–China relations 15
crises, protocols for handling 263
crisis management 261–7
currencies 229–30
cyberspace 141, 243

D

decarbonization 276–7
decolonization 34, 40–1
deconsolidation 212
decoupling 99
DeepSeek 119
Defence Telephone Link 262
deflation 150
democracy 206, 209–12
democratic backsliding 212, 213–14
democratic decline 214
democratic decoupling 212–13
Democratic Party (US) 100
Democratic Party of Japan (DPJ) 1, 3
democratic recession 213, 215
Democratic Republic of Vietnam 38

democratization 193, 209, 211, 215
Deng Xiaoping 54, 97, 128
Diamond, Larry 212
Diaoyu 1–2, 3, 144, 168–70
  map of *168*
Diem, President 218
digital currencies 230
digital infrastructure 146–7
digital media, and nationalism 204
disaggregated supply chain 70–1
'Doi Moi' market-based reforms 58
dollar, US 229–30
DPRK (Democratic People's Republic of Korea) *see* North Korea
'dual circulation' economy 110, 205
Dutch East India Company 19
Dutch East Indies 33, 35, 195
Duterte, Rodrigo 201, 214

E

earthquakes 219
East Asia 62, 65, 66
  and China–ASEAN Free Trade Agreement 74
  and supply chains 73
East Asia Summit (EAS) 88–9, 136, 176–7, 250, 265, 266
East China Sea 83, 138, 168–70
  and effects of climate change 221
  on 'standard national map' 144
East Pakistan 40, 51
East Vietnam Sea 173
economic capacity 5, 11, 31, 117
economic engineering 117–18
economic growth 4, 50, 60, 211, 251, 259, 272–3, 276
  China 71, 72, 83, 85, 97, 101, 122
  and the Cold War 44, 51
  and the Global Financial Crisis of 2007–08 103
  and globalization 67, 260
  India 157, 159, 202, 247
  US 78

INDEX

economic interdependence 4, 8, 14, 15, 66, 162, 260, 273
  China and the US 94, 95
  in Fractured Asia 239, 244
  in Northeast Asia 163
  with the PRC 78
  provides both mutual benefits but also interlocking vulnerabilities 115
  and social advancement 275
economic leverage 118
economic liberalization 275
economic nationalism 205–6
economic sanctions 118, 230
economic statecraft 114, 230
economy 65–75
EEZ (exclusive economic zone) 1–2, 174–5
EIC (British East India Company) 19–20, 22
electric vehicles (EVs) 121–2, 221, 242, 248
elites 201, 202, 208, 212, 271, 272
empathy, strategic 234–5, 241, 271
empire 19, 25, 29, 30, 34, 35, 40
entrepreneurship 50, 96, 278
era of markets 9, 15, 94, 258, 275
ethnonationalism 197, 202
EU
  and ARF 89
  and Central Asia 187
  and CPTPP 275
  and the PRC 75
  UK referendum to leave 11
euro 230
export-focused industrialization 10, 66, 91, 95
export-led industrialization 258

F

Ferdinand, Archduke Franz 267
Fergana Valley 185
First Indochina War 38
flooding 219
food production, and effect of climate change 221
Fordism 68
Fortyn, Pym 97
Fractured Asia 228, 239–44, 270
France 33
  and Indochina 24
  and Southeast Asia 28, 178
  and Southeast Asia Treaty Organization 47
  and Vietnam 38
Freedom House 211–12
free trade agreements 274
Fukuyama, Francis 211

G

G7 231
G20 231
Gandhi, Mohandas 39
GATT (General Agreement on Tariffs and Trade) 66, 68, 229, 274
GDP growth 10, 75
Geneva Accords 38, 47, 48
geoeconomics 114
geopolitical competition 42, 64, 95, 119, 126, 141, 160, 162, 218, 250, 251
  in Fractured Asia 239
  in Rebalanced Asia 244
  in Unified Asia 228, 249
  between the US and China 15, 111, 189
geopolitical rivalry 14, 54, 92, 222, 228, 256, 273
geopolitical stability 259, 273
geopolitics, definition 125–6
Global Civilization Initiative (GCI) 148
Global Development Initiative (GDI) 148
Global Financial Crisis (GFC) of 2007–08 8, 11, 97–8, 103
globalization 5, 6, 7–8, 9–10, 11, 13, 63–4, 66, 92, 258
  and China 100
  and the COVID-19 pandemic 95–6, 105, 109–10
  created an initial political backlash 97

and geopolitical stability 259
and political factors 260–1
and rapid industrial growth 67
recast 120, 121
global multipolar order 233
global production 242–3
Global Security Initiative (GSI) 148
Gracey, General Douglas 38
grand bargain 236–8
Great Game 189
great power competition 8, 89, 92, 113, 115, 122, 127, 161, 171, 172, 190, 270
and ASEAN 175–6
and climate change 222
and military expenditure 130
and Trump 81
great powers 132–3, 136, 141–2, 161, 236–7, 268
green technology 220–1, 223, 248
grey zone tactics 140
Gulf states 187
Gulf War 1990–91 58

H

Hansen, Pauline 97
Hatta, Mohammed 38
Hawaiian Islands 25
hegemony 268, 270
Helsinki Final Act 265
high technology 141, 242, 247–8
Hindu nationalism 202
Hindus 40
Hindutva 202
Ho Chi Minh 195
Hong Kong 30, 49–50, 57, 71
Honshu 220
hotlines 262
household expenditure 102
Huawei 118, 121, 141, 271
hydrocarbon reserves 186

I

illiberalism 193
illiberal states 207, 208, 215, **216**
Imperial China 2
imperialism 18, 25, 28, 30, 31, 258

India 19–21, 39–40, 41, 60, 63, 64, 66, 157–60, 195, 217
and Bangladesh 51–2
and Central Asia 187
and China 74, 139, 179–82, 205, 221
and democracy 212
and democratic backsliding 213
and democratic recession 215
and disputed border with China 144
and East Asia Summit 89
in Fractured Asia 240–1
and liberties 208
map showing disputed territories *181*
and maritime space 138
military power 250
and nationalism 200–1, 202–3, 204, 205–6
and Pakistan 178, 179
part of 'second wave' of democratization 209
and the Quad mechanism 119
and Raisina Dialogue 90
in Rebalanced Asia 247
and rice 220
and the Shanghai Cooperation Organization 89
and Southeast Asia 178
swing state 135
and the US 155, 241
and the USSR 58–9
Indian Military 182
Indian Navy 182
Indian Ocean 137, 138, 160, 182, 219–20, 221
Indochina 24, 29, 31, 33, 35, 37–8, 41, 195
Indochina Wars 40, 172
Indonesia 29, 31, 38–9, 40, 217
and ASEAN 52, 87, 172, 176
and the Asian financial crisis of 1997–98 96
created out of the various elements of the Dutch East Indies 24, 195

and democracy 206, 211, 212
and democratic backsliding 213
and Malaysia 47
and patronage networks 215
and protectionism 206
and value-add 73
Indo–Pacific 137, 138
INDOPACOM (United States Indo-Pacific Command) 81–2
industrialization 67, 95, 258
industrial policy 50, 51, 67, 116, 247, 273
industrial production 49, 68, 69
inflation 116, 120, 243, 251
Inflation Reduction Act (US) 121–2
infrastructure investment 140
interdependence 14, 15, 115
  and China 4, 78–9, 94, 95
  and decoupling 99
  vulnerabilities of 120
International Institute for Strategic Studies 90
International Monetary Fund (IMF) 229, 231
international production 67–8, 69–70
Iran 89
Ishihara Shintaro 169
Israel 133–4, 233

J

Jammu 183
Japan 25–7, 30, 45–6, 55, 205
  and ASEAN+ 3 88
  during the Cold War 48, 51
  and democracy 212
  economic growth 50
  and export-focused industrialization 10, 66
  and the Korean War 50
  military capability 241
  military power 250
  and nationalism 203–4
  part of 'second wave' of democratization 209
  and the Philippines 37
  and the Quad mechanism 119
  and Senkaku Islands 1–2, 3, 168–9
  signed instrument of surrender on 2 September 1945 34
  and Southeast Asia 178
  and South Korea 217
  and supply chains 73
  and Taiwan 37
  and Tokugawa Ieyasu 18
  tourism market 3
  and the US 134, 152
  in World War II 28–9, 31, 32, 33
Japanese Empire 26, 35, 196, 258
  map of extent 27
Japanese Navy 29
Java 220

K

Kan Naoto 1
Kashmir 180, 183
Kazakhstan 89, 135, 185
Khmer Rouge 60
Kim Il-sung 36
Kingdom of Cambodia 38
Kingdom of Laos 38
Kingdom of Siam 25
Kissinger, Henry 53
Korea 26, 28, 35–6, 40
  and the Second Indochina War 50 *see also* North Korea; South Korea
Korean Peninsula 41, 45, 165, 167–8, 245, 246–7
  map of 166
Korean War 41, 44–5, 50, 167
Kuomintang (KMT) 32, 33–4, 37
Kyrgyzstan 89, 135, 185, 190

L

Labour Party (UK) 97–8
Lai Ching-te, President 255
landslides 219
Laos
  and the Geneva Accords 47
  and Indochina 195
  and Indochina Wars 172

Leninist regime 206
swing state 135
left-wing socialism 202
Leninism 197, 198, 206
Liberal Democratic Party (LDP)/
　Japan 1, 203
liberal internationalism 233–4
liberalism 193, 224
liberalization 57, 74, 88, 274, 275
liberals 208
liberal states 207, 215, **216**
lockdowns 102
long littoral 137

M

Mahan, Alfred 125
Makinder, Halford 125
Malaya 24, 29, 32, 35
Malaysia 41, 49–50, 195
　and ASEAN 52, 87, 172
　and the Asian financial crisis of
　　1997–98 96, 211
　and democracy 212
　and Indonesia 47
　and the South China
　　Sea 173, 174–5
　swing state 135
　and value-add 73
Manchukuo 26, 28
Manchuria 26, 28
manufactured goods 68–9
Mao Zedong 53, 126–7
Marco Polo Bridge Incident 28–9
Marcos, Ferdinand 210
maritime zones 139
market efficiency 96, 113
market-led globalization 5,
　6, 9–10, 63–4, 66, 95–6,
　122, 235–6
　and economic growth 67
　and strategic system 7
markets, era of 9, 15, 94, 258, 275
Marshall Plan 119
Marxism–Leninism 197
Mekong Delta 220
microchip industry 13, 70,
　106, 108

Micronesia 25
middle-class interests 215
military competition 17, 46, 124,
　131, 160
military control zones 137
military dominance, American 62,
　76, 77, 93, 137, 231–2, 269
military equilibrium 191, 239,
　247, 269
military expenditure 130
military power 139, 177, 234, 253
　China 128, 239
　India 241, 250
military primacy 56, 240, 244, 245
minilateral arrangements 217
minilateral diplomacy 267
Mnuchin, Steve 12, 104
Modi, Narendra 157, 159,
　201, 202
Mohammad, Mahathir 209
monsoons 219–20, 276
Move Forward Party 212
Mughal Empire 20
multilateralism 87, 89, 147
multipolar geopolitical
　environment 33
multipolar global order 158–9, 229
Muslim League 39
Muslims 40, 205
Myanmar 135, 195, 213

N

narcotic smuggling 190
nationalism 193, 194–206, 224,
　251, 259, 260, 277–8
National Security Strategy 2017
　(US) 13–14
natural disasters 224
Navarro, Peter 99
navigation, freedom of 174–5
Nepal 184
Netherlands 33
　and Indonesia 24, 38–9
　and Southeast Asia 28
netizens 200
New Zealand
　in APEC 57

and East Asia Summit 89
and Southeast Asia Treaty
  Organization 47
and TPP 80
Ngo Dinh Diem 48
Nixon, President
  Richard 53, 126–7
non-alignment 46, 58
North Atlantic Treaty's Chapter V
  obligations 133
North Borneo 41
Northeast Asia 51, 56, 163–70
  and the Cold War 54
  links with Southeast Asia 61,
    63, 65
  and peace dividend 62
  security tensions 60
North Korea 36, 40, 45, 167, 168
  and China 135
  nuclear ambitions 78, 266–7
  part of the Japanese Empire 196
  and the USSR 58
North Pole 222
North Vietnam 52
Nuclear Non-proliferation
  Treaty 267
nuclear technology 155
nuclear weapons 165, 179
Nye, Joseph 77

O

Obama, President 79–81, 152,
  169, 182
Observer Research Foundation 90
Occupy Wall Street movement 11
oil prices 101
Olympics 102
One China policy 54
opium 22

P

Pacific Islands 25
PACOM (Pacific Command) 81
Pakistan 51, 195
  and authoritarianism 214
  and Central Asia 187
  disputed border with China 144
  and India 40, 41, 178, 179, 183–4
  and the Shanghai Cooperation
    Organization 89
  and Southeast Asia Treaty
    Organization 47
  and the US 52, 57, 135
patronage networks 215
Pearl Harbor bombings 29, 37
Pelosi, Nancy 144
Pence, Mike 99
People's Liberation Army–Navy
  (PLAN) 163, 182
People's Republic of China
  (PRC) 4, 10, 67, 97, 110
  in APEC 57
  and ASEAN+ 3 88
  benefited from disaggregated
    supply chain 71
  and 'dual circulation'
    economy 110–11
  and the four modernisations 54–5
  GDP 78
  and India 182
  and Japan 1–3
  military modernization 128
  most important two-way trade
    partner for more than 120
    countries 75
  'reform and opening up'
    period 122–3
  and the Soviet Union 48
  and Taiwan 191, 240
  and Vietnam 207
  see also China; US–China relations
performance legitimation 198, 200
Perot, Ross 97
Perry, Commodore 25, 26
personal protective equipment
  (PPE) 94–5, 106–7
pharmaceuticals 13, 107, 117
Philippines 47, 210, 217
  and ASEAN 52, 87, 172, 176
  and China 173
  colony of Spain 19, 25, 195
  and democracy 211–12
  and democratic backsliding 214
  and Japan 29, 35, 37

and populism 201
and the South China Sea 175
and the US 25, 37, 48, 134
Philippines Commonwealth 37
PLAAF fighter 255
political parties 214–15
political systems **216**
populism 201
populist nationalism 201
Portugal, in Goa and Macau 19
Powell, Jerome 12, 104
President-to-President hotline 262
production
  global 242–3
  international 67–8, 69–70
protectionism 206
protocols for handling specific
  crises 263
Puri, Samir 229
Putin, Vladimir 112
Puyi, emperor 26

Q

Qing dynasty 2, 21–3, 36
Quad 119, 136, 217
quantum computing 141

R

rainfall, heavy 220
Raisina Dialogue 90, 270
Rajapaksas 214
rare earth minerals 2, 3
Rebalanced Asia 228,
  244–9
renminbi 230
Republican Party (US) 201
revisionist powers 158
rice 220
rights 147–8
right-wing nationalism 202
rivalry, geopolitical 64
Rogoff, Ken 229–30
ROK (Republic of Korea) *see*
  South Korea
Roosevelt, President 25
'rules-based order' 217
Rusk, Dean 36

Russia 64
  and Central Asia 188–9
  and China 135, 144, 148, 151
  and East Asia Summit 89
  effect of economic
    sanctions 230–1
  and grey zone tactics 140
  and India 241
  invasion of Ukraine 187
  and Japan 26
  and the Shanghai Cooperation
    Organization 89

S

Samoa 25
sanctions 114, 118, 150,
  187, 230–1
Sarawak 41
SARS (severe acute respiratory
  syndrome) 100
Saudi Arabia 187, 234, 243
Second Indochina War 47, 50
'second wave' of democratization 209
security 61, 63, 162, 184, 224–5
  and ARF 88
  and ASEAN 176
  and Central Asia 190
  and China 112, 151
  and CICA 89–90
  and geopolitics 126
  and the Global Security
    Initiative 148
  and Huawei 118
  and Northeast Asia 60
  and South Asia 51
  and swing states 135
  of Taiwan 164–5
  and Trump 111
  and Xiangshan Forum 90
security dilemma 130–1, 264
seismic shocks 251–4
semiconductors 118–19, 121
Senkaku Islands 1–2, 3, 144, 168–70
  map of *168*
Seoul Metropolitan Area 167
Shanghai Cooperation Organization
  (SCO) 89, 136, 147, 186

INDEX

Shangri-La Dialogue (SLD) 90, 147, 265, 270
Sheikh Hasina 214, 217
Shimonoseki, Treaty of 2, 26, 168–9
Siam 25
  see also Thailand
Singapore 24, 30, 41, 49–50, 195
  and ASEAN 52, 87, 172
  and democracy 212
  illiberal state 208
  and TPP 80
  and the US 134–5
Sino-Japanese War, 1894–95 2, 26, 36–7, 168–9
Sino-Russian partnership 187–8, 218
Six Party Talks 170, 246–7, 266–7
'small garden high walls' approach 247–8
social media, used to spread misinformation to advance an illiberal agenda 217
South Asia 60–1, 63, 178–84
  and the Cold War 51
  and international trade 65
  United Nations map of *179*
South Asian Association for Regional Cooperation (SAARC) 87–8
South China Sea 83, 172–5
  disputes 131, 138, 205
  and effects of climate change 221
  and India 241
  map showing territorial claims in *174*
  with the nine-dashed line 145, *145*
  on 'standard national map' 144
Southeast Asia 23–5, 28, 41, 47, 51, 170–8
  and AFTA 74
  and the Cold War 54
  colonial holdings 1914 *24*
  links with Northeast Asia 56, 61, 63, 65
  and peace dividend 62
  political map *171*
Southeast Asian Command (SEAC) 32–3, 37, 39

Southeast Asia Treaty Organization (SEATO) 47
South Korea 10, 36, 40, 49–50
  and ASEAN+ 3 88
  and the Asian financial crisis of 1997–98 96
  and democracy 210, 212
  and Japan 51, 217
  and microchips 108
  military power 250
  part of the Japanese Empire 196
  and the US 48, 134, 167
  and value-add 73
South Sea 129
Southwest Pacific Area Command 32
sovereign capability 107–8, 117
sovereignty 207–8
Soviet Union
  and Central Asia 28
  and the PRC 48
  see also USSR
Spain, and the Philippines 19, 25, 195
Spanish–America War of 1898 25, 37
special economic zones (SEZs) 71, 72
spheres of influence 136, 156, 233
Sri Lanka 40, 184
  and the Rajapaksas 214
  swing state 135
state building 56, 195
state-led globalization 247
State of Vietnam 38
status quo powers 158
strategic balance 87, 137, 184, 191, 270
  after the Vietnam War 52
  and Bangladesh 51
  and China 143, 163–4, 169
  and Concert system 237
  and geopolitics 126
  and grand bargain 236
  in Rebalanced Asia 244
  in Unified Asia 228
  for the US 44–5, 54, 56, 130, 154–5, 259

strategic competition 16, 75–87, 162, 172, 177–8, 262–4, 264
strategic depth 138
strategic empathy 234–5, 241, 271
strategic equilibrium 130, 191, 228, 249, 250, 267
strategic imagination 16, 87, 92, 191
strategic stability 170, 264
strategic system 7, 91, 113, 260
Subianto, Prabowo 213
Suharto, General 52, 96, 211
Sukarno 38, 52
Sumatra 32
Sun Yat-sen 22
super typhoons 220, 253
supply chains 15, 73, 74, 95, 106, 120–1
swing states 135
Syngman, Rhee 36

T

Taiwan 10, 49–50, 66, 138, 163–5
  in APEC 57
  and China 41, 78, 83, 191, 199, 206, 240, 255
  during the Cold War 51
  and COVID-19 pandemic 106
  and India 160
  introduced democratic reforms in 1992 210
  map of the Taiwan Strait *164*
  and microchips 108
  part of the Japanese Empire 26, 28, 36–7, 196
  in Rebalanced Asia 245, 246
  'repatriated' on 'standard national map' 144
  and the Second Indochina War 50
  and the US 53, 54, 55, 126, 134
Taiwan Relations Act 54
Tajikistan 89, 135, 185, 190
tariffs 68–9, 81, 99, 114, 153, 260
technology, high 141, 242, 247–8
terrorism 189
Tet Offensive 52

Thailand 25, 47, 49–50, 210–13, 273
  and ASEAN 52, 172
  and the Asian financial crisis of 1997–98 96
  and democratic recession 215
  swing state 135
  and value-add 73
  youth protests 217
third-party relationships 178, 187
'third wave' of democratization 209, 212
TikTok 117
Timor Leste 211, 212
Timurid Empire 185
Tokugawa Ieyasu 18, 26
'Track 1' gatherings 91
'Track 1.5' processes 90–1, 147, 265
'Track 2' meetings 91
trade 65–6, 73, 75
  as a proportion of GDP 120
  and the US 155–6
trade agreements 274
trade flows 120
trade routes 75
transnational problems 222–3
Trans-Pacific Partnership (TPP) 80, 153
Treaty of Shimonoseki 2, 168–9
Trump, Donald 11, 81, 82, 98–100, 155, 252–3, 256, 273
  and China 92, 99, 112, 153
  and COVID-19 pandemic 111
  and populism 201
  and travel bans 102
TSMC 108
tsunamis 219
Turkey 187
Turkmenistan 135, 185
typhoons 219, 220, 253, 276

U

UK
  Labour Party 97–8
  referendum to leave the EU 11
  and Southeast Asia 178
  and Southeast Asia Treaty Organization 47

INDEX

Ukraine 112, 187
unemployment, and COVID-19 pandemic 102, 104
Unified Asia 228, 249–51
United Nations (UN)
 and Korea 36
 UN system 228–9
United Nations Convention on the Law of the Sea (UNCLOS) 173
US 31, 151–7
 2017 National Security Strategy 13–14
 after World War II 32
 and the AIIB 90
 alliances 76, 77, 134–5
 in APEC 57
 in Asia in the 19th century 25
 and Central Asia 189
 Cold War strategy 76, 77–8, 218
 congagement 79
 and the contested maritime space 138
 and COVID-19 pandemic 12, 104–5
 and East Asia Summit 89
 global production zone 242
 as great power 132
 and high technology 242
 and Huawei 118–19, 141
 and India 182–3, 240–1
 invasion of Afghanistan 186
 and Israel 133–4
 and Japan 3, 29, 33, 45–6
 and Korea 36
 military dominance 55–6, 76, 77, 137, 231–3, 239–40
 naval supremacy 138
 and Pakistan 52
 and the Philippines 37, 195–6
 PLAAF fighter incident 255
 possibility of departing from the region 252–3
 primacy in Asia 125, 129–30, 256, 259, 268, 271
 and the Quad mechanism 119
 in Rebalanced Asia 245–6
 and Southeast Asia 28, 178
 Southeast Asia Treaty Organization 47
 and South Korea 167
 and Taiwan 164–5
 and TikTok 117
 and Trump 99–100
 and the USSR 34–5, 43, 266
 and Vietnam War 48
 see also US–China relations
US–Central Asia summit 187
US–China relations 14, 44, 64, 129–30, 150–1, 152, 154, 182–3, 238–9, 271–2
 China rejects US military primacy 245
 and congagement 78–9
 during COVID-19 pandemic 15
 and economic interdependence 94, 95
 have incompatible visions of the future 268–9
 recognized the PRC 53–4, 126–7
 and tariffs 153
 and Trump 99, 111
US–Japan mutual security treaty 169
US Navy 142
USNS Impeccable 129
USS Missouri 34
USSR 31, 185, 269–70
 after World War II 32, 33, 34
 and China 52
 collapse of 57–8
 invasion of Afghanistan 57
 and Korea 36
 and the US 34–5, 43, 266
Uzbekistan 89, 135, 185

V

value-add 73
value chain 69–70, 72, 73, 258–9
value network 69–70
victimization 204–5
Vietnam 38, 273
 and ASEAN 176
 and China 173, 207

and Indochina 195
and Indochina Wars 40, 172
Leninist regime 206
and the US 135
and the USSR 58
Vietnam–Cambodia conflict 60
Vietnam War 47–8
vigilantism 214

W

Wake Island 25
war, risks of 244, 254
war on terrorism 189
water, and climate change 221
Weibo 200
Western Pacific 137, 138, 160, 219, 240, 253, 271
West Pakistan 40
WHO (World Health Organization) 100
Widodo, President Joko 213
World Economic Forum 5, 91
World War II 28, 29, 30, 31, 32–3, 39
WTO (World Trade Organisation) 11, 273–4

X

Xiangshan Forum 90, 147, 270
Xi Jinping 83–4, 85, 128, 151
    and foreign policy 64, 129
    plausible shock of the CPC removing him from power 253
    in Rebalanced Asia 245
    speech at Davos 100
    and Taiwan 144, 163

Y

Yasuhiro Nakasone 55

Z

Zhan Qixiong 1, 2, 3
ZTE 121, 141

www.ingramcontent.com/pod-product-compliance
Lightning Source LLC
Chambersburg PA
CBHW031138020426
42333CB00013B/433